Table For Two

BACK FOR SECONDS

Table For Two

BACK FOR SECONDS

WARREN CATERSON

 Winfield & Scott Press

Most Winfield & Scott Press books are available at special quantity discounts for bulk purchasers for sales promotions, premiums, fundraising, and educational needs. Special books, book excerpts, or promotional materials can also be created to fit specific needs. For more information please e-mail us at sales@WinfieldAndScottPress.com.

Winfield & Scott Press LLC
3501-B North Ponce De Leon Boulevard, Suite 255
St. Augustine, FL 32084
www.WinfieldAndScottPress.com

Library of Congress Cataloging-in-Publication Data

Caterson, Warren.
        Table for two : back for seconds / Warren
        Caterson.
        p. cm.
        Includes index.
        LCCN 2013952405
        ISBN-13: 978-0-9801568-7-4
        ISBN-10: 0-9801568-7-4

        1.   Cookery for two. I. Title.

TX652.C38 2009   641.   5'612
                        QBI08-600229

Cover Design: Rebecca Anne Russo
Author Photograph: Darice Michelle Photography
Interior Design: BecCreative, LLC.

Printed in the United States of America

DEDICATION

To St. Lawrence, patron saint of chefs, and to St. Jude, patron saint of lost causes. I've asked for their prayers more times than I can count.

Often on the very same night - depending on what I was cooking and who I was cooking for…

Table of Contents

Preface

Since my first cookbook came out and started doing well at Barnes & Noble, Amazon, and Big Bob's Diner and Truck Tire Repair, I've heard lots of people tell me how lucky I am to have achieved my dream.

I thank them, sign their book, and smile. Because I know I'm lucky.

Why?

I was born into a family of immigrant entrepreneurs who spun gold from hardship.

I went to a public high school where I learned algebra, studied Chaucer, and read Langston Hughes. I attended a college where I sat side-by-side with brilliant young men and women who went on to launch brilliant careers.

I married a wonderful woman who gave birth to six incredible kids. We built a new house and planted a garden. We owned a Porsche. We sold everything and moved to the inner city to work with young people. I learned to remodel and live in three Victorian homes.

I made a lot of money. I lost a lot of money. I may have made some of it back.

I wrote a novel that didn't sell and a cookbook that did. Very well, in fact.

Some would say it was all a massive stroke of luck. That I was one of the 'chosen few'.

Yeah... Right...

I remember going to the Fireman's Parade as a child in my hometown of Mamaroneck, New York in the early sixties. It was a big deal. This was the era of three TV stations, sandlot baseball, circus under a real tent, and pizza by the slice. My dad hoisted me on his shoulders to see the parade. I know I saw more than he did. But I'm convinced we both had a great time.

Flash-forward to the Mid-90's. I took my wife and kids to Chicago to see the Thanksgiving Day Parade. Crowds swarmed along the curb. The older kids nudged their way to the front. I hoisted my young son Aaron up on my shoulders so he could revel in a parade that I would never see. But I certainly enjoyed his squeals of laughter as floats, clowns and marching bands drifted by.

I'm convinced we both had a great time.

And you're 'lucky' too. 'Cuz someone, somewhere. let you climb on their shoulders to see The Parade. I don't care if you were raised in Beverly Hills or Bed-Stuy. We all stood on someone's shoulders to see a parade that they could only hope to see. It might've been a parent, grandparent, uncle, aunt, teacher, coach, neighbor, rabbi, or priest. Someone stooped low enough to allow us to scramble onto their shoulders to see something remarkable.

Now it's time for each one of us to lift someone up on our shoulders. To let them fully see what you and I have only caught a glimpse of.

This is how the world changes…..For the good.

I bet you're wondering, 'What does this have to do with a cookbook?'

Easy. I'm gonna give you some recipes that'll knock your socks off. Some of them are mine. Some I gleaned from other great chefs and tweaked. Yep, I'm standing on their shoulders.

Now pull out that skillet and climb up on mine.

Then share them with someone else.

Bon appétit,

Warren

PS. This book wouldn't be possible if I had not climbed up on some non-chef shoulders. So here's a big shout out to my cover designer, Becky Russo, my editor Amber Hanna Forbes, cooking studio owner Andrea Rosenblatt (okay, she's a chef), and last, but certainly not least, Mill Aller, Janis Smeal, and Ron and Cathy Marshall. Your faith in this project helped bring it to light. Slainté!

MEASURMENTS

Liquid Measure Volume Equivalents

1 teaspoon	= 1/3 tablespoon
1 tablespoon	= 3 teaspoons
2 tablespoons	= 1 fluid ounce
4 tablespoons	= 1/4 cup or 2 ounces
5 1/3 tablespoons	= 1/3 cup or 2 2/3 ounces
8 tablespoons	= 1/2 cup or 1 teacup or 4 ounces
16 tablespoons	= 1 cup or 8-ounces
1/4 cup	= 4 tablespoons
3/8 cup	= 1/4 cup + 2 tablespoonss
5/8 cup	= 1/2 cup + 2 tablespoonss
7/8 cup	= 3/4 cup + 2 tablespoonss
1 cup	= 1/2 pint or 8 fluid ounces
2 cups	= 1 pint or 16 fluid ounces
1 pint	= 2 cups or 16 fluid ounces
1 quart	= 2 pints or 4 cups
1 gallon	= 4 quarts

Cooking Terms

COOKING TERMS

Note: For additional definitions of cooking terms and ingredients along with helpful kitchen tips and cooking hints, sign up for my email newsletter at www.tablefortwocookbooks.com.

BLANCHING OR PARBOILING

A technique to partially cook a food in boiling water in preparation for later completion in a dish. Blanching will also loosen the skin of vegetables and will set their color, particularly if the item is immediately plunged into a bowl of ice water. When using this technique, begin your timing the moment the food hits the water. Do not wait for the water to return to a boil.

BRAISING

An ideal method of cooking larger chunks of meat or vegetables that require some tenderizing. Simply brown the meat in a little butter or olive oil then add a little bit of broth or water to the pan and simmer over low heat. This is also an excellent way to cook chicken or fish to keep them from drying out.

BROWNING MEAT

Browning meat in a bit of oil over high heat will not only give it an appealing brown or bronze appearance, it will provide a deeply rich flavor as well. You may have to brown cubed meat in batches to ensure that they brown. Overcrowding the pan will lower the heat and will result in the meat being steamed, rather than browned. Some cookbooks suggest that you dredge the meat in flour before browning. I avoid this because it's the flour that gets browned and not the meat. After all, the purpose of this technique is to brown the natural sugars in the meat and a coating of flour will prevent that from happening.

DEGLAZING

After your meat or vegetable has been browned, you should pour a little wine, stock or water into the pan over high heat and scrape up the rich brown bits that remain. Add this to your soup, stew or sauce for extra flavor.

DREDGING

Thin meats and fish are rolled or tossed in flour or breadcrumbs, which are often seasoned with salt and pepper, before frying or sautéing.

JULIENNE OR MATCHSTICK CUT
Simply cut your vegetable into thin slices, stack the slices then cut them into thin sticks. The sticks may then be cut to your desired length.

MARINATING
This is a technique whereby meats or vegetables are soaked in a flavoring liquid for added pizzazz. However, contrary to popular belief, marinades do little to tenderize tough and inexpensive cuts of meat. The only remedy for that is braising or stewing.

PINCH OR DASH
Start with less than an 1/8 teaspoon and season to taste.

POACHING
A method that gently cooks fish, meat or eggs in stock or water at just below a simmer. This will give the food a delicate and balanced flavor.

REDUCING
Boil a liquid over medium-high or high heat until it is reduced in volume and becomes concentrated.

ROUX
This is a term that describes equal parts of fat and flour which are used to thicken sauces and gravies. For a white roux, the mixture will need to be whisked for at least 4 or 5 minutes; less than that and the sauce will have an off taste. For a brown roux, the mixture will have to be cooked longer, up to an hour, depending on the flavor desired. The longer a roux cooks, the nuttier the flavor.

SAUTÉING
You'll see this term used a lot in this book. It's derived from the French word meaning 'to jump' and is a technique used to cook food quickly with a minimum amount of fat. It's important that you use a heavy skillet that can hold the food in one layer. Here are a few helpful hints for a perfect sauté:

1.   Heat the pan and then add the fat. Your food will be less apt to stick.

2.   Your food should be at room temperature and patted dry.

3.   Parboil dense vegetables like carrots, potatoes, turnips and rutabagas if you're sautéing them with other quicker cooking vegetables like onions, celery, peppers or squash.

4.   Salt slows the browning process. Season after sautéing if possible.

STEAMING

Steaming is one of the simplest and most nutritious ways to cook food. Unlike boiling, steaming will retain more of the food's vitamins and minerals. You can find a wide variety of steamers on the market but you may use a colander or sieve as well. To keep foods from becoming too wet, drape a towel over the basket before replacing the pot lid. This will keep the condensation that normally collects on the lid from falling back onto the food. This technique is particularly effective when you want light and puffy steamed rice.

STIR-FRYING

I use this term interchangeably with sautéing. It's simply the oriental method for cooking food quickly in a minimum amount of fat. Some cooks insist upon using a wok. If you already have one, by all means use it. But for the amount of food we will be cooking throughout this book, a good skillet or sauté pan will do just fine.

Ingredients

INGREDIENTS

BROTH/STOCK

Homemade broth is certainly hard to beat, but many of us don't have the time, inclination, or freezer space to create our own broth or stock from scratch. This is where a good soup base comes to the rescue. Available on-line and in many supermarkets, soup bases are seasoned, paste-style concentrates of freshly cooked meat, poultry, seafood and vegetables. There are several excellent soup bases and stocks on the market including, but not limited to, Tones, Minor's, Better than Bouillon, and Glory Foods. These are all superior to bouillon cubes, which you should avoid at all costs. Whatever brand you choose, be sure to examine the ingredients – the first item listed for beef base should be beef, chicken should be chicken, ham should be ham, and so on. You may be able to save additional money by purchasing larger containers of often-used base from one of the club stores, like Costco or Sam's. That's where I purchase my chicken and beef base.

BUTTER

Although this staple has gotten a bad rap for the last 30 or so years, I feel it is totally undeserved. When used in moderation and primarily as a flavoring, butter is a delicious addition to many dishes and will not be detrimental to your health. Those who still insist on margarine as a healthier alternative have not read the latest research. But remember, the key is to use it as a flavoring enhancer; for sautéing I recommend olive oil.

CAPERS

Sun-dried flower buds, which are usually pickled in brine and jarred, add a piquancy to any dish. Find them in the pickle section of your supermarket.

COCONUT MILK

Found canned or frozen in most supermarkets. Use unsweetened.

CREAM

I'm referring to half and half or regular whipping cream in the recipes that follow. Heavy whipping cream would be too thick.

HERBS & SPICES

Fresh or dried? It depends. I try to use fresh herbs when available but many times I have to rely on dried, when I use 1/3 the amount. Herbs with woody stems and strong aromatics, such as thyme and oregano, intensify in flavor once dried and may be used in many soups, stews, roasts and other cold-weather dishes. Summer herbs like parsley, cilantro, chives, and basil are best used fresh because they lose too much flavor when dried. Fresh herbs are best when added toward the end of a recipe while dried should be added toward the beginning. When using dried herbs, crumble them between your fingers to release their oils before you add them to your recipe. As far as spices go, most will be dried because fresh spices can be rare. Below are some recommendations:

Basil (best fresh)	Chives (best fresh)
Coriander Seeds (best dried)	Cumin (best dried)
Dill (best fresh)	Ginger (best fresh)
Oregano (best dried)	Parsley (best fresh)
Rosemary (fresh or dried)	Sage (fresh or dried)
Tarragon (best fresh)	Thyme (fresh or dried)
Turmeric (best dried)	

The recipes that follow use dried herbs, unless it is absolutely essential to use fresh, because this is what many of us have at our disposal. I do encourage you to use fresh whenever possible, just remember to triple the amount.

LEMON, LIME, AND ORANGE JUICE

You'll notice that I use quite a bit of citrus in my cooking. Living in Florida, who wouldn't? Hands down, fresh is optimal, but it is not always convenient. I keep some Minute Maid Frozen Lemon Juice® on hand when I'm in a pinch and avoid bottled lemon juice because the taste is substantially different from fresh. However, I do keep a bottle of Nellie and Joe's Key Lime Juice® in the fridge – it's a good substitute for fresh squeezed lime juice. When it comes to orange juice, I often opt for the not-from-concentrate bottled variety when I don't have any fresh oranges on hand. Ditto for grapefruit juice.

OILS

You'll find that I use olive oil in most of these recipes. It has a wonderful flavor and, because it is mono-unsaturated, it is easy on the heart. I use the less expensive 'pure' olive oil for basic sautéing and reserve extra virgin when I want the flavor of the oil to shine through. Of course, you may use canola oil in place of pure olive oil. I use other oils, like sesame and walnut, when I feel their distinctive flavor is necessary for the dish.

PINE NUTS
These expensive little nuggets actually come from a large species of pinecone in Italy. Like many nuts and seeds, their flavor improves with toasting.

PROSCIUTTO
This Italian ham has been seasoned and air-dried. Sliced razor thin, this richly delicious meat will go a long way. Buy in small batches from your butcher or in many supermarkets.

SHALLOTS
A cross between the garlic and the onion, these are sometimes unavailable. A simple mix of a little onion with garlic will yield a similar flavor.

VINEGARS
I try to keep a bottle of each of these in my cupboard:

Red Wine Vinegar	White Wine Vinegar
Cider Vinegar	Rice Wine Vinegar
Balsamic Vinegar	Malt Vinegar

These should do for most of the recipes you're likely to come across. As for the wide variety of flavored vinegars on the market, i.e. Tarragon Vinegar, I often make my own, which is cheaper, or I simply add that particular herb to the dish.

WINE
I have one simple rule when cooking with wine: If you can't drink it, don't cook with it. The cooking wines found next to the vinegar at the grocery store are loaded with salt. You're better off buying an inexpensive red or white wine from your wine merchant. (This goes for Sherry, Madeira, and other fortified wines as well.) For white wine I recommend Sauvignon Blanc and for red wine I recommend Burgundy.

Soups

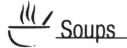 ## Soups

Hungry for some soup? I know you can open a can of condensed soup and plop it into a saucepan with a can of water. 5 or 10 minutes later you'll have yourself a steaming bowl of vegetable, chicken noodle, or tomato soup. It sure is convenient and may work in a pinch. But have you read any soup labels recently? Do you really want all that salt and other additives? Me neither.

If you look at the following soup recipes I think you'll be surprised that some of them won't take much more time than preparing a batch of condensed soup. As an added bonus, you'll know the quality of ingredients and you'll be able to adjust the salt content. For instance, my Shrimp and Coconut Soup takes all of 10 minutes to prepare.

As in my first book, *Table for Two - Back for Seconds*, these soup recipes might serve 2 hungry adults if served as an entrée. All you'll need for a complete meal is a light salad and warm crusty bread. But as in my first book, I really planned on serving 4 with these recipes. Why? Because as we all know, soup tastes better the next day.

If you're up to it, you can double many of these recipes and freeze the leftovers in either 1-pint containers or zip lock bags so that you can reheat them for those days when you want lunch or dinner fast.

"Wait," you say. "Did you just say store my soup in zip lock bags?" Yep. You'll save lots of precious room in your freezer if you do so. Here's how: Let the soup cool a bit and pour 2 cups into quart-size (or smaller) freezer bags and label them. Lay them flat on a small baking sheet and place them in the freezer. When they are frozen, remove the baking sheet and stack frozen soup one on top of the other. This way they'll take up much less room than freezing the soup in big blobs in a bag or in containers.

• SHRIMP AND COCONUT SOUP •

With 3/4-pound of shrimp, this lightning-quick soup for two could almost double as a stew. Whenever you pine for an evening in the islands, whip up a pot of this, warm some bread, pour a cold beverage of choice, then snuggle up and stream "South Pacific" from Netflix.

PREP: Under 5 minutes   COOK: 5 minutes

INGREDIENTS
    1 cup canned unsweetened coconut milk
    1 cup water
    1/2 teaspoon red curry paste
    1/4 teaspoon kosher salt
    1 (2 x 1/2-inch) strip lime peel
    3/4 pound large shrimp, peeled and deveined
    1/4 cup julienne-cut fresh basil
    Lime slices to garnish (optional)

DIRECTIONS
Combine the coconut milk, water, curry paste, salt and lime peel in a large saucepan over medium-high heat. Bring to a boil and reduce heat to medium. Stir in shrimp, cover, and cook until shrimp just turns pink, about 3 minutes. Remove lime peel and stir in basil. Serve with lime garnish if desired.

• WHITE BEAN AND SAUSAGE SOUP •

PREP: 10 minutes   COOK: 20 minutes

INGREDIENTS

    1 tablespoon olive oil
    3/4 pound smoked beef sausage or kielbasa
    3 carrots, peeled and sliced into 1/4-inch pieces
    1 rib celery, sliced thin
    1/2 medium onion, chopped (about 1/2 cup)
    1 (15-ounce) can northern white beans, drained
    1 (14.5-ounce) can stewed tomatoes, undrained
    1-1/2 teaspoons dried rosemary
    1/2 cup dry white wine
    4 cups chicken broth
    1/2 teaspoon cayenne pepper, or to taste
    1/4 teaspoon freshly ground black pepper
    1-1/2 cups shredded Muenster or pre-packaged bag of five Italian cheese

DIRECTIONS

1. Heat a large saucepan over medium-high heat. Add oil and swirl to coat. Stir in sausage, carrots, celery and onion. Sauté until sausage is brown and vegetables soften, about 6 to 8 minutes.

2. Add beans, tomatoes, rosemary, wine, and chicken broth. Bring to a boil over high heat then reduce heat to medium-low. Cook, uncovered until soup reduces and thickens a bit, about 10 - 12 minutes. Season with cayenne and black pepper.

3. Ladle into warm bowls and sprinkle with shredded cheese.

• SOUTHERN GREENS, BEANS AND BACON SOUP •

Having grown up just outside New York City, my introduction to Southern Cuisine came from watching The Andy Griffith Show and The Beverly Hillbillies on TV. It wasn't 'til I spent a number of years in southeast Tennessee that I actually got to savor the food of the Deep South. While some items are an acquired taste - I still avoid okra in most forms, and I have yet to eat certain parts of mammals (hog jowls anyone?) - I did fall in love with the complex flavors that much of Southern Cuisine offers. This is one such dish.

PREP: Under 5 minutes   COOK: 35 minutes

INGREDIENTS
    4 slices smoked bacon, chopped into 1/4-inch pieces
    1 medium onion, chopped (about 1 cup)
    3 cups chopped kale
    4 cups chicken or vegetable broth
    1 (15-ounce) can cannellini or great northern beans, rinsed and drained
    1/4 teaspoon freshly ground black pepper
    2 - 3 dashes hot sauce, or to taste
    Kosher salt to taste

DIRECTIONS
1. Cook bacon in a large saucepan or medium Dutch oven over medium-high heat until crisp, about 7 - 8 minutes. Pour off all but 1 tablespoon bacon fat.

2. Stir in onions and sauté until they just begin to soften, about 5 minutes. Add kale and sauté until it begins to wilt, about 3 minutes. Turn heat to high, add remaining ingredients and bring to a boil. Reduce heat to medium-low, cover and simmer for 20 minutes.

• COCONUT CHICKEN CORN CHOWDER •

In my previous book, *Table for Two - The Cookbook for Couples*, I featured a chicken corn chowder recipe that my wife learned to make growing up in Lancaster County, Pennsylvania, and it was a big hit for those who tried it. Now I'd like to introduce an interesting twist on this Pennsylvania Dutch classic. I imagine this is the soup the Amish would've made famous if only they'd settled in the South Seas instead of Eastern Pennsylvania.

PREP: 10 minutes   COOK: 20 minutes

INGREDIENTS
    2 cups cubed red potatoes
    1 tablespoon unsalted butter
    1 small onion, finely chopped (about 1/2 cup)
    1 clove garlic, minced or pressed
    2 cups fresh or frozen corn kernels
    1 (13.5-ounce) can unsweetened coconut milk
    3 cups diced cooked chicken breast or thighs
    1/4 teaspoon kosher salt
    1/4 teaspoon freshly ground black pepper
    1/4 cup chopped fresh cilantro, chives, or green onions to garnish

DIRECTIONS
1.   Place the potatoes in a large saucepan and cover with water. Bring to a boil and cook until potatoes are soft, about 8 - 10 minutes, drain and set aside. (Or you can place potatoes in a microwave-safe bowl, cover with plastic wrap, make a small slit in the wrap to vent, then nuke on high for 3 minutes).

2.   Rinse the saucepan then add the butter and melt over medium-high heat. Add the onions and sauté until soft and translucent, about 6 - 8 minutes. Add the garlic and sauté for 1 additional minute. Stir in the corn, coconut milk, chicken, salt and pepper and bring to a boil. Stir in the potatoes and return to a boil. Reduce heat and simmer for 2 minutes. Ladle into bowls and garnish with cilantro, chives, or green onions.

• CORN AND ROASTED RED PEPPER SOUP •

You must think I am crazy about corn. I am. In just about every incarnation. Frozen corn is available year round but there's nothing like fresh corn on the cob during the height of the summer. Of course, we here in Florida can enjoy fresh corn on the cob in the fall, winter and spring (I'm not gloating, just stating facts).

PREP: 5 minutes   COOK: 15 minutes

INGREDIENTS
    2 tablespoons olive oil
    1 medium onion, chopped (about 1 cup)
    1 clove garlic, minced or pressed
    5 cups frozen corn kernels, defrosted
    4 cups chicken or vegetable broth, divided
    1 (7-ounce) jar roasted red peppers, drained, patted dry, and chopped
    1/8 teaspoon ground nutmeg
    1/4 teaspoon hot sauce
    3/4 cup plain yogurt

DIRECTIONS
1.   Heat large saucepan over medium-high heat. Add oil and swirl to coat. Stir in onion and sauté until soft and translucent, about 6 - 8 minutes. Add garlic and sauté 1 additional minute.

2.   Add corn and 2 cups broth. Bring to a boil, reduce heat to medium-low and cover. Cook until corn is tender, about 6 - 8 minutes.

3.   Pour corn mixture into a blender or food processor and puree. Return to saucepan and add remaining broth and roasted peppers. Return to a boil over medium-high heat and cook for 1 minute. Season with nutmeg and hot sauce.

4.   Ladle into warm bowls and top with yogurt.

HOT SAUCE

Several of my recipes call for bottled hot sauce. For many of us, that means reaching for a bottle of Tabasco®, a popular and widely available product. But like many bottled products, people's personal tastes will determine what they will purchase. Some folks swear by locally made sauces with limited distribution (we brag about our datil pepper sauces in my neck of the woods). But since I'm trying to use nationally available products, here are my personal favorites:

Franks Hot Sauce® - This cayenne pepper-based sauce is the go-to sauce for hot wings. However, I use it in just about every recipe that calls for hot sauce.

Sriracha Hot Chili Sauce® - Chili-laced Sriracha (or Red Rooster Sauce) is a staple in Thai cuisine, but it's the new poster boy in many American kitchens due to raves received in magazines like *Cooks Illustrated*. This is a clean tasting hot sauce that, due to its thickness, clings well to anything it's brushed on.

Texas Pete Hot Sauce® - Although this great sauce originated in North Carolina, and not the Lone Star State, Texas Pete has wowed consumers since the 1940's.

• MEXICAN TORTILLA SOUP •

Believe it or not, this is actually quite a good dish for breakfast if you have any leftovers from the night before. You may want to fry some eggs and slide them onto each reheated bowl of soup.

PREP: 10 minutes   COOK: 20 minutes

INGREDIENTS
   1 tablespoon olive oil
   1 medium onion, chopped (about 1 cup)
   2 cloves garlic, minced or pressed
   1 teaspoon ground cumin
   4 cups chicken broth
   2 (14.5 ounce) cans Mexican stewed tomatoes
   1 tablespoon minced jalapeño pepper, remove ribs and seeds for less heat
   1/4 teaspoon freshly ground black pepper
   2 cups Monterey jack cheese
   1 (9-ounce) bag tortilla chips, coarsely crushed

DIRECTIONS
   1. Heat a large saucepan over medium-high heat. Add olive oil and swirl to coat. Stir in onion and sauté until soft and translucent, about 6 - 8 minutes. Add garlic and cumin and sauté for an additional 1 - 2 minutes.

   2. Add chicken broth, tomatoes, and jalapeño peppers. Bring to a boil, reduce heat to medium-low and cook uncovered for 10 minutes.

   3. Season with pepper then ladle into warm bowls. Sprinkle with cheese and tortilla chips.

• MEXICAN POSOLE SOUP •
(Tomatillo, Chicken and Hominy Soup)

This soup is a Northwestern Mexican tradition that can be served anytime of the year. You can make this using fresh tomatillos (simply husk about 1/2-pound and boil in a pot of water until tender, then puree with a cup of chopped onions and 2 garlic cloves in a blender until finely chopped), but we want to speed things up a bit so we'll use bottled salsa verde. If you use leftover chicken, you can have this delicious soup on the table in less than 15 minutes.

PREP: 5 minutes   COOK: 10 minutes

INGREDIENTS
    3 cups chicken broth
    1 (15.5-ounce) can white hominy
    3/4 cup prepared salsa verde (tomatillo salsa)
    2 cups chopped cooked chicken breasts or thighs
    1-1/2 teaspoons ground cumin
    1/4 cup chopped fresh cilantro
    Kosher salt and freshly ground black pepper, to taste
    Fresh lime wedges (optional)

DIRECTIONS

1.   Combine the broth, hominy, and salsa verde in a large sauce pan and bring to a boil over medium-high heat.

2.   Meanwhile, toss the chicken with the cumin in a small bowl until coated. Add the chicken to the broth mixture and reduce heat to medium-low. Simmer until chicken is hot, stirring occasionally. Remove pan from heat and stir in the cilantro. Season with salt and pepper to taste. Serve with fresh lime wedges to garnish.

• POBLANO PEPPER AND CORN SOUP •

While we're on the subject of delicious soup from south of the border, I need to share this spicy one with you. Poblano peppers are often categorized as a mild pepper. Don't believe it. To me, green bell peppers are mild. Poblanos on the other hand can range from medium to surprisingly hot. So I would suggest removing the ribs and seeds from the peppers before adding them to the dish. If the soup doesn't pack enough punch, add a few drops of hot sauce and when you make it the next time, leave the ribs intact.

PREP: Under 5 minutes   COOK: 10 minutes

INGREDIENTS
    1 tablespoon olive or canola oil
    1 medium onion, chopped (about 1 cup)
    4 poblano peppers, seeded and chopped
    3 cups frozen white or yellow corn, divided
    2 cups whole milk, divided
    3/4 teaspoon kosher salt
    1/2 cup shredded sharp cheddar cheese
    Hot sauce to taste

DIRECTIONS

1. Heat a 10-inch skillet over medium-high heat. Add oil and swirl to coat. Stir in onions and chilies and sauté until the onions are soft and translucent, about 6 - 8 minutes.

2. Meanwhile, place 1 cup corn and 1-1/2 cups milk in a Dutch oven. Bring to a boil over medium-heat.

3. Place remaining corn and milk in a blender and process until smooth. Add corn and milk puree to the Dutch oven. Stir in the chili/onion mixture and salt; reduce heat to medium and cook for 5 - 6 minutes. Ladle into warm bowls and top each serving with 2 tablespoons cheese and hot sauce.

• SPINACH AND POTATO SOUP •

I like soups like this one because you couldn't get it in a can even if you wanted to. You can use a 10-ounce box of frozen leaf spinach in a pinch, but since bagged baby spinach is available year-round in most supermarkets, I recommend using the fresh.

PREP: 5 minutes   COOK: 15 minutes

INGREDIENTS
   2 teaspoons olive oil
   I large onion, chopped (about 1-1/2 cups)
   3 cups chicken or vegetable broth
   1 cup diced red or Yukon gold potatoes
   1/2 teaspoon kosher salt
   1/4 teaspoon freshly ground black pepper
   1 (6-ounce) bag fresh baby spinach
   1/2 cup sour cream
   1 teaspoon lemon zest
   Additional sour cream to garnish

DIRECTIONS

1.   Heat a large saucepan or a Dutch oven over medium heat. Add olive oil and swirl to coat. Add onions and sauté until soft and translucent, about 8 - 10 minutes. Increase heat to high and add broth, potatoes, salt and pepper. Bring to a boil, then reduce heat to medium-low. Cover and simmer until the potatoes are tender, about 6 - 8 minutes. Stir in spinach and cook until spinach wilts, about 2 - 3 additional minutes.

2.   Pour half the soup and sour cream into a blender or food processor and puree until smooth. Return the soup to the saucepan and heat through. Serve in warm bowls and sprinkle each bowl with 1/4 teaspoon lemon zest. Spoon additional sour cream on top.

• HAM AND SWEET POTATO SOUP •

This traditional soup is usually served in late fall or winter and is a particularly popular way to use up whatever ham and sweet potatoes are left over from Thanksgiving or Christmas feasts. Some folks also prepare it using leftovers from their Easter feasts in the spring. To me, though, it is delicious any time of the year. If you don't have leftovers and don't have time to prepare the sweet potatoes from scratch, feel free to use canned sweet potatoes. Just simmer them until they are heated through in step 2 and proceed as directed. It will cut about 10 minutes off of your cooking time.

PREP: 5 minutes   COOK: 30 minutes

INGREDIENTS
   1 tablespoon olive or canola oil
   1 cup diced cooked ham
   1-1/2 cups sliced leek, white parts with some green
   3 cups peeled and diced sweet potatoes (about 2 medium)
   3 cups chicken broth
   2/3 cup half & half (or evaporated milk)
   1/4 teaspoon fresh cracked pepper
   Sliced green onions to garnish (optional)

DIRECTIONS
   1. Heat a Dutch oven over medium heat. Add oil and swirl to coat. Add diced ham and sauté until lightly brown, about 3 - 4 minutes. Remove ham with a slotted spoon and set aside.

   2. Add leeks and sauté until tender, about 5 minutes. Add sweet potatoes, chicken broth, half & half, and pepper. Bring to a boil then reduce heat to medium-low. Cover and simmer until potatoes are tender, about 15 minutes.

   3. Pour half the potato soup into a blender or food processor and puree until smooth. Pour into a bowl. Pour the other half of the soup into the blender and puree until smooth. Return pureed soup to the Dutch oven and stir in ham. Cook until heated through. Serve in warm bowls with sliced green onions to garnish.

• CHARLESTON SHE CRAB SOUP •

My friend Michael manages one of the top private clubs in Northeast Florida. One of the most popular items on their menu is Charleston She Crap Soup. They must make gallons of it each day. But the folks from Charleston who visit whisper that, although the soup is delicious, it really does not completely measure up to the real thing. I'm thinking it's because authentic Charleston She Crab soup contains crab roe (hence the name She Crab Soup) and crab roe is not readily available in these parts. It's probably not available where you live either. So I'm offering up a version, which is close to what Michael's establishment serves. If you have access to crab roe, by all means use it!

COOK: 10 minutes   COOK: 25 minutes

INGREDIENTS

3 tablespoons unsalted butter
1 small onion, chopped
  (about 1/2 cup)
3 tablespoons all-purpose flour
3 cups milk
1 cup heavy cream
2 cups lump crab meat
3 tablespoons crab roe,
  if available, divided
1 teaspoon lemon zest

1/2 teaspoon Worcestershire sauce
1/2 teaspoon kosher salt
1/8 teaspoon ground nutmeg
1/8 teaspoon freshly ground
  black pepper
1/8 teaspoon cayenne pepper
3 tablespoons sherry
1 tablespoon chopped chives,
  (optional)

DIRECTIONS

1. Heat a large saucepan over medium heat. Add butter and swirl to coat. Stir in onion and sauté until soft and translucent, about 8 - 10 minutes.

2. Add flour and cook, stirring for 2 - 3 minutes. Turn heat to high and slowly whisk in milk and cream. Bring to a boil and cook, stirring until thickened, about 2 - 3 minutes.

3. Reduce heat to medium-low and add crab meat, 2 tablespoons roe, lemon zest, Worcestershire sauce, salt, nutmeg, pepper and cayenne. Cook uncovered, stirring occasionally, for 10 minutes.

4. Stir in sherry and ladle into warm bowls. Sprinkle with chopped chives and remaining crab roe if using.

• BOSTON FISH CHOWDER •

It seems that every coastal city in America (and the world, for that matter) serves up a fish chowder that it calls its own. And I've loved every one that I've ever tasted. Some use only one variety of locally caught fish and some use a variety of local fish. Some use potatoes and some don't. Some add tomatoes. Some throw in some shellfish. Here I'm offering this version that's popular in Boston. In the next recipe, I'll offer another equally delicious, but lesser-known, version from Southeast Florida.

PREP: 10 minutes   COOK: 30 minutes

INGREDIENTS
    2 teaspoons olive oil
    3 slices bacon, chopped
    1 medium onion, chopped (about 1 cup)
    1 teaspoon thyme
    2 medium red or Yukon gold potatoes, peeled and diced
    1 cup bottled clam juice
    2 cups fish or chicken broth
    2 cups half and half
    1 pound firm white fish (cod, haddock, monkfish) cut into 1-inch pieces
    Kosher salt and freshly ground black pepper, to taste

DIRECTIONS

1. Heat a large saucepan over medium heat. Add olive oil and swirl to coat. Stir in bacon and sauté until brown and barely crisp, about 5 minutes. Remove bacon with a slotted spoon and drain on paper towels.

2   Raise heat to medium-high and add onions to saucepan. Sauté until soft and translucent, about 6 - 8 minutes. Add thyme and potatoes and sauté for 5 minutes. Stir in clam juice and broth and bring to a boil. Reduce heat to medium and cook until potatoes are just tender, about 10 minutes.

3. Add half and half and bring to a simmer. Lower heat to medium and add fish. Cook until fish is opaque, about 2 - 3 minutes. Season with salt and pepper.

4. Ladle into warm bowls and sprinkle with reserved bacon.

• BISCAYNE BAY YACHT CLUB FISH CHOWDER •

The storied origins of this famous chowder grows out of one Charlie Frow, keeper of the Florida Cape lighthouse in Southeast Florida in the 1870's. Old Charlie took on the job of "handyman" at the newly opened Biscayne Bay Yacht Club, evidently a better situation with a man with a family. Since food wasn't served at the club at the time, someone asked Charlie to prepare a chowder for the first Washington's Birthday Regatta in 1887. He evidently got a recipe from his friend Charlie Peacock at the nearby Peacock Inn. Mr. Peacock, most likely, was inspired by seafood chowders popular in the Bahamas. Chowder like this is served to this day at the annual regatta.

PREP: 10 minutes   COOK: 35 minutes

INGREDIENTS
  1/4 pound salt pork, skin removed, diced
  1 large onion, chopped (about 1-1/2 cups)
  2 tablespoons diced red or green pepper
  1 cup diced fresh or canned tomatoes
  2 cups shrimp, chicken or vegetable broth
  1 teaspoon kosher salt
  1 small bay leaf, crumbled
  Pinch dried thyme
  Pinch mace
  Dash hot pepper sauce
  2 large red potatoes (about 3/4 pound) peeled and cubed
  1-3/4 pounds grouper (or other firm white fish like cod,
    halibut, or snapper), cubed
  1-1/2 cups whole milk
  2 teaspoons unsalted butter
  1 cup heavy cream

DIRECTIONS
  1. Heat a Dutch oven or large saucepan over medium-high heat. Add the salt pork and sauté until crisp, about 5 minutes. Stir in the onions and peppers and sauté until the onions are soft and translucent, about 6 - 8 minutes. Stir in the tomatoes and sauté for 1 additional minute.

2. Add the broth, salt, bay leaf, thyme, mace, and hot pepper sauce. Bring to a boil and add the potatoes. Cover and reduce heat to medium-low. Cook until the potatoes are cooked but still firm, about 12 - 15 minutes.

3. Lay fish on top of the potatoes and broth. Cover and simmer until fish is opaque and flakes easily with a fork, about 10 minutes.

4. Add the milk and butter and simmer (do not boil) to heat through. Stir in cream and cook until heated though.

Serve in warm bowls with oyster crackers to garnish.

Table For Two Tips

BUTTER BASICS

I'm so glad that we're returning to real butter after a few decades of margarine and a host of 'almost as good as butter' in sticks and tubs. Why? Because nothing tastes like a pat of good, sweet butter. Besides, research shows that margarine may be more detrimental to our health than real butter. And when used in moderation, butter will add not only flavor, but texture and nuance to any dish. Welcome home butter!

My Three Butter Rules:

1. Use unsalted butter. Why? Because we're all trying to cut down on our sodium intake and the amount of salt added to butter can vary from brand to brand and salted butter almost always contains more water than unsalted. And the primary reason manufactures add salt to butter is to extend its shelf life. So buy unsalted. It's fresher and will taste better. Besides, you can always add salt if needed as you cook.

2. Don't store butter in that convenient butter compartment in the fridge door. Instead, store it in the back of the fridge where it's the coldest. Your butter will keep for 2 to 3 weeks. If you need to keep it longer, pop it in the freezer. Oh, and regardless of where you store it, keep it tightly wrapped. Butter is notoriously known to absorb all kinds of flavors in your fridge because of its high-fat content.

3. Save your money when cooking with butter and purchase Land O' Lakes or Cabot Creamery unsalted butter. For a delicious pat on a warm bun or piece of good toast, go ahead and spring for Lurpack or Kerrygold.

• CREAMY ROASTED RED PEPPER SOUP •

This soup from Southern France is often served during the hot air balloon festivals that are held in the fall. You can prepare this by roasting your own red peppers, but I usually opt for jarred roasted red peppers to expedite things. If you go with the vegetable broth, this makes for a wonderful vegetarian meal. If you forgo the cream cheese as well, your vegan friends will adore you.

PREP: 5 minutes   COOK: 15 minutes

INGREDIENTS
   1 tablespoon olive oil
   I medium onion, chopped (about 1 cup)
   2 cups jarred roasted red peppers
   1 cup vegetable or chicken broth
   1/4 teaspoon freshly ground black pepper
   1 (15-ounce) can cannilloni beans, drained
   1/2 cup light cream cheese (about 4 ounces)
   1 tablespoon chopped chives to garnish

DIRECTIONS

1. Heat a small skillet over medium-high heat. Add oil and swirl to coat. Stir in onions and sauté until soft and translucent, about 6 - 8 minutes.

2. Place onions, red peppers, broth, pepper and beans into a blender or food processor and blend until smooth.

3. Pour the pepper-broth mixture into a medium saucepan over medium-high heat and bring to a simmer, stirring occasionally. Add cream cheese and stir until melted and smooth. Garnish with chives and additional pepper to taste.

Salads

Salads

I sure took a lot of heat for only including a handful of salad recipes in *Table for Two - The Cookbook for Couples*. Looking back, I see it was sort of ridiculous. But I thought with the plethora of pre-packaged salads in most produce departments along with shelves and shelves of salad dressings, most people would go for that option.

Boy was I wrong.

So many folks wrote and told me how much they enjoyed the Strawberry and Spinach salad they wondered why I didn't include more like it.

I hope the recipes I've included here will make up for it. I've even included some recipes for popular salad dressings, should you choose to make them from scratch at home.

And by the way, there's nothing wrong with opening a bag of organic spring mix greens and drizzling a good bottled salad dressing over it them when you're in a time crunch. I do it all the time.

However, if you have some time on your hands waiting for a meat to marinate or if you are baking something that will take some time, creating your own salad from scratch is a great way to use that time.

• SPINACH SALAD WITH STRAWBERRIES •
AND BUTTERMILK DRESSING

As I mentioned in the salad introduction, I included a recipe for a strawberry and spinach salad in my previous book. It recieved a lot of compliments and has since become a staple of my personal chef business. So I decided to try spinach and strawberries with a different dressing. It's a keeper. I think you'll agree. Feel free to use a good buttermilk dressing from the grocery store, but I've also included a recipe for homemade.

PREP: 15 minutes

INGREDIENTS
    2 cups fresh baby spinach
    1-1/2 cups hulled and quartered strawberries
    6 fresh mint leaves, chopped
    3 tablespoons sliced almonds
    Buttermilk dressing

DIRECTIONS
Divide spinach between two salad plates. Add strawberries and sprinkle with mint leaves. Drizzle buttermilk dressing over all to taste and garnish with almonds.

BUTTERMILK DRESSING
INGREDIENTS
    1 cup buttermilk
    1 cup mayonnaise
    3 tablespoons fresh lemon juice
    3 tablespoons sugar
    1/4 cup minced fresh parsley
    1/4 teaspoon garlic powder
    1/4 teaspoon onion powder
    1/2 teaspoon kosher salt
    1/2 teaspoon freshly ground black pepper
    Pinch cayenne pepper, or to taste
    6 scallions, chopped (both green and white parts)

DIRECTIONS
        Combine all ingredients in a small bowl and whisk until smooth.

• HONEYDEW MELON WITH PROSCIUTTO SALAD •

I like the contrast in color between the green honeydew melon and the pink prosciutto, but feel free to use cantaloupe or any ripe melon that's available. And don't feel you have to serve this as a salad; if you omit the greens and dressing and chop the melon into 1-inch squares then wrap each square with a bit of prosciutto and secure with a toothpick, you'll have a wonderful, no-cook appetizer or dessert.

PREP: 15 minutes

INGREDIENTS
　　4 slices prosciutto
　　2 wedges honeydew melon, peeled (about 1/4 of the melon)
　　2 cups mixed salad greens
　　Balsamic vinaigrette

DIRECTIONS

1.　In a medium bowl, toss greens with salad dressing to taste and divide between two salad plates.

2.　Wrap two pieces of prosciutto around each melon wedge and place on the bed of greens. Drizzle with additional dressing.

SIMPLE BALSAMIC VINAIGRETTE
INGREDIENTS
　　1/4 cup balsamic vinegar
　　2 teaspoons dark brown sugar (you may not need this if you use very good quality balsamic vinegar)
　　1 tablespoon chopped garlic
　　1/2 teaspoon kosher salt
　　1/2 teaspoon freshly ground black pepper
　　3/4 cup extra virgin olive oil

DIRECTIONS
In a small bowl, whisk the vinegar with the sugar (if using), garlic, salt and pepper until sugar and salt dissolves. Slowly add the oil, whisking constantly. (Or you can put all the ingredients in a screw-top jar or cruet and shake to combine.) Taste and adjust the seasonings.

• SPINACH SALAD WITH PEARS, CHEDDAR CHEESE, • AND APPLESAUCE DRESSING

PREP: 15 minutes   COOK: 2 minutes

INGREDIENTS
- 4 cups baby spinach
- 1 ripe pear, peeled, cored and diced
- 2 tablespoons diced red bell pepper
- 2 tablespoons chopped pecans, toasted
- 1 cup applesauce
- 1 cup cottage cheese
- 1/2 cup shredded medium cheddar cheese

DIRECTIONS

1. In a medium bowl, toss the spinach, pears, and bell peppers and divide into two salad bowls or plates.

2. In a small skillet, sauté pecans over medium-high heat until lightly toasted, about 2 - 3 minutes.

3. Meanwhile, warm applesauce in small saucepan or a microwave oven for 1 minute.

4. Pour applesauce over salad and add a scoop of cottage cheese to each. Sprinkle with cheddar cheese and pecans, and serve.

• ARUGULA SALAD AND GRAPEFRUIT •

PREP: 15 minutes

INGREDIENTS
    3 cups baby arugula
    1/2 large pink grapefruit, peeled, sectioned and chopped
    1/2 avocado, peeled, pitted, and diced
    1 tablespoon chopped fresh cilantro
    Honey Lemon Dressing

DIRECTIONS
Combine ingredients in a medium bowl and toss. Divide between 2 plates
and serve.

HONEY LEMON DRESSING
INGREDIENTS
    6 tablespoons extra virgin olive oil
    3 tablespoons fresh lemon juice (about 2 lemons)
    1-1/2 teaspoons lemon zest
    1-1/2 tablespoons honey
    1/2 teaspoon thyme
    Kosher salt and black pepper to taste

DIRECTIONS
Combine ingredients in a medium bowl and whisk until well-mixed.

• ICEBERG WEDGES WITH BLUE CHEESE DRESSING •

PREP: 10 minutes   COOK: 10 minutes

INGREDIENTS
    2 slices bacon
    1/2 head iceberg lettuce cut into 2 wedges
    1/2 pint cherry or grape tomatoes
    1/2 green or yellow bell pepper, cored, seeded and cut into thin strips
    Blue cheese dressing
    1 scallion sliced

DIRECTIONS

1. Heat a small skillet over medium-high heat and sauté bacon until brown and crisp, about 8 - 10 minutes. Remove bacon to paper towels and pat dry. Crumble and reserve.

2. Place a wedge of lettuce on a salad plate and scatter the tomatoes and pepper slices around the wedges.

3. Ladle 1/2 cup of dressing over each wedge and sprinkle with bacon and scallions.

BLUE CHEESE DRESSING
PREP: 5 minutes

INGREDIENTS
    3 cups crumbled blue cheese
    2 cups mayonnaise
    2 cups buttermilk
    9 tablespoons lemon juice (about 3 lemons)
    Kosher salt and black pepper to taste

DIRECTIONS
Combine ingredients in a medium bowl and whisk until well-mixed. Or combine ingredients in a food processor and mix until smooth, about 30 seconds.

• CRANBERRY AND SPINACH SALAD •

PREP: 10 minutes

INGREDIENTS
   1 teaspoon butter
   3 tablespoons almonds, blanched and slivered
   1-1/2 teaspoons toasted sesame seeds
   3/4 teaspoon black poppy seeds
   2 tablespoons white sugar
   1/2 teaspoon minced onion
   1/8 teaspoon paprika
   1 tablespoon white wine vinegar
   1 tablespoon cider vinegar
   2 tablespoons extra-virgin oil
   2 cups baby spinach, rinsed and torn into bite-size pieces
   1/4 cup dried cranberries

DIRECTIONS
1. Heat a small skillet over medium heat. Add butter and melt. Add almonds and sauté until lightly toasted. Remove from heat, and let cool.

2. In a medium bowl, whisk together the sesame seeds, poppy seeds, sugar, onion, paprika, white wine vinegar, cider vinegar, and olive oil.

3. Add the spinach, toasted almonds and cranberries and toss.

• SHRIMP LOUIS •

The origin of this famous salad (and its cousin, Crab Louis) is shrouded in mystery. Some folks claim it was created around the turn of the last century at the St. Francis Hotel in San Francisco. Others are certain it originated in the kitchen of the Olympic Club in Seattle. But there's one thing almost everyone is unanimous about: Who the heck is Louis? (Although the locals in Spokane insist it was created by Llewellyn "Llewellyn "Louis" Davenport at the renowned Davenport Restaurant).

PREP: 5 minutes   COOK: 10 minutes

INGREDIENTS
    1 egg
    1/2 cup mayonnaise
    1 tablespoon heavy cream
    1 tablespoon chili sauce
    1/4 teaspoon Worcestershire sauce
    1/8 teaspoon hot sauce
    1 tablespoon minced onion
    4 teaspoons fresh lemon juice
    3/4 cup shredded lettuce
    1/2 pound cooked medium shrimp, shelled and deveined
    1 fresh ripe tomato, quartered or 8 cherry tomatoes
    2 tablespoons chopped fresh chives

DIRECTIONS
1. Place egg in a small sauce pan and cover with water. Bring to a boil over high heat and remove from heat. Let egg rest for 10 minutes. Shell and slice the egg.

2. Meanwhile, in a small bowl, combine the mayonnaise, cream, chili sauce, Worcestershire, hot sauce, onion, and lemon juice.

3. Arrange lettuce on two salad plates and arrange half the shrimp on each plate. Spoon sauce over shrimp and arrange egg slices around the shrimp. Place tomatoes on each plate. Garnish each plate with chives.

• FRESH TOMATO AND FETA CHEESE SALAD •

When fresh, plump tomatoes are available at your local farmer's market, there's no better, or simpler, salad to make than this one.

PREP: 10 minutes

INGREDIENTS
  2 ripe tomatoes, sliced
  1/2 small Vidalia or other sweet onion, sliced
  1/2 cup crumbled feta cheese
  1/4 cup sliced green olives with pimentos
  2 tablespoons extra virgin olive oil
  1 tablespoon balsamic vinegar
  1 tablespoon chopped fresh parsley
  2 fresh basil leaves, slivered
  1/8 teaspoon kosher salt
  Pinch of freshly ground black pepper, or to taste

DIRECTIONS
  1.   Arrange tomato and onion slices on a small, deep serving platter. Sprinkle slices with crumbled cheese and olive slices.

  2.   In a small bowl, whisk together the olive oil, vinegar, parsley, basil, salt, and pepper. Drizzle oil mixture over tomato slices and serve.

• CHERRY TOMATOES AND PINE NUTS •

PREP: 5 minutes   COOK: 5 minutes
SET: 1 hour

INGREDIENTS
  14 cherry tomatoes, halved
  1/3 cup pitted and sliced green olives
  1/2 cup sliced black olives
  1 green onion, minced
  1/4 cup pine nuts
  3 tablespoons extra-virgin olive oil
  2 teaspoons balsamic vinegar
  1 teaspoon white sugar
  1/4 teaspoon dried oregano
  Kosher salt and freshly ground black pepper, to taste

DIRECTIONS

1. In a medium bowl, combine cherry tomatoes, green olives, black olives, and green onion.

2. Heat a small skillet over medium heat. Add pine nuts and sauté until golden brown, turning frequently. Stir into tomato mixture.

3. In a small bowl, mix together olive oil, balsamic vinegar, sugar, and oregano. Season to taste with salt and pepper. Pour over salad, and gently toss to coat. Chill for 1 hour.

• BROCCOLI, TANGERINE, AND OLIVE SALAD •

This delightful salad can be prepared in less than 10 minutes, but the results are stunning. If you don't have tangerines, feel free to use a small orange (or even canned mandarin oranges). It's important, though, that you use Kalamata olives; California black olives lack the rich, nutty taste of their Greek cousins.

PREP: 5 minutes   COOK: 5 minutes

INGREDIENTS
   1/2 pound broccoli florets (about 3 cups)
   2 tablespoons chopped Kalamata olives
   1 tangerine, peeled and segmented, plus 1-1/2 teaspoons finely grated zest
   1 tablespoon extra virgin olive oil
   1/4 teaspoon kosher salt
   1/8 teaspoon freshly ground black pepper

DIRECTIONS
   1.   Steam broccoli until crisp tender, about 5 - 7 minutes. Remove and rinse with cold water to cool. Set on a plate lined with paper towels to drain.

   2.   In a medium bowl, toss the broccoli with the olives, tangerine segments and zest, oil, salt, and pepper.

Chilis and Stews

CHILIS AND STEWS

I originally thought about including these in the soup chapter and calling it Soups, Stews and Chilis. Then I thought that you might want to consider a soup as one course of a multi-course dinner. In that case, chilis and stews would not do. So I decided to give them their own chapter.

Some of these may already be familiar to you, others may be brand new. I hope you'll try them all and will tweak them as you see fit. All of these recipes should feed 4, which is good, because like soup, most chilis and stews taste better the next day.

A good stew requires little more than warm crusty bread and a glass of wine or beer and, during the fall or winter, it's really hard to beat. Especially if you have a fire going in the fireplace.

If you are looking for vegetarian chilis or stews, you'll find several wonderful recipes in the Vegetarian chapter.

• SIMPLE BEEF AND BEAN CHILI •

Chili purists will be quick to let you know that there aren't any beans in real chili. Whenever one accosts me while I'm dishing this out I just smile and say, "You are probably correct." Then I add, "Now hand me your bowl, I think you're gonna like this."

PREP: 5 minutes   COOK: 25 minutes

INGREDIENTS
    2 tablespoons olive or canola oil
    1 large onion, chopped (about 1-1/2 cups)
    3 tablespoons chili powder
    4 garlic cloves, minced or pressed
    2 teaspoons ground cumin
    1/2 teaspoon oregano
    1-1/2 pounds lean ground beef
    2 (14.5-ounce) cans diced tomatoes
    2 (15-ounce) cans red kidney beans, drained and rinsed
    Kosher salt and freshly ground black pepper, to taste
    2 cups shredded cheddar cheese

DIRECTIONS
    1.   Heat a Dutch oven over medium-high heat. Add olive oil and swirl to coat. Stir in onions and sauté until they are soft and translucent, about 6 - 8 minutes. Add chili powder, garlic, cumin and oregano and sauté until fragrant, about 30 seconds.

    2.   Stir in beef and cook, breaking up chunks with a spoon until no longer pink, about 5 minutes. Add tomatoes and beans and cook until thickened, about 15 minutes. Season with salt and pepper. Sprinkle with cheese and serve.

• WHITE BEAN CHICKEN CHILI •

This recipe will sneak up on your taste buds. Because it's white and not the traditional red, folks assume it will be mild. Trust me it isn't. I usually use more cayenne pepper when I make this, but I want you to try it the way it is first. You can always add more pepper.

PREP: 10 minutes   COOK: 20 minutes

INGREDIENTS
- 1 tablespoon olive or canola oil
- 1 medium onion, chopped (about 1 cup)
- 3 cloves garlic, minced or pressed
- 1 (4-ounce) can diced jalapeño peppers (or 3 fresh jalapeño peppers chopped)
- 1 (4-ounce) can chopped green chili peppers
- 2 teaspoons ground cumin
- 1 teaspoon ground coriander
- 1 teaspoon oregano
- 1/2 teaspoon cayenne pepper, or more to taste
- 3-1/2 cups chicken broth
- 3 cups chopped cooked chicken breasts or thighs
- 3 (15-ounce) cans great northern beans
- 1 cup shredded Monterey Jack cheese
- Sour cream and chopped fresh cilantro to garnish (optional)

DIRECTIONS

1. Heat a Dutch oven over medium-low heat. Add oil and swirl to coat. Stir in the onion and sauté until tender and translucent, about 8 - 10 minutes. Stir in garlic and sauté 1 additional minute. Stir in the jalapeños, green chili peppers, cumin, coriander, oregano and cayenne. Continue to sauté until peppers are tender, about 3 minutes.

2. Stir in the chicken broth, chicken and white beans. Simmer until heated through, about 10 - 15 minutes.

3. Remove the mixture from heat. Slowly stir in the cheese until melted. Serve warm with a dollop of sour cream and a sprinkle of cilantro if desired.

• MOLE CHILI •

I love it when I can whip up a pot of chili in around 20 minutes. That's why this is perfect for weeknights. You can adjust the heat of this traditional Mexican chili by reducing or adding chili powder. This recipe also works well with diced lean beef, it will increase your prep time a little, but some folks prefer diced beef over ground beef. Try it both ways to see which you prefer.

PREP: Less than 5 minutes   COOK: 20 minutes

INGREDIENTS
1 pound ground round or other lean beef (1 pound diced
   lean beef can be used as well)
1 tablespoon olive oil
1 medium onion, chopped (about 1 cup)
1 clove garlic, minced or pressed
1 (14.5-ounce) can diced tomatoes, undrained
1 cup water or beef broth
2 tablespoons chili powder
1 ounce semi-sweet chocolate, coarsely chopped
1 teaspoon ground cumin
1 teaspoon kosher salt
1/2 teaspoon oregano
Sour cream and fresh chopped cilantro to garnish (optional)

DIRECTIONS

1. Heat a 10-inch skillet over medium-high heat. Add olive oil and swirl to coat. Add beef and cook, stirring often, until brown, about 5 minutes. Drain fat from skillet.

2. Stir in onion sauté until tender, about 5 minutes. Add the garlic and sauté 1 additional minute. Stir in the tomatoes, water or broth, chili powder, chocolate, cumin, salt and oregano. Reduce heat to medium. Cover and simmer until heated through, about 10 minutes. Serve in warm bowls with a dollop of sour cream and a sprinkle of cilantro if desired.

• LAMB STEW WITH WHITE BEANS •

When most of us think of lamb stew, we immediately think of Irish Stew. And for good reason, there's nothing like a piping hot bowl and a glass of Guinness on a cold winter's night. I included a wonderful recipe in my first book, but I would be remiss if I didn't share how other cuisines combine lamb, vegetables and spices to create equally delicious lamb dishes. Here are two of them.

PREP: 10 minutes   COOK: 2 hours

INGREDIENTS
2 pounds lamb shoulder, bone-in and cut into 3-inch pieces
   (your butcher will do this for you)
2/3 cup all-purpose flour
5 tablespoons olive oil, divided
1 large onion, sliced thin (about 1-1/2 cups)
3/4 teaspoon dried sage
Kosher salt and freshly ground black pepper, to taste
3/4 cup dry white wine
1-1/2 teaspoons tomato paste
3/4 cup beef broth
3 cups canned cannellini beans, rinsed and drained
3 cloves garlic, minced or pressed
2 tablespoons chopped fresh Italian parsley

DIRECTIONS
1.   Preheat oven to 350°. Dredge lamb in flour until coated. Shake off excess.

3.   Heat a Dutch oven over medium-high heat. Add two tablespoons olive oil and swirl to coat. Add lamb and sauté until brown on all sides, about 5 minutes. You may want to do this in batches so they don't steam. Remove lamb with a slotted spoon to a plate.

4.   Add the remaining olive oil to the pot. Stir in the onions and sage and sauté until the onions are soft, about 6 - 8 minutes. Return the meat to the pot and season with salt and pepper. Add the wine and bring to a boil and cook until the wine has nearly evaporated, about 10 minutes.

5.   Dissolve the tomato paste in the beef broth and stir into the pot. Place the Dutch oven in the oven, and cook, stirring occasionally, until meat is tender, about 1-1/2 hours. Stir in the beans and cook for another 15 minutes (add more broth if the stew is too dry). Stir in the garlic and parsley and serve with lots of crusty warm bread.

• LAMB TAGINE •

Lamb Tagine is a traditional Moroccan stew that's slow-cooked and served in an earthenware pot called, well, a tagine. This pot features a shallow base and conical-shaped lid that keeps the food moist while cooking and can be used in the oven. I don't have a tagine in my cupboard and you probably don't either. So we're going to use our trusty Dutch oven. However, tangines are available for under $25 at most pier-something type of stores.

PREP: 10 minutes   COOK: 1 hour, 10 minutes

INGREDIENTS
- 1 pound boneless leg of lamb, trimmed of fat and cut into 1/2-inch cubes
- 1 tablespoon olive oil
- 1/2 teaspoon kosher salt, divided
- 1 large onion, chopped (about 1-1/2 cups)
- 1 teaspoon ground cumin
- 1/2 teaspoon ground cinnamon
- 1/2 teaspoon cayenne pepper, or to taste
- 6 cloves garlic, chopped
- 2 tablespoons honey
- 1 tablespoon tomato paste
- 1/2 cup dried apricots, quartered
- 1-3/4 cups beef broth

DIRECTIONS

1. Heat a medium Dutch oven over medium-high heat. Add olive oil and swirl to coat. Sprinkle lamb with 1/4 teaspoon salt and toss. Add lamb to pan and sauté until lightly brown on all sides, about 5 minutes. Remove lamb from the pan and set aside.

2. Add onions to the pan and sauté until soft, about 6 - 8 minutes. Add remaining salt, cumin, cinnamon, cayenne pepper and garlic. Sauté for 1 additional minute. Stir in honey and tomato paste and sauté 30 seconds.

3. Return lamb to the pan and stir in the apricots and broth. Bring to boil then reduce heat to medium-low. Cover and simmer, stirring occasionally, until lamb is fork-tender, about 1 hour. Serve over Steamed White Rice or Couscous.

• BEER BRAISED CHICKEN STEW •

Like many stews, this seems to have too many ingredients to be bothered with, but trust me, they all come together to make a wonderfully fragrant and delicious entrée. Use a good lager for this; it'll add depth.

PREP: 10 minutes   COOK: 1 hour, 20 minutes

INGREDIENTS
   1/3 cup all-purpose flour
   1 teaspoon kosher salt
   1/2 teaspoon freshly ground black pepper
   1/2 teaspoon Hungarian sweet paprika
   4 chicken legs and 4 chicken thighs, bone in
   1/3 cup olive or vegetable oil
   1 clove garlic, peeled
   1 medium onion, chopped
   1 medium green bell pepper, seeded and chopped
   2 celery stalks, chopped
   2 (14.5 - ounce) cans diced tomatoes
   1 (12-ounce) can of beer
   3 tablespoons tomato paste
   1/2 teaspoon dried thyme
   1/2 teaspoon dried marjoram
   1 bay leaf

DIRECTIONS
   1.   Preheat oven to 350° (175° C).

   2.   Combine flour, salt, pepper, and paprika in a paper or plastic bag. Add chicken pieces one at a time and shake to coat well. Shake off excess and set aside.

   3.   In a Dutch oven, heat the oil over medium heat. Add the clove of garlic and chicken. Cook, turning, until chicken pieces are brown, about 10 minutes. Remove chicken to a plate.

   4.   Add onions, peppers, and celery. Sauté until the onions are soft and translucent, about 8 - 10 minutes. Return chicken to pot and toss with vegetables.

   5.   In a large bowl, combine the tomatoes, beer, tomato paste, thyme, marjoram, and bay leaf. Pour over chicken and bake, covered, for 1 hour until chicken is tender. Serve over Steamed White Rice.

• WEEKNIGHT BEEF STEW •

Most of us will wait for the weekend to create a great beef burgundy stew because it is so time-consuming. But what if we have a hankering for stew on a Tuesday night? This stew will more than rise to the challenge.

PREP: 10 minutes   COOK: 30 minutes

INGREDIENTS

8 ounces baby Portobello or white mushrooms, quartered
2 tablespoons olive oil
1-1/2 pounds boneless top sirloin steak, cut into 1-inch cubes
Kosher salt to taste
2 medium carrots, cut into 1/4 inch thick slices
1 medium onion, cut lengthwise into thin wedges
2 garlic cloves, sliced thin
1/2 cup dry white, red wine or beef broth
1 (16-ounce) can Great Northern or cannellini beans, rinsed and drained
1 (14.5-ounce) can diced tomatoes, undrained
Chopped fresh parsley for garnish

DIRECTIONS

1. Heat a 10-inch skillet over high heat. Add the mushrooms and cook, shaking the pan from time to time to prevent the mushrooms from sticking. Sauté them until they being to release their moisture and begin to brown, about 5 minutes. Remove to a bowl and set aside.

2. Add olive oil to the skillet and turn the heat down to medium-high. Add the beef in 1 or 2 batches and brown each batch on all sides, about 5 minutes per batch. As you finish cooking each batch, remove the meat from skillet, add to the bowl with the mushrooms, and sprinkle salt over them.

3. Add the carrots to the skillet and sauté 3 - 4 minutes. Add the onions and sauté another 5 minutes. Add the garlic sauté 1 additional minute. Stir in the wine or broth and bring to a boil. Return the beef and mushrooms to the pan. Continue cooking 3 more minutes.

4. Stir in the beans and tomatoes and cook 5 minutes more. Serve, garnished with chopped parsley.

• MEDITERRANEAN CLAM STEW •

Every stew need not feature beef, lamb or chicken. Here's a Mediterranean stew featuring clams that will be sure to satisfy the seafood lover in you. And look at all the veggies! This has to be one of the healthiest stews on the planet. For a vegetarian/vegan version, just omit the clams.

PREP: 10 minutes   COOK: 30 minutes

INGREDIENTS
  2 tablespoons olive oil
  2 large onions, chopped (about 3 cups)
  4 cloves garlic, minced or pressed
  1 red bell pepper, seeded and chopped
  1 green pepper, seeded and chopped
  1-1/2 cups asparagus cut into 1-inch pieces
  1 cup dry red wine
  2 yellow squash or zucchini, diced (about 2 - 2-1/2 cups)
  1 (14.5-ounce) can diced tomatoes, undrained
  1/3 cup chopped fresh basil
  1 teaspoon dried oregano
  1 (16-ounce) can cannellini beans, rinsed and drained
  1 teaspoon kosher salt
  1/4 teaspoon freshly ground black pepper
  2 (6-ounce) cans chopped clams, undrained

DIRECTIONS
  1. Heat a Dutch oven over medium heat. Add the olive oil and swirl to coat. Add the onions and sauté until soft and translucent, about 8 - 10 minutes. Stir in the garlic and sauté for 1 additional minute. Stir in the peppers, asparagus and wine. Simmer until vegetables are crisp tender, about 5 minutes.

  2. Stir in the squash, tomatoes, basil, oregano, beans, salt and pepper. Cover and simmer for 10 - 12 minutes. Stir in the clams and simmer until heated through, about 3 more minutes.

Sandwiches

 Sandwiches

I didn't have any sandwiches in my first book. What was I thinking? Sandwiches have served households and armies since the legendary Earl of Sandwich leant his name to the gloriously simple concoction of meat, veggies, cheese and condiments nestled between two slices of bread.

Now, I'm not going to go into the legend of how the sandwich came into existence. Several cultures claim credit for it. Bottom line? Whichever culture was responsible, they'll surely bask in the glory and praises of generation after generation who've savored this simple meal.

As I've traveled the country I've had the pleasure of munching on sandwiches that make use of regional ingredients while reflecting the tastes of each respective location. Here's a handful of some regional classics.

If I've left out the sandwiches that reflect and define your neighborhood or city, I offer profuse apologies. E-mail me your favorites and I'll do my best to include them in the next Table for Two cookbook.

These recipes are good all by their lonesome for a mouth-watering lunch. To make them a quick dinner, just add a cup of soup and a fruity dessert.

• TOMATO, BASIL AND MOZZARELLA SANDWICH •
(Boston, Massachusetts)

You can serve this North End staple either as a traditional sandwich or as an open-faced sandwich. It's important you use a good mozzarella cheese because it will shine in this dish.

PREP: 10 minutes

INGREDIENTS
    1/2 loaf Parmesan focaccia or Italian ciabatta bread
    4 fresh basil leaves, chopped
    1 tomato, sliced
    2 ounces fresh mozzarella cheese, sliced
    1/4 cup balsamic vinegar
    2 tablespoons extra virgin olive oil
    1/8 teaspoon red pepper flakes

DIRECTIONS
Slice the loaf of bread in half lengthwise. Layer the basil, tomato slices, and mozzarella cheese between the two halves of bread. Cut into two sandwiches. In a small dish, stir together the balsamic vinegar, olive oil and red pepper flakes. Use as a dipping sauce.

• PROSCIUTTO, MOZZARELLA AND •
OLIVE FOCACCIA SANDWICH
(San Francisco, California)

Here's another wonderful Italian sandwich that you can make with the half loaf of bread you have leftover from the recipe above. Waste not, want not.

PREP: 10 minutes   SET: 2+ hours

INGREDIENTS
  1 medium plum tomato, sliced
  2 tablespoons sliced Kalamata or black olives
  2 tablespoons chopped fresh basil leaves
  2 cups trimmed arugula, coarsely chopped
  1 tablespoon extra-virgin olive oil
  Kosher salt and freshly ground black pepper, to taste
  1/2 loaf Parmesan focaccia or Italian ciabbatta bread
  1/2 pound fresh mozzarella, thinly sliced
  1/4 pound thinly sliced prosciutto (or if unavailable, cooked, un-smoked ham)

DIRECTIONS
  1. In a medium bowl stir together tomato, olives and basil. In another medium bowl toss the chopped arugula with the oil, salt and pepper to taste.

  2. Halve the focaccia horizontally and spread bottom half with olive mixture. Top olive mixture with mozzarella, prosciutto, arugula, and remaining focaccia half. Press focaccia gently and cut in half and to make 2 sandwiches. Cut sandwiches diagonally in half and wrap tightly in plastic wrap.

  3. Chill sandwiches at least 1 hour or up to 1 day before serving.

• GROWN-UP GRILLED CHEESE •
(Wisconsin or Vermont)

Gone are the days when we slice off a hunk of processed cheese and slap it between two slices of Wonderbread before tossing it in a skillet greased with margarine from a tub. Maybe that's the way Mom made it, but we're going to tweak it a bit here. It's still a very simple sandwich but feel free to experiment with different cheeses. I'm not sure which state produces the best cheese, Wisconsin or Vermont. I'll let the fromagers sort it out. Me? I'm just glad we make really good cheese here in the States. So I listed them both.

PREP: Under 5 minutes   COOK: 15 minutes

INGREDIENTS
> 1 cup tightly-packed grated cheddar cheese (mild or medium), divided
> 4 slices firm, white sandwich bread
> 2 tablespoons unsalted butter, melted

DIRECTIONS

1.   Sprinkle cheese evenly between two bread halves. Add top half and press down. Brush sandwich tops with melted butter.

2.   Heat a 10-inch skillet over medium-high heat. Add sandwiches, butter side down, to the skillet and brush remaining side of sandwich with remaining butter. Cook sandwiches until crisp and deep golden brown (do not burn), about 5 - 8 minutes per side. Turn sandwich over one last time for half a minute for final crisping.

• CLASSIC REUBEN SANDWICH •
(Miami Beach, Florida)

I remember how awesome it was to sit at the counter in Wolfies in Miami Beach back in the mid-70's. It was like stepping through a time-warp into the late 40's. The interior may have been pure Florida kitsch, but the food and serving sizes were dead serious. Unfortunately, this South Beach landmark closed a couple of decades ago, but I've tried to replicate this famous sandwich. Although Russian dressing is traditional, it may be hard to find at the grocery store, so feel free to use a good thousand island dressing in its place. Oh, and two other things: Make sure you really squeeze the moisture out of the sauerkraut and be sure to follow the stacking directions exactly. It really does make a difference.

INGREDIENTS
- 6 tablespoons Russian or thousand island dressing, divided
- 4 (1/2-inch thick) slices rye bread
- 3 ounces sliced Swiss cheese, divided
- 1 cup sauerkraut, drained and squeezed of excess moisture (use jarred or bagged sauerkraut, not canned), divided
- 8 (1/4-inch-thick) slices pastrami or corned beef (about 4 ounces), divided
- 2 tablespoons unsalted butter, softened

DIRECTIONS
1. For each sandwich, spread 1 tablespoon of the dressing on one piece of bread and top with half of the cheese, half of the sauerkraut, and all of the meat. Spread another tablespoon of the dressing over the meat and top with the remaining sauerkraut and cheese, in that order.

2. Spread the remaining tablespoon of dressing on the remaining piece of bread and place it on top of the cheese. Press firmly to close the sandwich. Brush the butter on the outside of the sandwich.

3. Heat a 10-inch skillet over medium heat, place the sandwich in the pan, and press down on the sandwich with a spatula. Cook until the bread is crisp and golden brown, about 4 minutes. Flip and cook until the second side is golden brown, the cheese is melted, and the sandwich is warmed through, about 4 more minutes.

• MUFFULETTA SANDWICH •
(New Orleans, Louisiana)

Although the Sicilian-inspired muffuletta (or muffaletta) can be found in delis, sandwich shops, pool halls, and high-end restaurants throughout the region, The Central Grocery claims to be the spot where it originated. Most food historians agree, noting that Lupo Salvatore, an Italian immigrant, began serving this to blue-collar workers who wandered in from the nearby wharves and produce markets back in 1906. Plus, the sign above the store states that it's home of "The Original Muffuletta." Hey, if the sign says so…

PREP: 15 minutes

INGREDIENTS
- 1/2 pound loaf muffaletta or round Italian bread
- 3 tablespoons extra virgin olive oil
- 3 tablespoons grated Parmesan cheese
- 1-1/2 teaspoons dried basil
- 1-1/2 teaspoons dried oregano
- 6 Kalamata olives, pitted and chopped
- 6 pitted green olives, chopped
- 1/4 pound thinly sliced Genoa salami
- 1/4 pound thinly sliced ham
- 1/4 pound thinly slice mortadella
- 1/4 pound sliced provolone cheese
- 1/4 pound sliced mozzarella cheese

DIRECTIONS

1. Slice bread in half lengthwise. Drizzle olive oil on both sides. Sprinkle both sides with Parmesan cheese, basil, and oregano.

2. On the bottom half, layer olives and chopped green olives, then the salami, ham, provolone, mortadella, and mozzarella. Cover with top layer, and cut in half.

• PRIMANTI BROTHERS CLASSIC BEEF SANDWICH •
(Pittsburgh, Pennsylvania)

Yet another depression-era sandwich. This one, created by shop owner Joe Primanti, was served to truckers delivering goods to the nearby warehouses and produce yards. Since the truckers ate on the run, they needed a sandwich they could eat with one hand. Joe obliged. Since then, Primanti Brothers' shops populate the city and suburbs and have even found a home in South Florida. Of course, this delicious sandwich can no longer be eaten with one hand, as you'll find out after making one.

PREP: 30 minutes   COOK: 15 minutes

INGREDIENTS
FOR THE SLAW:
- 1-1/2 cups shredded cabbage
- 1 tablespoon olive oil
- 1 tablespoon apple cider vinegar
- 1 tablespoon white sugar
- 1/2 teaspoon freshly ground black pepper
- 1/2 teaspoon adobo seasoning (Goya® is good)

FOR THE FRIES:
- 2 cups vegetable oil for frying
- 1 large russet potato
- 1/2 tablespoons olive oil
- 1/2 pound sliced corned beef (divided)
- 2 slices provolone cheese
- 4 slices tomato
- 4 thick slices Italian bread

DIRECTIONS

1. In a medium bowl, mix the cabbage, olive oil, vinegar, sugar, black pepper, and adobo seasoning until thoroughly combined. Cover and refrigerate.

2. Heat oil in a deep-fryer or large saucepan to 375°. Cut the potatoes into 1/4-inch thick fries, and fry until they float and are golden brown, 4 to 5 minutes. Set fries on paper towels to drain.

3. Heat olive oil in 10-inch skillet over medium heat. Add corned beef and cook, turning once, until warmed through and the edges just starting to curl. Place cheese on top of the corned beef and cook until it begins to melt.

4. Place 1/4 of the beef and cheese on 4 bread slices, then top with French fries, cole slaw, 2 tomato slices, and the top pieces of bread.

• HOT BROWN SANDWICH •
(Louisville, Kentucky)

This open-face sandwich originated in Louisville's Brown Hotel in the mid 1920s. The Brown Hotel was much more than a place to rest your head; the hotel drew as many as 1200 people to its evening dinner dances. Because the dance usually ran from 10 pm to 1 am, guests usually took a break at midnight to grab a bite to eat. The popular option was ham and eggs. That changed when the chef decided that ham and eggs were too pedestrian and he came up with this offering. The rest, they say, is history.

PREP: 10 minutes   COOK: 20 minutes

INGREDIENTS
- 1 tablespoon unsalted butter
- 2 tablespoons all-purpose flour
- 1 cup milk
- 1/4 teaspoon kosher salt
- 1/4 teaspoon Worcestershire sauce
- 2 tablespoons grated sharp cheddar cheese
- 2 tablespoons grated Parmesan Cheese

- 1/2 tablespoons olive oil
- 4 strips bacon
- 1/2 pound thinly-slice cooked turkey
- 4 slices firm white bread, crusts trimmed
- 2 slices fresh, ripe tomato
- 1/4 cup grated Parmesan cheese

DIRECTIONS

1. In a small pot, melt butter over medium-high heat. Add flour and whisk until smooth and bubbly, about 5 minutes. Slowly add milk and stir until mixture begins to thicken. Add salt, Worcestershire sauce, Cheddar and Parmesan cheese. Cook, whisking constantly, until thick and bubbly.

2. Meanwhile, heat olive oil in a 10-inch skillet over medium-high heat. Add bacon and cook until crisp.

3. Toast bread slices until brown in a toaster or toaster oven.

4. Preheat broiler. Place toast on a baking sheet, arrange turkey slices on top and cover with cheese sauce. Top with tomato slices and bacon strips then sprinkle with 1/4 cup Parmesan cheese. Place under broiler until hot and bubbly.

• CUBAN SANDWICH •
(Tampa, Florida)

This recipe is made with ingredients found in most Cuban neighborhoods from the Keys, to Miami, to Tampa. However, some shops in the Ybor City neighborhood of Tampa also include a few slices of Genoa salami. This is most likely due to the fact that Ybor City was also home to a thriving Italian community as well. It's a nice touch, but Miamians would frown on it. This sandwich is made with a sandwich press called a plancha. It's similar to a panini press without the grooves. If you don't have a sandwich press, just use a heavy skillet or plate to press the sandwich while it cooks.

PREP: 10 minutes   COOK: 8 minutes

INGREDIENTS
    1/2 loaf Cuban bread or 2 sweet bread rolls
    1/4 cup mayonnaise
    2 tablespoons prepared mustard
    1/2 pound sliced Swiss cheese
    1/2 pound thinly sliced cooked ham
    1/2 pound thinly sliced fully cooked pork
    1/2 cup dill pickle slices
    1 tablespoon butter, melted

DIRECTIONS
1. Cut the bread or sandwich rolls in half (if using Cuban bread, cut to make two sandwiches). Spread mustard and mayonnaise liberally onto the cut sides. On each sandwich, place equal amounts of Swiss cheese, ham and pork in exactly that order. Place a few pickles onto each one and put the top of the roll onto the sandwich. Brush the tops with melted butter.

2. If you have a sandwich press, cook each sandwich for 5 - 8 minutes at medium-high heat. If a sandwich press is not available, place each sandwich in a large skillet over medium-high heat, and press the sandwiches down using another skillet or heavy plate. Cook for 5 -8 minutes, turning once. Slice diagonally and serve hot.

• ITALIAN BEEF SANDWICH •

(Chicago, Illinois)

The exact origin of this messy, dripping sandwich is dubious, but we know it did rise in popularity during the depression when meat was scarce and folks had to make a little bit of beef go a long way. Now this sandwich is served throughout the city whether in sandwich shops or from steam-spewing carts on the corner. Serve with plenty of napkins.

PREP: 5 minutes   COOK: 2 hours
SET: Overnight

INGREDIENTS

2 pounds boneless top round, bottom round, eye of round or rump roast
3 cloves garlic, slivered
1/2 cup beef broth
1-1/2 teaspoons salt
1-1/2 teaspoons coarsely ground black pepper
1-1/2 teaspoons crushed red pepper
1-1/2 teaspoons dried oregano
Jarred sweet peppers or giardiniera peppers (hot), sliced

DIRECTIONS

1. Preheat oven to 250°.

2. Make slits in roast with a sharp knife, and insert garlic slivers. Place roast in a dutch oven not much larger than the roast. Pour broth into pan, and season roast with salt, black pepper, red pepper, and oregano.

3. Cover, and bake for 2 hours, basting occasionally. Remove from oven, and let cool in roasting pan. Meat should be very rare. Cover and refrigerate overnight.

4. The next day, remove roast from pan and slice as thinly as possible. Add a little beef broth to roasting pan, and heat gently over medium-high heat, stirring to blend seasonings. When sauce is hot, add sliced beef just long enough to heat through. Serve on crusty Italian bread with peppers and the sauce on the side for dipping.

• PHILLY CHEESESTEAK •
(Philadelphia, Pennsylvania)

Like the Italian Beef Sandwich above, the Philly Cheesesteak rose in popularity during the Great Depression when folks needed to create a good meal using a minimum amount of beef, especially the more inexpensive cuts. Today we usually make it with better cuts of beef like roast beef or rib eye. However, it's still one of the best ways to stretch your beef budget.

PREP: 10 minutes   COOK: 10 minutes

INGREDIENTS
   2 large hoagie rolls or 2 large sub rolls, cut in half
   1 tablespoon extra virgin olive oil
   1 medium onion, thinly sliced
   1 green bell pepper, thinly sliced
   2 cloves garlic, minced or crushed
   1/2 lb deli roast beef (very rare, sliced wafer thin) or you use a frozen
     Rib-Eye steak shaved on an electric slicer
   Kosher salt and freshly ground black pepper, to taste
   1/2 lb provolone cheese (thinly sliced)
   Marinara sauce or ketchup (optional)

DIRECTIONS
1. Heat a griddle or 10-inch skillet over medium-high heat. Add olive oil, and when heated, add the onions and bell pepper and cook, stirring, until onions are soft and translucent, about 6 to 8 minutes. Add garlic, salt and pepper, and sauté for 1 minute.

2. Remove vegetables to a warm plate and add the meat to the griddle or pan. Cook, continuously flipping the meat over and slightly chopping the meat into slightly smaller pieces with 2 spatulas, until the meat is no longer pink, about 2 minutes.

3. Return the vegetables to the pan and mix with the meat. Season with salt and pepper to taste. Divide the meat and vegetable mixture into 2 portions, and top with the cheese to melt. Place mixture on each roll and serve with marinara sauce or ketchup.

Pasta

 # PASTA

If you purchased *Table for Two - The Cookbook for Couples* you noticed that I had a dearth of pasta recipes. Of course, in this case, dearth means none.

As in zero, nada, nil.

It wasn't that I didn't enjoy a good pasta dish and it wasn't because I couldn't create a good pasta dish.

It's just that there are so many good prepared pasta sauces on the market that both my editor and I said, "What's the use? Folks can pick up a good jar of marinara or even vodka sauce nowadays, why try to reinvent the wheel?"

We thought we were right on track with our thinking.

But we were wrong.

Soon after the first book hit the bookshelves I started getting feedback from readers and fans. Comments like: "I know I can buy bottled or canned marinara. I want more." Or "I'm not into tomatoes tonight. What can you do for me?" Or even, "That garlic-oil thing we had at your house last Friday? It rocked. Now tell me where I can find that in a jar on Aisle 12."

Man, let me tell you. I was humbled.

So in this book I've included some killer pasta recipes. Simple. Quick. And friggin' delicious. If you want a red pasta sauce, feel free to pull a jar off the grocer's shelf. There are so many good one out there. Just find a brand that tickles your taste buds and roll with it. It will be a perfectly simple mid-week meal.

But if you're looking for something different? These recipes should help.

And just so you know. Even though I'm the one who writes these *Table for Two* cookbooks, they are still somewhat of a collaboration. You have an idea or correction? Send it along. I listen. Really, I do. This chapter is an example.

Now let's pour some Chianti and eat.

• PASTA ALL'AMATRICIANA •

Originating from the town of Amatrice nestled in the mountains just north of Rome, this pasta dish is one of the most well-known and beloved dishes in Italian cuisine. While a truly authentic recipe calls for cured pork cheek and Pecorino Romano cheese, I know these two ingredients may not be available in your local market, so we'll substitute salt pork and regular Romano cheese. No one will know we made the switch. Trust me.

PREP: Less than 5 minutes   COOK: 30 minutes

INGREDIENTS
    1/2 pound spaghetti
    4 ounces salt pork, rind removed, rinsed, and patted dry*
    1/3 cup water
    1 tablespoon tomato paste
    1/4 teaspoon red pepper flakes
    2 tablespoons red wine
    1 (14.5-ounce) can diced tomatoes, undrained
    1 ounce (1/2-cup) grated Pecorino Romano cheese

DIRECTIONS
1. Slice the pork into 1/4-inch strips, then cut each strip crosswise into 1/4-inch pieces (chill the pork in the freezer to make it easier to slice).

2. Place pork and water into a 10-inch skillet and bring to a simmer over medium heat. Cook until water evaporates and the pork begins to sizzle a bit, about 5 - 7 minutes. Turn heat to medium-low and sauté pork until the fat renders and the pieces turn golden, about 5 - 7 minutes longer (do not brown or burn). Remove pork to a bowl with a slotted spoon and pour off most of the fat from the skillet.

3. Return skillet to medium heat and add the tomato paste, red pepper flakes, and wine. Cook, stirring constantly for 30 seconds. Add the tomatoes and pork and bring to a simmer. Cook, stirring frequently, until thickened, about 12 - 15 minutes.

4. Meanwhile, bring a large pot of salted water to a boil over high heat. Add the spaghetti and cook, stirring often, until al dente, according to the directions on the box.

5. Drain spaghetti and toss with the sauce. Sprinkle with cheese and toss again. Serve on warm plates.

*Feel free to use 3 or 4 slices of thick-cut bacon cut into 1/4-inch dice if you don't want to use the salt pork.

• PENNE ALL'ARRABBIATA •

This is another very popular classic Italian dish. Penne All'Arrabbiata translated is "enraged penne" due to the prodigious use of hot pepper. Of course you may adjust the amount of pepper to suit your taste, but I recommend you first make it as listed below so you can experience the real deal.

PREP: 5 minutes   COOK: 25 minutes

INGREDIENTS
  1/2 pound penne pasta
  2 tablespoons olive oil
  1/2 cup thinly sliced onions
  1 clove garlic, minced or pressed
  1/2 teaspoon crushed dried red pepper
  1 (14.5-ounce can) diced tomatoes, undrained
  2 or 3 fresh basil leaves, torn
  2 tablespoons freshly grated Parmesan cheese.
  Kosher salt and freshly ground black pepper, to taste

DIRECTIONS
  1.   Heat a 10-inch skillet over medium-high heat. Add olive oil and swirl to coat. Add the onions and sauté until soft and translucent, about 6 - 8 minutes. Add garlic and sauté 1 - 2 additional minutes. Add the red pepper and tomatoes; reduce heat to medium-low, and simmer, stirring occasionally, until thickened, about 10 - 15 minutes.

  2.   Meanwhile, bring a large pot of salted water to a boil. Add penne and cook, stirring often, until the pasta is al dente, according to the directions on the box.

  3.   Drain pasta and toss with the sauce. Sprinkle with basil leaves and cheese and toss again. Serve on warm plates, passing more cheese. Season with salt and pepper.

• SPAGHETTI WITH TOMATOES, BACON, AND ONIONS •

PREP: 10 minutes   COOK: 20 minutes

INGREDIENTS
1/2 pound spaghetti
2 slices bacon, cut into 1/4-inch pieces
2 tablespoons olive oil
1 medium onion, chopped (about 1 cup)
1 clove garlic, minced or pressed
1/2 (14.5-ounce) can diced tomatoes, undrained
Kosher salt and freshly ground black pepper, to taste
1 tablespoon chopped fresh Italian flat leaf parsley
Grated Parmesan cheese

DIRECTIONS

1. Sauté bacon in a 10-inch skillet over medium-high heat until partially brown, about 4 - 5 minutes.

2. Pour off most of the grease and add olive oil. Turn heat to low and add onions. Sauté until soft and translucent, about 6 - 8 minutes. Add garlic and sauté 1 additional minute. Add tomatoes and cook until sauce is slightly thickened, about 10 minutes. Season with salt and pepper to taste. Stir in parsley.

3. Meanwhile, bring a large pot of salted water to a boil. Add pasta and cook, stirring often, until the pasta is al dente, according to the directions on the box. Drain then toss with the sauce. Serve and sprinkle with Parmesan cheese.

• SPAGHETTI WITH GARLIC OIL •

I'd be lying if I didn't tell you that this is one of the favorite dishes in our house. My kids love it, my wife loves it, and company loves it. The fact that it only takes about 10 minutes to make with a handful of ingredients makes it that much more attractive. Besides, it also serves as a base for a number of delicious variations. Whoever coined the phrase "More isn't necessarily better" obviously had never whipped up a bowl of Spaghetti with Garlic Oil.

PREP: Less than 5 minutes   COOK: 10 minutes

INGREDIENTS
   1/2 pound thin spaghetti
   3 tablespoons extra virgin olive oil
   1-1/2 teaspoons minced or pressed garlic
   1 tablespoon finely chopped fresh Italian flat leaf parsley
   Kosher salt and freshly ground black pepper, to taste

DIRECTIONS
   1.   Heat a small skillet over low heat. Add the olive oil and swirl to coat. Add the garlic and cook, stirring often, until the garlic is golden, about 3 - 5 minutes (do not burn).

   2.   Meanwhile, bring a large pot of salted water to a boil over high heat. Add the spaghetti and cook, stirring often, until al dente, according to the directions on the box.

   3.   Drain pasta and toss with the garlic oil. Sprinkle with parsley and season with salt and pepper to taste.

SPAGHETTI WITH GARLIC OIL AND BLACK OLIVES
Add two tablespoons coarsely chopped imported black olives to the garlic oil and heat through.

SPAGHETTI WITH GARLIC OIL AND ANCHOVIES
Finely chop 1 ounce blotted anchovy fillets (about 1/2 can) and cook with the oil and garlic until fillets are dissolved.

SPAGHETTI WITH GARLIC OIL AND HOT RED PEPPER
Add 1/4 teaspoon crushed hot red pepper to the garlic oil for the final minute.

• FETTUCCINE WITH RED PEPPER •
AND CARAMELIZED ONIONS

Not every pasta dish has to feature tomatoes. This and the several that follow are proof. Not that I'm prejudiced against tomatoes. Heck, some of my best friends are tomatoes.

PREP: 5 minutes   COOK: 15 minutes

INGREDIENTS
   1/2 pound fettuccine
   1/4 cup olive oil
   1 large red or Spanish onion, thinly sliced
   2 red bell peppers, seeded, cored and cut into 1/4-inch strips lengthwise
   1 clove garlic, minced or pressed
   1/4 cup chopped Italian flat leaf parsley
   Kosher salt and freshly ground black pepper, to taste

DIRECTIONS

1.   Heat a 10-inch skillet over medium-low heat. Add the olive oil and swirl to coat. Add the onions and sauté until very soft, about 8 - 10 minutes. Raise the heat to medium and add red peppers. Sauté until peppers wilt, about 5 minutes. Add the garlic and sauté for 1 additional minute. Stir in parsley and salt and pepper to taste.

2.   Meanwhile, bring a large pot of salted water to a boil. Cook fettuccine until al dente according to the directions on the box.

3.   Drain pasta and toss with sauce.

A NOTE ON PASTA SERVING SIZES

If you read the back of most pasta boxes or peruse the recipes in cooking magazines or cookbooks, you will find that a pound of spaghetti should feed eight people. (That comes out to a mere two ounces per person). My question, when I read things like that is, "What universe are you cooking in?" Because in my house a pound of spaghetti wouldn't feed four people, let alone eight. Okay, maybe we love pasta too much in our house.

In the pasta recipes I've outlined here, I call for 1/2 pound for two people. That may be too much for you, especially if the sauce is heavy. If that's the case, you can save whatever is left over for lunch the next day (doesn't spaghetti, like soup, taste better the next day anyway?) or you can cut back on the amount of pasta in the recipe while keeping the sauce the same. Either way works for me.

• SPAGHETTI WITH BACON, BUTTER •
AND PARMESAN CHEESE

PREP: 10 minutes   COOK: 10 minutes

INGREDIENTS
- 1/2 pound spaghetti
- 2 strips bacon, cut into 1/4-inch pieces
- 3 tablespoons unsalted butter
- 1/4 cup grated Parmesan cheese
- 1 tablespoon chopped fresh Italian flat leaf parsley

DIRECTIONS

1. Sauté the bacon until brown in a 10-inch skillet over medium-high heat, about 5 - 6 minutes. Remove bacon with a slotted spoon and drain on paper towels. Pour off bacon grease.

2. Meanwhile, bring a large pot of salted water to a boil. Add pasta and cook, stirring often, until the pasta is al dente, according to the directions on the box. Reserve 2 tablespoons of the pasta water then drain pasta.

3. Melt butter in the pasta pot then add the pasta, reserved water, and cheese. Toss until pasta is evenly coated with sauce. Sprinkle with bacon and parsley then toss once more.

• SPAGHETTI WITH TUNA AND OLIVE SAUCE •

This is my version of the popular Italian dish known as Spaghetti al Tonno. I like the addition of lemon juice at the end, but you may forgo that ingredient.

PREP: 15 minutes   COOK: 10 minutes

INGREDIENTS
  1/2 pound spaghetti
  2 tablespoons olive oil
  3 medium garlic cloves, minced or pressed
  1/4 teaspoon hot red pepper flakes
  1/4 cup dry white wine
  1 (5.5-ounce) can tuna, packed in olive oil, drained and broken into fine pieces
  2 tablespoons minced Kalamata olives
  1-1/2 teaspoons capers, drained and chopped
  2 tablespoons chopped fresh Italian flat leaf parsley
  2 teaspoons unsalted butter butter
  1 tablespoon fresh lemon juice (optional)
  Kosher salt and freshly ground black pepper, to taste

DIRECTIONS
1.   Heat a 10-inch skillet over low heat. Add the olive oil swirl to coat. Add garlic and red pepper flakes, and sauté until fragrant but not browned, about 3-4 minutes. Add the wine, bring to a simmer, and cook for 1 minute. Add the tuna, olives, capers, and a sprinkle of salt, and cook until heated through, 1 minute.

2.   Meanwhile, bring a large pot of salted water to a boil. Add pasta and cook, stirring often, until the pasta is al dente, according to the directions on the box. Reserve 2 tablespoons of the pasta water then drain pasta.

3.   Return pasta to the pot and add tuna sauce, parsley, butter, lemon juice, a generous sprinkle of salt, several grinds of black pepper, and the reserved water. Toss until pasta is evenly coated with sauce. Serve immediately, with additional grinds of black pepper if desired.

• SHRIMP FETTUCCINE ALFREDO •

Prep time: 20 minutes   Cook time: 20 minutes

INGREDIENTS
   1/2 pound fettuccine pasta
   1 tablespoon unsalted butter
   2 cloves garlic, minced or pressed
   1/2 pound large medium shrimp peeled and deveined
   1/2 cup half-and-half
   3 tablespoons grated Parmesan cheese
   1-1/2 teaspoons chopped fresh parsley
   Kosher salt and freshly ground black pepper, to taste

DIRECTIONS

1.   Bring a large pot of lightly salted water to a boil. Add pasta and cook, stirring often, until the pasta is al dente, according to the directions on the box; drain.

2.   Meanwhile, heat a 10-inch skillet over medium hight heat. Add butter and swirl to melt. Add garlic and sauté until fragrant, about 1 - 2 minutes. And shrimp and sauté' until just barely pink, about 3 - 4 minutes.

3.   Reduce heat to medium, pour in half and half and stir. Sprinkle Parmesan cheese in one tablespoon at a time, stirring constantly, until well-incorporated. Stir in parsley, salt and pepper and stir frequently until sauce thickens, about 1 - 2 minutes. Do not boil.

3.   When sauce has thickened, pour over pasta and toss. Serve with crusty Italian bread.

• LINGUINE WITH TROPICAL FRUIT AND SHRIMP •

If you've spent any time reading my first cookbook, blog or newsletter, you are well-aware that I love to cook with fruit. That's why I had to end this chapter with a recipe that features pasta and tropical fruit. Unusual? Perhaps. Delicious? You bet!

PREP: 20 minutes   COOK: 20 minutes

INGREDIENTS
   8-ounces linguine pasta
   1/4 cup extra virgin olive oil
   1/4 cup pineapple juice
   1/4 cup no-pulp orange juice
   2-1/2 teaspoons grated orange zest
   2-1/2 teaspoons lemon zest
   1/2 teaspoon kosher salt
   1/2 teaspoon freshly ground black pepper
   2 cloves garlic, minced or pressed
   1/2 pound medium shrimp - peeled and deveined
   1 tablespoon chopped Italian flat leaf parsley
   1 tablespoon grated Parmesan cheese

DIRECTIONS
   1. Bring a large pot of lightly salted water to a boil over high heat. Add pasta and cook, stirring often, until the pasta is al dente, according to the directions on the box.

   2. Meanwhile, combine the olive oil, pineapple juice, orange juice, orange zest, lemon zest, salt, pepper, and garlic in a blender. Blend on high speed until smooth.

   3. Pour sauce into a 10-inch skillet over medium-high heat. Bring to a simmer and cook for 2 minutes. Add the shrimp and parsley; cook until shrimp are pink and cooked through, 3 to 5 minutes.

   4. Drain the linguini, and place in a warm bowl or serving platter. Spoon the shrimp and sauce over the pasta and toss. Sprinkle Parmesan cheese over pasta and serve hot.

Seafood

⌒⌇⌇⌁ Seafood

If our great grandparents could see what is available at the fish counter in our local supermarket they would be amazed. Salmon from Alaska and Chile. Cod from the North Atlantic. Shrimp from the Gulf. Catfish from the Deep South. Mahi-mahi, snapper, swordfish, and orange roughy. And what would they make of a fish called tilapia? Some of it fresh, much of it flash frozen aboard ship. And that's not a bad thing. Because it is flash frozen soon after it's caught, frozen fish can be 'fresher' than so-called fresh fish because some fresh fish could've been sitting out in the boat or dock for who knows how long. That's why you need to find a reputable fish monger for your fresh fish.

The variety would astound our elders and all of those who had to resign themselves to feast on what was caught locally or regionally.

Fortunately for us (and future generations) there is an increased emphasis on sustainable fishing and great strides are being made in the area of farm fisheries. I'm particularly excited with the advances made in urban fish aquaculture. But that's a whole 'nother chapter.

In the meantime, the following recipes feature fish that can be found in just about any market in the country. If you have a broader selection, please take advantage of the chart below because you can use a variety of fish for these recipes.

I hope this chapter will help you navigate through the range of choices available at your market. I've tried to include fish that are fairly common in all parts of the country. If you find a recipe that sounds intriguing, but the particular fish is unavailable, feel free to substitute using the chart below:

Grouper: striped bass, black sea bass (flakier texture), mahi-mahi, pompano, lemonfish, catfish, red snapper (flakier texture).

Mahi-mahi: orange roughy, red snapper, swordfish, tuna, catfish (fattier), tilefish (flakier texture, not as sweet), monkfish (not as sweet),

Tuna: swordfish, sturgeon, marlin, halibut, salmon, kingfish, mackerel.

Cod: pollock, halibut, sole, flounder, orange roughy, haddock, whiting, ocean perch, tilapia.

Flounder: sole, orange roughy, cod, haddock, tilapia.

Orange roughy: flounder, sole, red snapper, ocean perch, grouper.

Salmon: swordfish, mahi-mahi, albacore tuna, marlin, striped bass, trout.

Swordfish: tuna, halibut, marlin, mahi-mahi.

Snapper: sea bass, striped bass, grouper, rockfish.

Don't feel that you have to get all fancy when cooking fish. Sometimes a little butter, lemon juice, and salt and pepper will do the trick. Whether you grill, pan-fry, bake or roast, follow the Canadian Cooking Theory on page 76 for a quick and delicious entrée.

Table For Two Tips

A SPECIAL NOTE ABOUT SHRIMP

In the shrimp recipes that follow, I suggest using 1 pound shell-on shrimp because you'll lose a bit of weight with shelling. If you purchase the shrimp already shelled, figure on 12 ounces. But then again, we're big shrimp-eaters in our house so 1 pound of shell-on shrimp is always the minimum. Should you desire less shrimp, the marinade and sauce amounts will remain the same.

• BASIC BAKED COD •

This recipe is simplicity in itself. Depending on the thickness of your fillets, you can have this ready in around 5 minutes. Although we're using cod, this simple recipe will work with any firm-fleshed fish like halibut or striped bass.

PREP: Less than 5 minutes   COOK: Less than 10 minutes

INGREDIENTS
   2 (4 - 6 ounce) thick cod fillets
   2 teaspoons unsalted butter, divided
   Kosher salt and freshly ground black pepper to taste

DIRECTIONS
1.   Preheat oven to 425°.

2.   Place fillets on a lightly oiled baking dish. Dot with butter and season with salt and pepper to taste. Bake according to the Canadian Cooking Theory as described below.

Serve with a steamed vegetable of your choice and boiled red potatoes.

Table For Two Tips

THE CANADIAN COOKING THEORY
Many people are threatened when faced with a fresh fish fillet or steak, wondering how the heck they are going to grill, bake or poach the darn thing. Have no fear, after extensive testing, the Department of Fisheries in Canada came up with a cooking guideline that applies to any fish, in any cut, and in any method. Here it is:

Simply measure the fish at its thickest point then cook it for 10 minutes per inch. If the fish is 1-1/2 inches, that would mean 15 minutes. 1/2-inch? That would be 5 minutes.

Try it. It works!

• SAVORY BAKED COD WITH TOMATOES •

Now we'll take our basic cod recipe up a notch with the addition of some spices and tomatoes.

PREP: 5 minutes   COOK: 20 minutes

INGREDIENTS
    2 (4 - 6 ounce) cod fillets
    Kosher salt and freshly ground black pepper, to taste
    1-1/2 tablespoons olive oil
    3 tablespoons fresh lemon juice
    1 clove garlic, minced or pressed
    1-1/2 teaspoons ground cumin
    1/8 teaspoon cayenne pepper, or to taste
    1 medium tomato, sliced
    Lemon slices and fresh parsley to garnish (optional)

DIRECTIONS

1.   Preheat oven to 375°.

2.   Lightly oil a baking dish. Add fillets, skin side down (if they have skin) and sprinkle with salt and pepper to taste.

3.   In a small bowl, combine the olive oil, lemon juice, garlic, cumin and cayenne pepper.

4.   Layer the tomato slices on each fillet and spoon the olive oil mixture over all. Cover with tin foil and bake until fish is opaque and flakes easily with a fork, about 15 - 20 minutes depending on the thickness of the fillets. Top with lemon slices and parsley to garnish.

Serve with Rice Pilaf.

• ROAST COD WITH RED POTATOES •

What's the difference between roasting and baking? Temperature. Roasting will produce a golden brown color to the fish. You can prepare the fish and the potatoes in the same oven, just add the fish after the potatoes have roasted for 10 minutes or so.

PREP: 10 minutes   COOK: 25 minutes

INGREDIENTS
- 1/2 pound small red potatoes (about 6), sliced 1/4 inch thick
- 4 teaspoons olive oil, divided
- 1/4 teaspoon chili powder, or to taste
- 1/2 teaspoon kosher salt, divided
- 1/4 teaspoon freshly ground black pepper, divided
- 4 (4 - 6-ounce) cod fillets
- 1 bunches scallions, chopped, white with some green parts
- 1 fresh lemon

DIRECTIONS

1. Preheat oven to 425°.

2. In a medium bowl, toss the potatoes with 2 teaspoons olive oil, chili powder, 1/4 teaspoon salt, and 1/8 teaspoon pepper. Place potatoes on a lightly-oiled rimmed baking sheet.

2. Roast, tossing once, until golden brown and tender, about 20 to 25 minutes.

3. Meanwhile, place the fish on a second lightly-oiled rimmed baking sheet. Sprinkle the scallions on top of the fillets; drizzle with the remaining olive oil and season with 1/4 teaspoon salt and 1/8 teaspoon pepper.

4. Using a vegetable peeler, peel strips of zest from the lemon. Thinly slice them and sprinkle on the fish; reserve the lemon.

5. After the potatoes have cooked for 10 minutes, place the fish in the oven and roast until opaque and the scallions are tender, about 12 to 15 minutes.

6. Cut the reserved lemon in half and squeeze over the fish.

Serve with Sautéed Broccoli with Red Peppers and Almonds.

• BAKED COD WITH SOUR CREAM •

As with all baked fish recipes, you may want to check the fish after 10 or 15 minutes because fillets vary in thickness and oven temperatures aren't always accurate.

PREP: 5 minutes   COOK: 25 minutes

INGREDIENTS
    2 (4 - 6 ounce) cod fillets
    4 teaspoons lemon juice
    2 teaspoons chopped fresh dill (or 3/4 teaspoon dried)
    Kosher salt and freshly ground black pepper, to taste
    1/3 cup (or 1/2 cup if using larger fillets) sour cream
    2 thick slices red or sweet onion

DIRECTIONS
1.   Preheat oven to 375°.

2.   Place the fillets, skin side down (if they have skin), on a lightly-oiled baking pan. Sprinkle with lemon juice, dill, salt and pepper. Spread the sour cream evenly over each fillet. Break the onion slices into rings and press them into the sour cream.

3.   Cover pan with tin foil and bake until fish is opaque and flakes easily with a fork, about 25 minutes.

Serve with Pan-Roasted Rosemary Carrots and Boiled New Potatoes.

• PANKO CRUSTED BAKED GROUPER •

Grouper is a favorite for those who don't really care for fish because the flavor is so mild. Since it is such a firm-fleshed fish, it takes to baking well.

PREP: 5 minutes   COOK: 15 minutes

INGREDIENTS
    1/2 cup panko breadcrumbs
    2 tablespoons chopped fresh parsley
    1 clove garlic, minced or pressed
    1 teaspoon lemon zest
    1/4 teaspoon kosher salt
    2 (6 -8 ounce) grouper fish fillets
    2 teaspoons olive oil
    Lemon wedges to garnish (optional)

DIRECTIONS
1.   Preheat oven to 400°. Lightly oil a rimmed baking pan.

2.   In a small bowl, combine bread crumbs, parsley, garlic, lemon zest, and salt. Pour mixture onto a plate.

3.   Brush the top of each fillet with olive oil then press fillet into the crumb mixture coating one side. Place fillets in baking dish, crust-side up. Bake until fish easily flakes with fork, about 10 -15 minutes. Garnish with lemon wedges.

Serve with Sautéed Broccoli with Tomatoes and Bacon and Boiled New Potatoes.

• GRILLED SALMON WITH RASPBERRY GLAZE •

Chicken is not the only entrée that benefits from the addition of fruit. I think you'll enjoy the interplay of the sweetness of the jam and the tartness of the vinegar. If you're unable to grill this, you can also roast it in a 425° oven for 20 minutes.

PREP: 5 minutes   MARINATE: 1 hour
COOK: 15 minutes

INGREDIENTS
   1 cup fresh or frozen raspberries
   1-1/2 tablespoons raspberry jam
   1/2 tablespoons raspberry vinegar
   1/2 tablespoons balsamic vinegar (increase to 1 tablespoon
    if you do not have raspberry vinegar)
   2 tablespoons olive oil
   2 teaspoons fresh lemon juice
   1/2 teaspoon lemon zest
   2 (6-ounce) salmon fillets or steaks
   Kosher salt and freshly ground black pepper, to taste
   Fresh mint or Italian parsley leaves to garnish (optional)

DIRECTIONS
   1.   Place the raspberries in a small bowl and crush with a fork. Stir in the jam, vinegars, oil, lemon juice, and lemon zest until well combined.

   2.   Pat salmon dry and season with salt and pepper. Place fillets in a dish or zip lock bag then pour the raspberry marinade over the salmon. Place in the refrigerator for at least one hour, turning once.

   4.   Preheat grill to medium and lightly oil grill grate. Remove the salmon from the marinade and cook until the fish flakes easily with a fork, about 6 - 8 minutes per side.

   5.   In the meantime, transfer marinade to a small pan. Bring to boil over low heat, cook stirring constantly until lightly thickened.

   6.   Spoon the warm raspberry sauce over the salmon and garnish with fresh mint or parsley leaves. Decorate with fresh mint or parsley leaves.

Serve with Grilled Asparagus and Rice Pilaf.

• ROASTED SALMON WITH TANGY MUSTARD GLAZE •

Here is another wonderful roasted salmon dish. You can omit the mustard powder for a little less zing.

PREP: 10 minutes   COOK: 15 minutes

INGREDIENTS
    2 (6-ounce) salmon fillets
    Kosher salt and freshly ground black pepper, to taste
    1/4 cup Dijon mustard
    1/4 cup honey
    1 tablespoon water
    1 tablespoon fresh lemon juice
    1/2 teaspoon mustard powder
    3 cloves garlic, minced or pressed
    1 tablespoon fresh dill, chopped (or 1 teaspoon dried)

DIRECTIONS
    1.   Preheat the oven to 400°. Season both sides of salmon with salt and
          pepper and place in a lightly oiled baking dish.

    2.   In a small bowl, combine the Dijon mustard, honey, water, lemon juice,
          mustard powder and garlic. Reserve 1/4 cup, and pour remaining sauce
          over the salmon. Roast the salmon, uncovered, until fork-tender, about
          15 minutes.

    3.   Meanwhile, gently heat the remaining sauce in a small pan or in the
          microwave. Stir the dill into the reserved sauce and serve along with the
          salmon.

Serve with Steamed Green Beans and Orzo with Mushrooms.

• BAKED SALMON EN PAPILLOTE •

Fish cooked in paper (en papillote), or in foil, is a great way to ensure a melt-in-your-mouth entrée. The fish steams in its own juice along with the marinade.

PREP: 5 minutes   MARINATE: 1 hour
COOK: 45 minutes

INGREDIENTS
 6 tablespoons olive oil
 2 cloves garlic, minced or pressed
 1 teaspoon dried basil
 1 teaspoon kosher salt
 1 teaspoon freshly ground black pepper
 1 tablespoon fresh lemon juice
 1 tablespoon fresh Italian flat leaf parsley, chopped
 2 (6-ounce) salmon fillets

DIRECTIONS
1. In a medium bowl, combine the olive oil, garlic, basil, salt, pepper, lemon juice and parsley. Place salmon fillets in a zip lock bag and add the garlic mixture. Marinate in the refrigerator about 1 hour, turning occasionally.

2. Preheat oven to 375.

3. Place each fillet on a 12-inch square of aluminum foil, cover with marinade, and seal. Place sealed salmon in glass baking dish, and bake until fish easily flakes with a fork, about 35 to 45 minutes.

Serve with Zucchini with Tomatoes and Boiled Red Potatoes.

• SALMON CURRY •

This is my go-to dish when I want seafood with a minimum of fuss. If you have a can of Alaskan salmon in the cupboard and some white rice in the fridge or freezer, you can have this delicious dish on the table in just a matter of minutes.

PREP: 5 minutes   COOK: 20 minutes

INGREDIENTS
   1 small onion, chopped (about 1/2 cup)
   1-1/2 teaspoons unsalted butter
   1 (6-ounce) can wild Alaskan salmon, (about 1/2 cup)
   3 tablespoons curry powder, or to taste
   3/4 cup béchamel sauce
   White wine or white vermouth

DIRECTIONS

Heat a medium saucepan over medium high heat. Add the butter and swirl to coat. Add in the onion and sauté until it is soft, about 6 - 8 minutes. Stir in the salmon, curry powder and béchamel sauce (below). Heat to just the boiling point, about 3 - 5 minutes. Add white wine or vermouth to thin a little.

QUICK BÉCHAMEL SAUCE:

Heat a small saucepan over medium-low heat. Add 1 tablespoon butter and melt. Add 1 tablespoon flour and stir until smooth and light gold, about 6 - 7 minutes. Meanwhile, heat 1 cup milk in a separate saucepan over medium-high heat until just about boiling. Slowly whisk warmed milk into the butter flour mixture and stir until very smooth. Cook, stirring constantly until thickened, about 8 - 10 minutes. Season with salt, pepper and a pinch of nutmeg.

Serve over Steamed White Rice.

• PROSCIUTTO-ROASTED HALIBUT •

Once you start using prosciutto, I promise you'll be buying more from your local deli. It really adds a lot to meals like this, and a little goes a long way.

PREP: 5 minutes   COOK: 12 minutes

INGREDIENTS
   2 (5 - 6 ounce) halibut fillets
   3 teaspoons chopped fresh thyme, divided
   4 thin slices prosciutto
   2 tablespoons olive oil
   2 tablespoons chopped shallot
   1/2 cup white wine
   2 tablespoons unsalted butter
   Kosher salt and freshly ground black pepper, to taste

DIRECTIONS
   1.   Preheat oven to 400°.

   2.   Sprinkle 1 teaspoon thyme over each fish fillet then season with salt and pepper to taste. Place 2 slices prosciutto on a cutting board, overlapping slightly. Place a fish fillet in the center of the prosciutto crosswise. Fold ends of prosciutto over fish fillet and press down with the palm of your hand so the prosciutto sticks to itself. Repeat with the other fillet.

   3.   Heat a 10-inch oven proof skillet over medium-high heat. Add oil and swirl to coat. Add fillets, seam side down, and cook until prosciutto is brown, about 1 minute per side.

   4.   Place skillet in oven and roast fish until cooked through, about 6 - 8 minutes. Remove fish to a warm plate and cover loosely with tin foil.

   5.   Add shallot to skillet and sauté over medium-high heat for 1 minute. Add wine and remaining thyme and cook for 1 - 2 minutes. Whisk in butter until melted. Place each fillet on a plate and drizzle with the wine sauce.

Serve with Roasted Green Beans and Onions and Garlic Smashed Potatoes.

• NOT YOUR MAMA'S FISH STICKS •

Most of us grew up with fish sticks when we were kids. For many Catholic families, it was a Friday staple in the 50's and 60's. I even remember the school cafeteria serving it on Fridays. Here's a recipe that will allow you to enjoy them again. And you won't even have to wait for Friday.

PREP: 5 minutes   COOK: 10 minutes

INGREDIENTS
    12 ounces cod, halibut or other firm-fleshed fillets, cut crosswise
     into 3/4-inch wide strips
    Kosher salt and freshly ground black pepper, to taste
    1/3 cup mayonnaise
    2 tablespoons lemon juice
    3/4 cups seasoned panko bread crumbs
    2 teaspoons chili powder

DIRECTIONS
    1.   Preheat oven to 500°. Place rack in top 1/3 of the oven.

    2.   Lightly oil a baking sheet with vegetable oil. Season fish with salt and
          pepper to taste.

    3.   In a shallow bowl or dish, whisk the mayonnaise and lemon juice
          together. In a separate bowl or dish, whisk together the bread crumbs
          and chili powder. Dip fish in the mayonnaise and lemon mixture, then into
          the bread crumbs to coat.

    4.   Arrange fish on the baking sheet and bake until coating is golden, crisp
          and cooked through, about 10 minutes.

Serve with Savory Oven Fries and Steamed Corn.

• GRILLED TUNA WITH AIOLI SAUCE •

Talk about a lighting fast meal. Once the tuna marinates, it will only take a few minutes to grill. And I really mean only a few minutes. The tuna should be cooked to medium-rare for optimum flavor and texture.

PREP: 5 minutes   MARINATE: 1 hour
COOK: 5 minutes

INGREDIENTS
    2 tablespoons olive oil
    1 tablespoon red wine vinegar
    1 tablespoon chopped fresh basil
    1 teaspoon chopped fresh thyme
    1 teaspoon dried tarragon
    1 garlic cloves, minced or pressed
    3 tablespoons mayonnaise
    2 (5 - 7 ounce) tuna steaks, about 1-inch thick
    Kosher salt and freshly ground black pepper, to taste

DIRECTIONS
1. Whisk the first 6 ingredients in an 8-inch square baking dish to create the marinade. In a small bowl, whisk together the mayonnaise and 3 teaspoons of the marinade from the baking dish to create the aioli sauce.

2. Season the fish fillets with salt and pepper to taste then place in the baking dish and toss to coat. Allow to sit at room temperature for 1 hour, turning occasionally.

3. Prepare a grill for medium-high heat. Grill fish to desired doneness, (about 2 minutes per side for medium-rare.

4. Place a fillet on each plate and top with aioli.

Serve with Steamed Carrots and Orzo with Parsley.

• PAN-SEARED TUNA WITH SESAME OIL •

Here's another quick tuna recipe; one that you can make indoors. Because the tuna will only cook for a few minutes, you probably won't fill your kitchen up with smoke. But turn on the exhaust fan, just in case.

PREP: 5 minutes   COOK: 5 minutes

INGREDIENTS
    2 (5 - 7 ounce) tuna steaks, about 1-inch thick
    Kosher salt to taste
    1-1/2 teaspoons cracked pepper
    1 teaspoon sesame oil
    1 tablespoon soy sauce
    1/4 cup dry sherry
    1 tablespoon chopped chives or green onion tops to garnish

DIRECTIONS
    1.   Season both sides of the tuna steaks with salt and black pepper,
          pressing the pepper into the steak with the heal of your hand.

    2.   Heat a 10-inch skillet over high heat. Add the oil and swirl to coat. Add
          the steaks and brown on the surface but still pink in the center, about 2
          minutes per side. Remove steaks to a plate and cover loosely with tin foil
          to keep warm.

    3.   Add the soy sauce and sherry to the skillet and stir, scraping up any
          brown bits in the pan, for about 1 minute. Spoon over tuna steaks and
          sprinkle chives or green onion to garnish.

Serve with Green Beans and Cherry Tomatoes and Rice Pilaf.

• PAN-SEARED TUNA WITH BLACK PEPPERCORNS •

This is the seafood version of Steak au Poivre. Here we'll quickly pan-sear the tuna before removing from the heat to finish cooking.

PREP: 5 minutes   COOK: 6 minutes

INGREDIENTS
  2 (5 - 7 ounce) tuna steaks
  1/2 teaspoon kosher salt
  1/4 teaspoon cayenne pepper, or to taste
  1 teaspoon whole peppercorns
  1/2 teaspoon whole allspice berries
  1 tablespoon vegetable oil
  2 tablespoons unsalted butter, softened

DIRECTIONS
  1. Place the peppercorns and allspice in a small plastic bag and crush with a meat pounder, a can of vegetables, or the bottom of a saucepan. Combine in a small bowl with the salt and cayenne pepper.

  2. Brush both sides of each steak with the vegetable oil then sprinkle with the salt and pepper mixture using the palm of your hand to ensure that the cracked peppercorns adhere.

  3. Heat a 10-inch cast iron skillet over high heat until very hot, about 3 - 5 minutes. Place steaks in the pan and sear for about 1-1/2 minutes per side. Remove the skillet to a hot pad or trivet and cover. Let sit for about 2 - 3 minutes.

  4. Remove steaks to each plate and brush with softened butter.

Serve with Sautéed Potatoes and Mushrooms and Steamed Asparagus.

• GRILLED TERYAKI TUNA •

When many people think of tuna, this is the recipe that comes to mind. Unfortunately it's often overcooked, even in fine restaurants. You really only want to grill this for a minute or two per side depending on the thickness of the fillet or steak. Remember, the tuna will continue to cook after it's removed from the heat.

MARINATE: 30 minutes   COOK: 5 minutes
PREP: 5 minutes

INGREDIENTS
- 1/2 cup bottled teriyaki sauce
- 1/3 cup olive oil
- 3 - 4 cloves garlic, minced or pressed
- 1/2 teaspoon freshly ground black pepper
- 2 (5-ounce) tuna fillets

DIRECTIONS
1. Combine the teriyaki sauce, olive oil, garlic and pepper in a small bowl. Place the tuna in zip lock bag and pour in the sauce. Seal the bag with as little air in it as possible, then flip the bag to ensure the tuna fillets are well coated. Marinate for at least 30 minutes in the refrigerator, turning once.

2. Meanwhile, preheat an outdoor grill for high heat. Lightly oil grate.

3. Remove tuna from marinade, and place on grill. For rare tuna, grill for 1 to 2 minutes on each side for rare, or 3 to 6 minutes per side for medium.

Serve with Steamed Spinach and Quinoa Pilaf.

• GRILLED SWORDFISH WITH SPICY YOGURT SAUCE •

Since Greek-style yogurt has become all the rage, I thought I'd include a seafood recipe that makes good use of it. Because Greek yogurt is thicker than traditional yogurt, it clings to the steaks a little better. If you like this sauce, try it on other grilled items like beef, pork, lamb, or even veggies.

PREP: 10 minutes   COOK: 10 minutes

INGREDIENTS
    2 (5-ounce) swordfish steaks, about 1-inch thick
    1/2 teaspoon vegetable or canola oil
    1/2 teaspoon herbes de Provence (found in the spice section)
    Kosher salt to taste
    3 tablespoons finely-chopped fresh cilantro leaves
    2 tablespoons finely-chopped fresh mint leaves
    1 clove garlic, minced or pressed
    1/2 small jalapeño pepper, seeds removed and chopped
    1/4 teaspoon kosher salt
    1/2 cup plain Greek-style yogurt
    Chopped fresh parsley or chives to garnish

DIRECTIONS

1. Rub the steaks on both sides with the oil then sprinkle with the herbes de Provence and salt. Cover and place in the fridge until you're ready to grill.

2. Meanwhile, place the remaining ingredients in a small bowl and whisk until well-blended. (You can also put them in whole into a blender or small food-processor to blend).

3. Meanwhile, preheat an outdoor grill for high heat. Lightly oil grate.

4. Grill the steaks until lightly brown, about 2 minutes per side for medium-rare. Remove steaks to a warm plate and cover tightly with tin foil and let stand for 8 - 10 minutes.

5. Spoon enough sauce to coat the bottom of each plate, then place the steaks in the center of each plate. Spoon a little sauce over each steak and sprinkle with parsley or chives to garnish.

Serve with Quinoa with Green Peas.

• SAVORY GRILLED SHRIMP •

I love grilling shrimp because of the flavor grilling imparts and because it can be done so quickly. To make this, and any other grilled shrimp recipe nearly foolproof, thread the skewer through both the head and tail ends of the shrimp. That way they won't give you any problems when you turn them.

PREP: 5 minutes   MARINATE: 30 minutes
COOK: 5 minutes

INGREDIENTS
    2 cloves garlic, minced
    3 tablespoons olive oil
    2 tablespoons tomato sauce
    1 tablespoon red wine vinegar
    1 tablespoon chopped fresh basil (or 1 teaspoon dried)
    1/4 teaspoon kosher salt
    1/8 teaspoon cayenne pepper
    16 extra large shrimp, peeled and deveined
    4 bamboo skewers, soaked in water for 20 minutes
      (you may use 2 steel skewers as well)

DIRECTIONS
1.   In a medium bowl, mix together the garlic, olive oil, tomato sauce, and red wine vinegar, basil, salt, and cayenne pepper. Add shrimp, and stir to coat. Cover, and refrigerate for at least 30 minutes or up to 1 hour, stirring once or twice.

2.   Preheat grill for medium heat and lightly oil grate. Remove shrimp and discard marinade. Thread shrimp onto skewers by piercing once through the tail and once through the head.

3.   Grill until the shrimp turn pink, about 2 to 3 minutes per side.

Serve with Sugar Glazed Grilled Asparagus and Rice and Pasta Pilaf.

• GRILLED MARGARITA SHRIMP •

The only way to make Grilled Margarita Shrimp even better is to sip on an ice cold margarita while you're grilling them.

PREP: 15 Minutes   MARINATE: 30 minutes
COOK: 5 minutes

INGREDIENTS
    16 extra large shrimp, peeled and deveined
    2 cloves garlic, minced
    2 tablespoons fresh lime juice
    3 tablespoons olive oil
    2 teaspoons tequila
    3 tablespoons fresh chopped cilantro
    1/4 teaspoon cayenne pepper
    1/4 teaspoon kosher salt
    4 bamboo skewers, soaked in water for 20 minutes (you may use 2 steel
      skewers as well)

DIRECTIONS
1.   In a medium bowl, combine the shrimp, garlic, lime juice, olive oil, tequila, cilantro, pepper, and salt. Refrigerate 30 minutes. Meanwhile, soak the skewers if using bamboo.

2.   Preheat an outdoor grill for medium heat and lightly oil grate. Drain the marinade from the shrimp and discard; thread the shrimp on the skewers.

3.   Grill until the shrimp turn pink and opaque, about 2 to 3 minutes per side.

Serve with Grilled Corn and Rice Pilaf.

• BACON WRAPPED BAR-B-Q SHRIMP •

This is a wonderfully spicy dish that tastes like you made them on the grill. A perfect recipe for those days when you have a yen for spicy bar-b-q but it's raining out. It is also a great 'weekend meal' that can be thrown together on a weeknight. For ease of clean-up, line the bottom half of your broiling pan with aluminum foil.

PREP: 5 minutes   MARINATE: 15 minutes
COOK: 15 minutes

INGREDIENTS
   8 slices hickory smoked bacon, cut in half
   16 extra large shrimp, peeled and deveined
   8 toothpicks
   1 tablespoon Bar-B-Q Seasoning (I like Paul Prudhomme's), or to taste

DIRECTIONS
   1.   Preheat oven to 450°.

   2.   Wrap shrimp with bacon and secure with a toothpick.

   3.   Place the shrimp in a small bowl and toss with the Bar-B-Q Seasoning. Set the shrimp on a broiling pan and let sit for 15 minutes.

   4.   Cook the bacon wrapped shrimp for 10 to 15 minutes, or until bacon is crisp and shrimp is cooked through. Serve immediately.

Serve with canned Baked Beans and Grilled Corn.

• BAKED SHRIMP WITH DIJON MUSTARD •

In my first Table for Two cookbook I included a recipe for Garlic Baked Shrimp. The following recipe is an interesting variation of that company-pleasing, but oh-so-simple dish. Like the original recipe, this can be prepared in advance and popped into the oven at the last minute.

PREP: 10 minutes   COOK: 15 minutes

INGREDIENTS
    1 pound large shrimp, peeled and deveined
    1/2 cup butter
    1 tablespoon Dijon mustard
    1-1/2 teaspoons lemon juice
    2 cloves garlic, minced
    1-1/2 teaspoons chopped fresh Italian flat leaf parsley

DIRECTIONS
    1.   Preheat oven to 375°.

    2.   Arrange shrimp in a buttered baking dish.

    3.   Combine butter, mustard, lemon juice, garlic and parsley in a small
          saucepan and melt over medium heat. Pour over shrimp and toss to
          coat. Bake for 15 minutes until shrimp are pink and just cooked through
          (a little longer if dish was prepared ahead and chilled).

Serve with Rice Pilaf and Steamed Corn.

• GARLIC BAKED SHRIMP WITH SWISS CHEESE •

Here's yet another great baked shrimp recipe I know you're going to love.

PREP: 10 minutes   COOK: 25 minutes

INGREDIENTS
- 1 pound large shrimp, peeled and deveined
- 5 tablespoons unsalted butter, divided
- 2 scallions, chopped with some green1
- 1 clove garlic, minced or pressed
- 1/2 pound mushrooms, sliced (baby portobello or white button are fine)
- 1 cup grated Swiss cheese
- 1/4 cup dry white wine
- 4 thin slices Swiss cheese
- 1/2 cup panko bread crumbs

DIRECTIONS
1. Preheat oven to 375°.

2. Heat a 10-inch skillet over medium-high heat. Add 3 tablespoons butter and swirl to coat. Add scallions and sauté for 3 minutes. Add garlic and sauté 1 additional minute. Add mushrooms and sauté 3 minutes.

3. Place shrimp in a buttered casserole dish. Stir in scallions, garlic and mushrooms, then add grated cheese and wine. Toss to coat. Top with cheese slices and bread crumbs. Melt remaining butter and drizzle over the top.

4. Bake for 15 minutes until hot and bubbly. Broil for 2 additional minutes until top is browned.

Serve with Creamed Corn and Steamed Spinach.

• OLD FASHIONED STEAMED SHRIMP •

This classic recipe is great on a breezy summer day. If you don't like to cook with beer, feel free to replace it with another cup or two of water. This dish can be served hot or cold.

PREP: 5 Minutes   COOK: 10 Minutes

INGREDIENTS
   1 cup water
   1 bottle beer
   1 pound large shrimp, shell on
   2 to 3 tablespoons Old Bay Seasoning®
   1 (12-ounce) jar prepared cocktail sauce

DIRECTIONS

1.   In a large pot, bring water and beer to a boil.

2.   In a medium bowl, toss shrimp with the Old Bay. Place shrimp in a steamer basket and place on top of the pot and cover. (Do not submerge shrimp in the water). Steam shrimp until just pink.

Serve with cocktail sauce, Grilled Corn and Boiled Red Potatoes.

• CHARLESTON SHRIMP GRAVY •

In my book, *Cooking Outside the Lines*, I offer a version of my favorite shrimp gravy, one that has gotten rave reviews at seafood and shrimp festivals I've appeared at. My gravy was influenced by some that I've tasted in NE Florida and the panhandle and it goes particularly well over shrimp and grits. However, this Charleston Shrimp Gravy comes in a close second.

PREP: 20 Minutes   COOK: 20 Minutes

INGREDIENTS
   3 slices bacon
   2 tablespoons unsalted butter
   4 tablespoons all purpose flour
   1 medium onion, chopped (about 1 cup)
   1 green bell pepper, seeded and chopped
   1 clove garlic, minced or pressed
   1 pound large shrimp, peeled and deveined
   2 teaspoons seasoned salt
   Freshly ground black pepper, to taste
   1-1/4 cups chicken broth
   1/4 cup heavy cream
   1 green onion including the green, chopped

DIRECTIONS
   1.   Heat a 10-inch skillet over medium heat. Add bacon and sauté until crisp and browned, about 5 minutes. Remove bacon to paper towels to drain. Crumble and reserve.

   2.   Add the butter to the bacon grease. When the butter begins to sizzle, sprinkle 2 tablespoons of flour over it. Reduce the heat to medium-low, and cook for about 12 minutes, stirring frequently, to make a dark brown roux. Don't let it burn - reduce heat if necessary.

   3.   When the roux reaches dark brown, increase the heat to medium-high, and add the onions and bell pepper. Sauté for 3 minutes, just until softened. Add the garlic and sauté 1 additional minute.

   4.   Meanwhile, place the shrimp in a bowl, and toss with seasoned salt, pepper, and remaining flour. Pour into the skillet, and stir constantly for 1 minute.

Whisk in the chicken stock and cream and reduce the heat to low. Cook for 3 or 4 minutes until the shrimp is just pink and the broth thickens.

5.   Remove from heat and sprinkle the chopped green onion and bacon bits over it.

Serve over hot grits, warm biscuits, or Steamed White Rice and Sautéed Kale.

SHRIMP STOCK - DON'T TOSS THOSE SHELLS!

I usually buy my shrimp with the shells intact because it allows me to whip up batches of shrimp stock or broth. Although you can use chicken broth in a lot of shrimp recipes like bisque or shrimp gravy, nothing beats a good homemade shrimp stock. So next time you shell your shrimp, put the shells into a zip lock freezer bag and keep adding to it until you have enough shells to create your stock. Here's my recipe. It'll make about a quart of stock. Once made you can freeze 1 cup servings in zip lock freezer bags.

INGREDIENTS
1/2 tablespoon olive oil
1/2 cup chopped onion
1/4 cup chopped celery
1/4 cup chopped carrot
2 pounds shrimp shells
5-1/2 cups water

1 bay leaf
1/4 cup chopped fresh parsley
1/2 teaspoon thyme
6 whole peppercorns
1 teaspoon tomato paste

DIRECTIONS

1.   Heat a dutch oven over medium heat. Add the olive oil and swirl to coat. Add the onions, celery and carrots and sautè until the vegetables are soft, about 10 minutes.

2.   Turn heat to high and stir in the shrimp shells and sautè until the shells turn pink, about 1 - 2 minutes. Add the water, bay leaf, parsley, thyme, peppercorns and tomato paste. Bring to a boil, reduce heat to medium-low and simmer for 45 minutes.

3.   Drain the stock through a fine mesh strainer, pushing down on the shells to extract as much shrimp goodness as you can. Let cool, then freeze for up to 6 months.

• SHRIMP AND ANDOUILLE SAUSAGE •

This recipe was inspired by the wide variety of shrimp and sausage dishes that are so common in southern Louisiana. Andouille sausage is a staple in that part of the country and it's now available in most supermarkets. If you can't find it, substitute an equal amount of kielbasa. Serve this with cold beer and lots of warm, crusty bread.

PREP: 15 minutes   COOK: 20 minutes

INGREDIENTS
  3/4 pound large shrimp, peeled and deveined
  2 teaspoons Creole or Cajun Seasoning (like Zatarain's®)
  2 tablespoons olive oil, divided
  3/4 pound andouille sausage, sliced crosswise at a diagonal,
    about 3/4-inch thick
  1 medium onion, peeled, halved and thinly sliced
  1 red pepper, cored, seeded and sliced into 1/4-inch strips
  2 teaspoons chopped fresh thyme (or slightly less than 1 teaspoon dried)
  1 clove garlic, minced or pressed
  3/4 cup chicken or vegetable broth
  3 tablespoons Creole mustard (Zatarains is good) or deli style mustard
  1-1/2 teaspoons red wine vinegar
  Kosher salt and freshly ground black pepper to taste

DIRECTIONS

  1.   Toss shrimp with the Creole or Cajun seasoning in a medium bowl.

  2.   Heat a 10-inch skillet over medium-high heat. Add 1 tablespoon olive oil
        and swirl to coat. Add sausage and sauté until browed on both sides,
        about 5 minutes. Remove sausage to a bowl and add shrimp to skillet.
        Sauté until just pink, about 3 minutes. Remove to the bowl with
        the sausage.

  3.   Add remaining oil then the onion, bell pepper and thyme to the skillet.
        Sauté until vegetables are crisp-tender, about 5 minutes. Add garlic and
        sauté for 1 additional minute. Season with salt and pepper to taste.

  4.   Add broth, mustard and vinegar to the skillet. Stir until slightly thickened,
        about 2 - 3 minutes. Return sausage and shrimp to the skillet and
        simmer, stirring, until heated through, about 1 minute.

Serve over Steamed White Rice with Creole Corn.

• MUSSELS MARINIÈRE •
(Mussels in White Wine)

More and more supermarkets and fish markets are selling cultivated mussels that are grown on lines or nets. They are generally free of barnacles and have been de-bearded. This is a good thing for the home cook because a significant amount of time could be spent removing barnacles and other foreign items from the shells as well as the beard. If you do happen to purchase mussels that have beards, I've given instructions on how to remove them in the *Table for Two Tip* on the next page.

PREP: 10 minutes   COOK: 10 minutes

INGREDIENTS
- 2 pounds mussels, cleaned and debearded
- 1 clove garlic, minced
- 1 small onion, chopped (about 1/2 cup)
- 3 tablespoons chopped fresh Italian flat leaf parsley, divided
- 1/2 bay leaf
- 1/8 teaspoon dried thyme
- 1 cup dry white wine (I prefer Sauvignon Blanc)
- 2 tablespoons unsalted butter, divided
- 1/8 teaspoon freshly ground black pepper

DIRECTIONS

1. Wash mussels. If necessary, remove "the beard" (see *Table for Two Tip* on the next page).

2. Combine onion, garlic, 2 tablespoons parsley, bay leaf, thyme, wine, 1 tablespoon butter and pepper in Dutch oven with a lid. Bring to boil over medium-high heat. Lower heat, and sauté for 2 minutes. Add mussels, and cover. Cook just until shells open, about 5 to 6 minutes. Do not overcook. Remove mussels from sauce, discarding any that have not opened, and place in bowls. Add remaining butter and parsley to pan. Heat until butter melts. Pour over mussels.

Serve with a simple salad and lots of warm bread.

BUYING MUSSELS AND STORING MUSSELS

1. Purchase mussels that are fresh and alive. Live mussels will usually have closed shells, but undisturbed mussels may have slightly open shells. If a shell is open, tap it. If it closes, the mussel is still alive. If it doesn't, discard it. Do not rinse the mussels until you are ready to prepare them.

2. If you are not going to eat the mussels right away, store them in a bowl covered with a damp cloth or paper towel in the back of the refrigerator. Don't put them in a plastic bag or container; that will suffocate them. Mussels are best eaten right away, but they will last a few days in the fridge.

3. Most mussels sold today are farmed so they usually will not have any barnacles or a beard (a brown tuft located between the shells). If you purchase wild mussels you may opt to remove any barnacles or seaweed. You will also have to remove the beard by grasping it and pulling it off (use a knife or scissors if it gives you any problem). Don't de-beard the mussels until you are ready to cook them because the process will kill them.

4. Rinse the mussels under cold water then prepare them according to the recipe.

• PERFECT STEAMED CRAB LEGS •

So you were able to snag a deal on king crab, snow crab or Dungeness crab at the market this week. Good for you! I say that because there are not many deliciously succulent (and healthy) foods that can be cooked in 5 to 10 minutes. My portions here are pretty large. I feel if I have to do all the work of cracking and breaking, I may as well get as much as I can of this incredibly sweet meat. But remember, the crab has already been cooked, so we are just really re-heating here, so don't be tempted to over-steam. I usually figure on at least 1 pound of crab legs per person. I rely on grilled corn and simple boiled potatoes to complete the meal.

PREP: None   COOK: 8 minutes

INGREDIENTS
   2 or 3 pounds of crab legs

DIRECTIONS
Bring two cups of water to a boil in large pot over medium-high heat. Place crab legs in a colander or large steaming basket and place in the pot. Cover and steam until a sweet crab scent fills your kitchen, about 5 - 8 minutes depending on the crab (king crab will take longer). Don't over cook or the crab will be tough and rubbery. Serve with melted butter or freshly squeezed lemon and plenty of napkins.

Serve with Grilled Corn and Boiled Red Potatoes.

• OVEN ROASTED CRAB LEGS •

Okay. You've mastered steamed crab legs. Now let's try something different. It takes just a few minutes longer, but the results are worth it. You'll need an oven-proof skillet (just one more reason to get that iron skillet I've been telling you to get since my first cookbook).

PREP: 10 minutes   COOK: 20 minutes

INGREDIENTS
   2 - 3 pounds crab legs, cracked in a few places
   1/4 cup (1/2 stick) unsalted butter
   1/4 cup olive oil
   1 tablespoon minced shallot (or onion)
   1-1/2 teaspoons dried crushed red pepper
   6 cloves garlic, minced or crushed (about 2 tablespoonss)
   2 teaspoons thyme
   2 tablespoons chopped fresh Italian flat leaf parsley, divided
   Kosher salt and freshly ground black pepper
   1/2 cup orange juice
   1 teaspoon orange zest

DIRECTIONS
   1.   Preheat oven to 500°.

   2.   Melt butter with the olive oil in a large ovenproof skillet over medium-high heat. Add shallot and red pepper flakes and sauté for 2-3 minutes. Add garlic and sauté for an additional 1-2 minutes.

   3.   Add crab legs and toss to coat. Sprinkle with thyme and 1 tablespoon parsley. Season with salt and pepper. (Easy on the salt. Crabs are naturally salty). Toss again.

   4.   Place skillet in the oven and roast, stirring once, until the crab legs are heated through, about 10 - 12 minutes.

   5.   Remove crab legs to a warm serving platter and cover with tin foil. Add orange juice and zest to the skillet and bring to boil over high heat until reduced by half, about 5 minutes. Crack crab legs and spoon orange sauce over them then sprinkle with remaining parsley.

Serve with Bourbon Glazed Carrots and Boiled Red Potatoes.

• PAN-SEARED SEA SCALLOPS WITH CHERRY TOMATOES •

Sea scallops are available two ways in most markets: Dry and wet. It's important that you purchase dry scallops for any recipe that calls for searing or browning. Wet scallops have been treated with a solution of sodium tripolyphosphate (or STP) to prolong their shelf life. This treatment adds additional moisture to the scallops and you will find them almost impossible to brown or sear. If they aren't labeled, don't be afraid to ask.

PREP: 10 minutes   COOK: 15 minutes

INGREDIENTS
   3/4 pounds large sea scallops
   Kosher salt, to taste
   2 tablespoons olive oil, divided
   2 large green onions, chopped with the white and green parts separated
   1/2 pint basket cherry (or grape) tomatoes, approximately 6 ounces
   2 tablespoons chopped Italian flat leaf parsley, divided
   1-1/2 tablespoons fresh lemon juice
   1/4 teaspoon Hungarian sweet paprika
   Kosher salt and freshly ground black pepper, to taste

DIRECTIONS
   1.   Pat scallops dry and sprinkle with kosher salt.

   2.   Heat a 10-inch skillet over medium-high heat. Add 1 tablespoon olive oil and swirl to coat. Add scallops and cook until browned on the outside and slightly opaque in the center, about 2 minutes per side. Remove scallops to a warm plate and cover with tin foil.

   3.   Add remaining oil to the skillet and swirl to coat. Add white part of the onions and sauté until crisp-tender, about 1 - 2 minutes. Add tomatoes and green part of the onions and sauté until tomatoes begin to split and release their juices, about 5 minutes. Stir in 1-1/2 tablespoons parsley, lemon juice and paprika.

   4.   Return scallops and their juice to the skillet and sauté until just heated through, about 1 minute. Season with salt and pepper.

   5.   Transfer scallops and tomato mixture to a warm platter. Sprinkle with remaining parsley.

Serve with Roasted Asparagus and Buttermilk Mashed Potatoes

• CLASSIC SURF AND TURF •

I wasn't sure if I should put this in the beef or seafood chapter, but then I realized that the 'surf' precedes the 'turf' alphabetically. Problem solved. Many surf and turf recipes suggest that you toss a lobster tail and a steak on the grill with little more than salt and pepper as seasonings. I love the simplicity in that. But tonight we're going to have some fun with this by throwing in a good bit of butter, garlic, and cayenne pepper. I think you're going to love it.

PREP: 5 minutes   SET: 1 hour
COOK: 10 minutes

INGREDIENTS
    1/4 cup unsalted butter, room temperature
    1 tablespoon olive oil
    1 shallot, minced
    2 cloves garlic, minced or pressed
    1/3 teaspoon kosher salt
    1/3 teaspoon cayenne pepper
    Pinch freshly ground black pepper
    2 (6 - 8 ounce) New York strip steaks (about 3/4 to 1-inch thick)
    2 (3 - 4 ounce) uncooked lobster tails (defrosted if frozen)

DIRECTIONS
1. Place first 7 ingredients in a blender and puree until slightly smooth (or melt butter and place in medium bowl and whisk until slightly smooth).

2. Spread 1 heaping teaspoon of butter over each side of the steaks and the cut side of each lobster tail. Let steaks sit at room temperature and the lobster in the fridge for 1 hour. Transfer remaining butter to a small saucepan.

3. Preheat grill to medium-high heat. Grill steaks until cooked to desired doneness (about 3 - 4 minutes per side for medium-rare). Grill lobster, shell side down, for 5 minutes, then turn and grill until meat is opaque, about 3 more minutes. Meanwhile, set the saucepan on the grill to melt butter.

Serve steaks and lobster with the reserved melted butter.

Chicken

 # Chicken

Boy, we in the states sure love our chicken. Some recent studies show that the average American consumes a little over 60 pounds of chicken a year. Heck, we consume over 1.25 billion (yes, *billion*) chicken wings during super bowl weekend!

For most of us, chicken usually means boneless skinless chicken breasts, which can be a good, healthy choice, especially if you get it on sale. However, if we just limit our chicken options to this popular cut, I think we're doing ourselves (and our taste buds) a disservice. Chicken thighs, whether boneless or bone-in, may be the breast's less popular cousin, but when it comes to flavor, availability and price, chicken thighs are in many ways preferable to breasts, particularly if you want chicken flavor in your dish.

But, one might ask, aren't breasts healthier and easier on the heart and arteries? Not really. A 3.5-ounce piece of boneless, skinless chicken breast has .56 grams of saturated fat and 114 calories. The thigh? 1 gram of saturated fat and 119 calories. Not much difference, eh? (So why do we think otherwise? Perhaps we could chalk it up to marketing). In addition to more chicken flavor, dark meat also contains more iron, zinc, riboflavin, thiamine, and vitamins B6 and B12 than white meat.

So maybe it's time to rethink things.

If you're looking for a 'blank slate' for your recipe because you want to highlight certain spices or sauces, chickens breasts will do just fine. However, if you want to feature chicken for its flavor then chicken thighs are the way to go.

And about those wings? Man, I long for the days when they were relegated to bar food (in real bars, not the new upscale 'neighborhood' tavern chains) and could be had for 10¢ or 25¢. But enough of my whining. Wings are still fairly inexpensive if you make them at home. I've included a healthier version of the traditionally-fried Buffalo wings. I think you're gonna like them.

• SIMPLE SAUTÉED CHICKEN BREASTS WITH ONIONS •

Talk about a quick dinner. That's the beauty of chicken breasts; they cook in no time. And because they do, it's easy to over-cook them. And dried out chicken breasts are one of my least favorite entrees. So remember, my cooking times are suggestions. Your cooking time may be different depending on your stove. And I always remove the breast from the heat a little before they're done because they will continue to cook off heat.

PREP: 5 minutes   COOK: 15 minutes

INGREDIENTS
  2 boneless, skinless chicken breasts
  Kosher salt and freshly ground black pepper, to taste
  2 teaspoons olive oil
  2 teaspoons unsalted butter
  1 small or medium onion, peeled or sliced
  1/2 teaspoon fresh herb of choice (basil, thyme, rosemary, oregano,
    marjoram, etc)

DIRECTIONS
  1. Place chicken breasts between two pieces of wax paper or plastic wrap
      and pound to an even thickness of about 1/2-inch. Season with salt and
      pepper to taste.

  2. Heat a 10-inch skillet over medium-heat. Add the olive oil and butter
      and swirl to coat. Stir in the onions and sauté until they are soft and
      translucent, about 8 - 10 minutes. Add the chicken breasts to the pan
      and sauté along with the onions, turning often, until just barely opaque,
      about 6 minutes. Sprinkle breasts with your herb of choice.

Serve with Green Peas with New Potatoes.

• CHICKEN SEVILLE •
(Chicken with Oranges)

This is a lightning quick version of a dish that's usually roasted or braised. I may include one of those in a future book, but for now I want you to try one that can be made in about 20 minutes.

PREP: 5 minutes   COOK: 15 minutes

INGREDIENTS
   2 boneless, skinless chicken breasts
   Kosher salt and freshly ground black pepper, to taste
   1/3 cup orange juice
   1/3 cup heavy cream (or half & half for a lighter sauce)
   1-1/2 teaspoons sherry
   1/8 teaspoon ground ginger
   2 tablespoons butter
   1-1/2 teaspoons chopped fresh Italian flat leaf parsley

DIRECTIONS
1. Place chicken breasts between two pieces of wax paper or plastic wrap and pound to an even thickness of about 1/2-inch. Season with salt and pepper.

2. In a small bowl combine the orange juice, cream, sherry, and ginger.

3. Heat a 10-inch skillet over medium heat. Add the butter and swirl to coat. When the butter begins to bubble, add the chicken breasts and cook until lightly brown, about 2 - 3 minutes per side.

4. Reduce heat to medium-low and stir in orange juice mixture. Continue to cook, turning occasionally, until chicken is opaque throughout but still very moist, about 6 - 8 minutes. Remove chicken to a warm platter, spoon sauce over and sprinkle with parsley.

Serve with Pan-Roasted Asparagus and Roasted Red Potatoes.

• SAUTÉED CHICKEN WITH MUSHROOMS •
AND BLUEBERRIES

This dish is similar to the Chicken Veronique recipe I featured in my previous book. To me, there's something about cooking chicken with fruit that makes my mouth water just thinking about it. Try this with blackberries, raspberries, or concord or red grapes.

PREP: 10 minutes   COOK: 15 minutes

INGREDIENTS
   1/4 cup all-purpose flour
   Kosher salt and freshly ground black pepper, to taste
   2 boneless, skinless chicken breasts or 4 boneless, skinless thighs
   1 tablespoon olive oil
   2 slices Canadian bacon cut into strips (or 2 slices bacon, chopped)
   1/4 pound button mushrooms, sliced
   1-1/2 teaspoons Dijon mustard
   1/4 pound blueberries (frozen and thawed may be used)
   2 teaspoons fresh lemon juice
   1-1/2 teaspoons chopped fresh Italian flat leaf parsley
   Lemon wedges to garnish (optional)

DIRECTIONS

1. On a small plate, mix the flour with the salt and pepper. Dredge each chicken piece in the flour until coated well. Shake off excess.

2. Heat a 10-inch skillet over medium-high heat. Add oil and swirl to coat. Add chicken and cook until well-browned and crisp, about 2 - 3 minutes. Reduce heat to medium. Turn chicken and cook until brown and crisp on the other side and it is opaque in the center, about 4 - 5 minutes. Transfer the chicken to a warm plate and tent loosely with tin foil to keep warm.

3. Return heat to medium-high. Add the bacon to the pan and sauté until cooked and the fat renders out. Add the mushrooms and sauté for 2 - 3 minutes. Add the mustard and sauté for 1 minute.

4. Gently add the blueberries and lemon juice and remove from the heat before the blueberries turn too soft. Spoon blueberries sauce over each chicken breast and sprinkle with parsley. Serve with lemon wedges for a bit more bite. Serve over Smashed New Potatoes.

• CHICKEN BREASTS IN CAPER AND CORN SAUCE •

I came up with this when I wanted Chicken Piccata but didn't have any lemons. And like Chicken Piccata, this can be whipped up in about 20 minutes.

PREP: 5 minutes   COOK: 15 minutes

INGREDIENTS
    2 boneless, skinless chicken breasts
    Kosher salt and freshly ground black pepper
    1 tablespoon unsalted butter
    1 tablespoon finely chopped shallots
    1/4 cup dry white wine
    3 tablespoons drained capers
    1/2 cup heavy cream
    1 cup fresh or frozen corn kernels
    1 tablespoon chopped chives

DIRECTIONS
1. Season chicken with salt and pepper to taste. Heat a 10-inch skillet over medium-high heat. Add butter and swirl to coat. Add chicken and cook for 2 minutes. Turn chicken and sprinkle shallots into the skillet. Add the wine and bring to a boil and reduce heat to medium. Cover and cook for 3 minutes.

2. Add capers and cream and stir to mix. Cover and cook an additional 5 minutes.

3. Remove chicken to a plate and tent loosely with tin foil or another plate to keep warm. Add the corn to the skillet and cook, stirring, for 1 minute. Stir in the chives. Spoon the sauce over the chicken and serve.

Serve with Boiled Red Potatoes and Steamed Green Beans.

• CHICKEN SALTIMBOCCA •

This popular recipe is usually prepared with the breast either folded or rolled. Maybe I'll include the more traditional method in a future book. This version will take all of 10 minutes to prepare. By the way, saltimbocca literally means, "to jump in your mouth". This will.

PREP: 5 minutes   COOK: 10 minutes

INGREDIENTS
    2 skinless, boneless chicken breasts
    Kosher salt and freshly ground black pepper, to taste
    1/3 cup all-purpose flour
    1 tablespoon olive oil
    2 large, thin pieces prosciutto
    1 tablespoon unsalted butter
    1-1/2 teaspoons fresh chopped sage (or 1/2 teaspoon dried)
    2 teaspoons freshly grated Parmesan cheese
    1/3 cup Marsala wine

DIRECTIONS
1. Place a breast between two pieces of plastic wrap or waxed paper and pound carefully to about 1/4-inch without tearing. Repeat with the other breast.

2. Place flour on a plate. Season each breast with salt and pepper to taste. Dredge each breast in flour and shake off excess.

3. Heat a 10-inch skillet over high heat. Add olive oil and swirl to coat. Add the breasts in one layer and cook for 1 minute until golden brown. Turn and cook until golden brown, about 1 additional minute. Remove chicken to a plate and loosely cover with tin foil or another plate to keep warm.

4. Add the prosciutto to the skillet and sauté about 15 seconds to heat through. Place a piece of prosciutto on each chicken.

5. Add the butter to the skillet to melt. Return the chicken to the skillet and sprinkle with sage and Parmesan cheese. Pour the Marsala into the skillet, cover and cook for 1 or 2 minutes until cheese is melted. Remove chicken from pan and drizzle with the Marsala to serve.

Serve with Herb Crusted Broiled Tomatoes and Steamed Asparagus.

• SAUTÉED CHICKEN WITH GREEN BEANS •
AND RED PEPPERS

This is one dish where it is preferable to use fresh tomatoes over canned. This is because we won't actually be cooking the vegetables; we will only be 'threatening' them. We want them somewhat crisp when we serve this.

PREP: 10 minutes   COOK: 10 minutes

INGREDIENTS
  2 boneless, skinless chicken breasts
  Kosher salt and freshly ground black pepper, to taste
  1-1/2 tablespoons olive oil
  1 small onion, chopped (about 1/2 cup)
  1 garlic clove, minced or pressed
  1/4 pound green beans, cut into 2-inch pieces (frozen is fine) 1/2 red bell
  pepper, seeded and cut into thin strips length-wise
  2 plum tomatoes, quartered
  1/2 can anchovies stuffed with capers, drained and chopped
  1 tablespoon lemon juice
  1 tablespoon chopped fresh Italian flat leaf parsley to garnish

DIRECTIONS
  1.   Place a breast between two pieces of plastic wrap or waxed paper and pound carefully to about 1/2-inch without tearing. Repeat with the other breast. Season with salt and pepper.

  2.   Heat a 10-inch skillet over medium-high heat. Add oil and swirl to coat. Add onion and sauté until soft and translucent, about 6 - 8 minutes. Add garlic and sauté for 1 - 2 minutes. Add chicken and sauté, tossing frequently, until opaque, about 3 - 4 minutes. Remove chicken with a slotted spoon to a plate. Cover loosely with tin foil (or a plate) to keep warm.

  3.   Add green beans and red pepper to the skillet. Sauté until veggies are crisp tender, about 2 minutes. Add tomatoes, anchovies, and chicken. Sprinkle with lemon juice. Sauté until heated through, about 2 minutes. Garnish with parsley

Serve with pasta.

• CHICKEN BOLOGNESE •

Consider this a southern Mediterranean version of the traditional Chicken Cordon Bleu.

PREP: 5 minutes   COOK: 12 minutes

INGREDIENTS
    2 boneless, skinless chicken breasts
    3 tablespoons unsalted butter
    1/2 teaspoon dried oregano
    Kosher salt and freshly ground black pepper, to taste
    2 slices prosciutto
    2 slices smoked provolone cheese (or mozzarella)
    1/4 cup dry white wine

DIRECTIONS
1. Place a breast between two pieces of plastic wrap or waxed paper and pound carefully to about 1/4-inch without tearing. Repeat with the other breast.

2. Heat a 10-inch skillet over medium heat. Add butter and swirl to coat. Add chicken breasts and cook until golden brown on one side, about 1 - 2 minutes. Turn and cook an additional 1 - 2 minutes. Season with oregano, salt and pepper.

3. Place a slice of prosciutto and then a slice of cheese on each breast. Drizzle wine over chicken. Cover pan and cook until cheese is melted and the chicken is cooked through, about 5 minutes.

Serve with Pan-Roasted Asparagus with Parmesan Cheese and Orzo with Parsley.

FLAMBÉ LIKE THE PROS

A flambé is a stunningly sensual sight when done safely and properly. Here's how to accomplish both:

1. Since cold liquor will not ignite quickly, I always warm the required amount of cognac, brandy or rum in a cup or small bowl in the microwave for 30 or so seconds (you can also warm it in a small saucepan over medium heat).

2. When you're ready to flambé your dish, remove the pan from the heat source and add the designated amount of warm brandy, cognac or rum. NEVER pour any alcoholic beverage directly from the bottle, especially over the heat source - the flame could follow the alcohol stream up into the bottle, causing it to explode. Tragically, this has happened in restaurants that should've known better.

3. After adding the cognac, brandy or rum, return the pan to the stove over medium-high heat then step back and ignite the fumes with a long kitchen match. Don't try to ignite the liquid. It won't. Instead, set the match just above the liquid. The fumes will take it from there.

4. Cook the dish until the flames die out, then proceed with the recipe as directed.

• CHICKEN WITH CHAMPAGNE CREAM SAUCE •

This rich dish belies its simplicity. It will also allow you to impress your loved one with a flambé. Creating a flambé may take some practice, but it's a sight to behold. If you opt to flambé, reduce the brandy to 1/2 tablespoons or so and continue as directed.

PREP: 5 minutes   COOK: 30 minutes

INGREDIENTS
  2 bone-in chicken breasts, with skin
  Kosher salt and freshly ground black pepper, to taste
  3 tablespoons unsalted butter
  2 tablespoons brandy or cognac
  1/4 cup chicken broth
  1 cup champagne
  1-1/2 teaspoons tomato paste
  1/2 cup heavy cream, divided

DIRECTIONS
  1.   Season chicken with salt and pepper. Heat a 10-inch skillet over medium
       heat. Add butter and swirl to coat. And chicken and sauté until lightly
       browned, about 5 minutes per side. Pour fat from skillet. Meanwhile,
       warm the brandy in a small saucepan or in the microwave.

  2.   Remove pan from heat and add brandy or cognac. Return pan to stove
       and ignite brandy with a long kitchen match. When the flame subsides,
       add the chicken broth, champagne, tomato paste, and 1/4 cup cream.
       Simmer until chicken is tender, about 25 - 30 minutes. Remove chicken
       to a plate and loosely tent with tin foil or another plate to keep warm.

  3.   Add remaining cream to skillet. Bring to a boil and cook, stirring, until
       slightly thickened, about 3 - 5 minutes. Season with salt and pepper to
       taste. Pour sauce over chicken and serve.

Serve with Pan-Roasted Rosemary Carrots and Roasted Red Potatoes.

• CHICKEN BREASTS WITH PROSCIUTTO AND SAGE •

Cooking chicken with the bone in and skin intact will make for a very tender and flavorful dish. If you want to cut down on the fat, remove the chicken skin before you spoon the sauce over it.

PREP: 10 minutes   COOK: 20 minutes

INGREDIENTS
   2 bone-in chicken breasts with skin
   Kosher salt and freshly ground black pepper, to taste
   2 tablespoons olive oil
   1 small onion, chopped (about 1/2 cup)
   1/4 cup peeled and finely chopped carrots
   1/4 cup finely chopped celery
   1 clove garlic, minced or pressed
   1/2 cup dry white wine
   1/4 cup (packed) slivered prosciutto (about 1-1/2 ounces)
   1-1/2 tablespoons chopped fresh sage or 1-1/2 teaspoon dried

DIRECTIONS
   1.   Season chicken breasts with salt and pepper.

   2.   Heat a 10-inch skillet over medium-high heat. Add oil and swirl to coat. Add chicken and sauté until brown, about 3 minutes per side. Remove chicken to a plate.

   3.   Add onions, carrots, and celery to the skillet and sauté until the onions are soft and translucent, about 6 - 8 minutes. Add garlic and sauté 1 - 2 additional minutes.

   4.   Return chicken to the skillet along with any juices that have accumulated on the plate. Add the wine, prosciutto, and sage. Bring to a boil then reduce heat to medium-low. Cover and simmer, turning chicken once, until cooked through, about 6 minutes per side. Serve chicken and spoon sauce over each piece.

Serve with Mashed Potatoes with Carrots.

• DEVILED DELMONICO CHICKEN •

In *Table for Two - The Cookbook for Couples* I presented a recipe for shaked and baked chicken. This is a similar recipe but is geared to those whose palate leans toward more spicy dishes. You can use regular breadcrumbs, but I like using panko breadcrumbs for the extra crunch they give.

PREP: 10 minutes   COOK: 25 minutes

INGREDIENTS
  1/4 cup mayonnaise
  1/4 cup course grained mustard (deli mustard)
  2 teaspoons Worcestershire sauce
  1/4 teaspoon garlic powder
  3/4 cup seasoned panko breadcrumbs
  1 green onion, chopped
  4 large chicken drumsticks

DIRECTIONS

  1.   Preheat oven to 425°.

  2.   In a small bowl, whisk the mayonnaise, mustard, Worcestershire sauce, and garlic powder until well combined. In another bowl, mix bread crumbs and chopped onion until well-combined.

  3.   Dip each drumstick in the mayonnaise mixture and turn to coat. Then dip each drumstick in the breadcrumbs and turn to coat.

  4.   Place drumsticks on lightly oiled rimmed baking sheet and bake until brown and cooked through, about 25 minutes.

Serve with Green Beans and Shallots and Savory Oven Fries.

• BUFFALO WINGS TWO WAYS •

We Americans love our wings. Just look at the number of wing joints that dot our roadways. And for many of us, the only way to prepare wings is the way they've been doing it at the Anchor Bar in Buffalo, New York since 1964. I'm going to give you two recipes: the first one is the more traditional version and the second is a bit healthier. They're both delicious. Oh, and one other thing. Purists only use one hot sauce: Franks.

INGREDIENTS
    24 chicken wing pieces
    Kosher salt and freshly ground black pepper, to taste
    Canola oil for frying
    3 tablespoons unsalted butter
    3 tablespoons Franks Red Hot Original® hot sauce
    3 medium celery stalks, cut into 3-inch pieces
    1-1/2 cups blue cheese dressing

DIRECTIONS
IN THE SKILLET:

1. Heat 1/2-inch oil in a 10-inch skillet to 365°. Season wings with salt and pepper.

2. And chicken and fry, turning, until crisp and golden, about 10 - 12 minutes. Remove to drain on paper towels.

3. Meanwhile, melt butter in a small saucepan then add hot sauce to heat through. Add wings and toss to coat.

IN THE OVEN:

1. Preheat oven to 400°.

2. Season wings with salt and pepper then bake for 25 minutes.

3. Meanwhile, melt butter in a small saucepan then add hot sauce to heat through. Place wings in a warm bowl and toss with the sauce to coat.

Serve with celery and blue cheese dressing on the side.

• SAVORY BAKED CHICKEN WINGS •

Although Buffalo Wings are my favorite, this recipe (and the one for Looed Chicken Wings in my book *Cooking Outside the Lines*) run a close second.

PREP: 5 minutes   MARINATE: 30+ minutes
COOK: 1 hour

INGREDIENTS
    24 chicken wing pieces
    2 tablespoons soy sauce
    2 tablespoons dry sherry
    1 clove garlic, minced or crushed
    1 teaspoon freshly grated ginger
    1-1/2 teaspoons sugar
    2 green onions, chopped

DIRECTIONS
    1.   Preheat oven to 375°.

    2.   In a small bowl, combine the soy sauce, sherry, garlic, ginger and sugar. Place the wings in a large zip loc bag and pour the marinade over all. Let sit for at least 30 minutes.

    3.   Place the wings on a lightly oiled rimmed baking sheet and bake for 1 hour until cooked through. Sprinkle with green onions

Serve with Sautéed Snow Peas and Steamed White Rice

• CHICKEN CACCIATORE •

(Southern Italian)

This is the type of chicken cacciatore most of us are familiar with. I usually use canned diced tomatoes but if I have only canned whole, I'll use them instead. I just crush them in my fist before adding them to the pot.

PREP: 10 minutes   COOK: 50 minutes

INGREDIENTS
- 3 tablespoons olive oil
- 2 chicken legs and 2 chicken thighs
- 1 medium onion, sliced
- 1/2 pound mushrooms, sliced (baby portobello or white button)
- 3 garlic cloves, minced or pressed
- 1 green pepper, seeded and cut into 1-inch pieces
- 1 (14.5-ounce) can diced tomatoes, undrained
- 1/2 cup dry white wine
- 1 teaspoon dried oregano
- 1 teaspoon kosher salt
- 1/2 teaspoon freshly ground black pepper

DIRECTIONS

1. Heat a 10-inch skillet over medium heat. Add olive oil and swirl to coat. Add chicken pieces and brown on all sides, about 10 minutes. Remove chicken and drain on paper towels.

2. Add the onions, mushrooms, and green peppers to the skillet and sauté until onions are soft, about 6 - 8 minutes. Add garlic and sauté 1 - 2 additional minutes. Stir in remaining ingredients until well-combined.

3. Return chicken to the skillet and bring to a boil. Reduce heat to medium-low. Cover and simmer until chicken is cooked through and tender, about 20 - 30 minutes.

Serve with pasta.

• CHICKEN CACCIATORE •
(Northern Italian)

This northern version of Chicken Cacciatore utilizes butter along with the olive oil, and, like most northern Italian dishes, it doesn't contain tomatoes. After you make this, I think you'll agree that it's a nice change.

PREP: 5 minutes   COOK: 50 minutes

INGREDIENTS
    2 chicken legs and 2 chicken thighs
    Kosher salt and freshly ground black pepper, to taste
    5 tablespoons unsalted butter, divided
    3 tablespoons olive oil
    1/4 pound prosciutto, cut into bite-sized pieces
    1 tablespoon chopped fresh sage, or 1 teaspoon dried
    3/4 cup dry white wine

DIRECTIONS
    1.   Season chicken pieces with salt and pepper to taste. Heat a 10-inch skillet over medium heat. Add 3 tablespoons butter and the olive oil and swirl to coat. Add chicken pieces and brown on all sides, about 10 minutes.

    2.   Pour off most of the fat from the skillet and add the prosciutto, sage, and wine. Cover and cook until chicken is tender, about 20 - 30 minutes. Remove chicken to a warm plate and tent loosely with tin foil to keep warm.

    3.   Turn heat to medium-high and bring sauce to a boil and cook until slightly reduced. Remove skillet from the heat and swirl in the remaining butter. Spoon sauce over chicken and serve with pasta.

• CHICKEN CASSEROLE WITH SHERRY CREAM SAUCE •

When most of us think of chicken casserole, our mind travels back to a time when we stared down at chunks of chicken swimming in mixture of canned cream of mushroom soup and white rice. It wasn't bad when we were kids, but hardly something you'd serve today for your loved one. This version will awaken your taste buds in a way the old version couldn't. Don't let the long list of ingredients scare you off. It really does come together quickly.

PREP: 10 minutes   COOK: 35 minutes

INGREDIENTS

4 boneless skinless chicken thighs
Kosher salt and freshly ground
   black pepper, to taste
1 tablespoon olive oil
1/4 pound baby portobello
   mushrooms (halved if large)
1 medium onion, peeled and sliced thick
2 small turnips, peeled and quartered
1/2 pound very small new potatoes

8 peeled baby carrots
1-1/4 cups chicken broth
2 tablespoons sweet sherry
1/4 pound whole green beans
   (frozen is fine)
1-1/2 teaspoons cornstarch
1/2 cup plain low-fat yogurt
1/4 teaspoon lemon zest

DIRECTIONS

1. Season chicken thighs with salt and pepper to taste. Heat a small Dutch oven over high heat. Add oil and swirl to coat. Add chicken and sauté until brown, about 2 - 4 minutes per side. Remove chicken to a plate.

2. Add mushrooms to the pot and sauté for 1 - 2 minutes. Reduce heat to medium; push the mushrooms to the side, add the onions and sauté for 2 minutes. Spread the onions and mushrooms evenly across the bottom of the pan. Add the turnips, potatoes, and carrots in an even layer on top of the onions and mushrooms.

3. Add the stock and sherry to the pot and bring to a boil. Add the chicken and any accumulated juices and reduce the heat to medium-low. Cover and simmer for 10 minutes. Add the green beans and continue to simmer, covered, until chicken and vegetables are cooked through, about 5 minutes.

4. Remove chicken and vegetables to a serving platter or 2 shallow bowls/plates with a slotted spoon. Cover loosely with tin foil to keep warm.

5. Return the stock to a boil over high heat for 5 minutes until slightly reduced. Meanwhile, in a medium bowl, mix the cornstarch with the

yogurt and lemon zest until well combined. Slowly add about 3/4 of the stock to the yogurt mixture, stirring until thickened. Return the yogurt to the pot and bring to a boil until thickened. Season with salt and pepper to taste. Spoon sauce over chicken and serve.

Table For Two Tips

ONION AND GARLIC BASICS

As you may have noticed, I use onions and garlic a lot. I want you to get in the habit of using them a lot, too. They're available year round and add incredible flavor to just about any dish. Here are some of the questions I get when doing shows around the country. Hopefully the answers will encourage you to use more onions and garlic.

1. **How should I store onions, garlic and shallots when I get them home from the store?** I advise folks to store your onions and garlic (or any fresh produce for that matter) exactly the way your supermarket displays and stores them.

2. **How do I chop onions without crying?** Place the onion in the freezer to chill for 1/2 an hour. Then, using a very sharp chef's knife, cut off the onion top and peel the outer layers leaving the root end intact. The sharper your knife, the less you will cry.

3. **How long can I store my chopped onions?** If you place them in a sealed container or zip lock bag, they will keep in your refrigerator for 7 - 10 days. If you need to keep them longer, place them in the freezer.

4. **Can I store chopped garlic in olive oil?** I don't recommend it because you run the risk of botulism contamination. Chop or press your garlic as you need it.

5. **How do I peel garlic cloves?** Place the clove on your cutting board, lay the broad side of your chef's knife on top, then whack it gently with the palm of your hand. The peel will fall right off. Or better yet, invest in a good garlic press (I like Zyliss) and you won't even have to peel the garlic when you press it.

6. **How do I get rid of the onion or garlic smell on my hands?** You can remove the odor by rubbing your hands with salt (add a little water to make a paste) or lemon juice. However, I don't use these methods because I always seem to have at least one small cut on my hands and salt and lemon juice sting like crazy. Instead, I'll run my hands under water while rubbing them with a large stainless steel spoon. Oh, you can also purchase my wife's homemade coffee soap (hint-hint) which also works like a charm.

• CHICKEN AND SAUSAGE CASSEROLE •

Here is another chicken casserole that I know you will like. If you enjoy spicy food, you may substitute hot Italian sausage for the sweet Italian sausage.

PREP: 10 minutes   COOK: 1 hour

INGREDIENTS
    1/2 pound sweet Italian sausage
    3 tablespoons all-purpose flour
    1/2 teaspoon freshly ground black pepper
    1/2 teaspoon Hungarian sweet paprika
    2 chicken legs and 2 chicken thighs
    2 tablespoons olive oil
    1 small onion, sliced
    1/4 pound mushrooms, sliced
    1 (15.5 ounce) can diced tomatoes, undrained
    1/2 cup chicken broth or water
    1/4 teaspoon caraway seeds
    1/2 (10-ounce) package frozen peas or sliced green beans

DIRECTIONS
1. Pierce sausage in several places with a fork. In a small skillet, cook sausages over low heat until brown and cooked through, 20 minutes. Remove sausage to a plate lined with paper towels to drain, then cut into 1-inch chunks.

2. Place flour, pepper and paprika in a paper or plastic bag. Add chicken pieces one at a time and shake to coat. Reserve flour mixture.

3. Heat a Dutch oven over medium heat. Add olive oil and swirl to coat. Add chicken pieces and sauté until brown, about 5 minutes per side. Remove and drain on paper towels.

4. Add onions and mushrooms and sauté until onions are tender, about 8 - 10 minutes. Stir in reserved flour and cook for 2 - 3 minutes. Return chicken to the pot. Stir in chicken broth, tomatoes, and caraway seeds. Cover and simmer for 10 minutes.

5. Stir in sausages and peas and cook for 10 additional minutes until heated through.

• ROASTED CHICKEN WITH PEPPERS •
AND SWEET POTATOES

This is a wonderful all-in-one dish that makes good use of chicken thighs. However, you can also make this using two chicken thighs and two chicken drumsticks.

PREP: 15 minutes   COOK: 30 minutes

INGREDIENTS
    4 bone-in chicken thighs
    1 tablespoon deli-style mustard
    1 teaspoon cinnamon
    1/2 cup apple juice
    2 small sweet potatoes, peeled and cut into wedges (about 1 pound)
    2 medium onions, peeled and quartered
    1 red pepper, quartered lengthwise, seeds and ribs removed
    1 yellow or green pepper, quartered lengthwise, seeds and ribs removed
    Kosher salt and freshly ground black pepper, to taste
    1 tablespoon olive oil

DIRECTIONS
1. Preheat oven to 450°.

2. In a medium bowl, combine the mustard, cinnamon, and apple juice until well-mixed. And the chicken and turn to coat. Remove chicken to 9 x 13 inch baking dish.

3. Meanwhile, place the potatoes into a medium sauce pan and pour in boiling water to cover; cook over high heat for 5 minutes. Drain.

4. Add the potatoes, onions, and peppers to the bowl and turn to coat in the mustard sauce. Pour vegetables and sauce into baking dish. Season with salt and pepper to taste then drizzle olive oil over all.

5. Place baking dish in the oven and roast, tossing occasionally, until the chicken and vegetables are well-browned and the chicken is cooked through, about 45 minutes.

Serve with a green salad and warm, crusty bread.

• ARROZ CON POLLO •
(Chicken and Yellow Rice)

This classic dish of Spain, Latin America, and Puerto Rico is, to me, the ultimate chicken casserole. It seems there are as many variations as there are Latino kitchens. Here is my favorite recipe - a conglomeration of different ones I've tried over the years. I'm sure after you try mine, you'll begin to tweak it as well!

PREP: 15 minutes   MARINATE: 2+ hours
COOK: 50 minutes

INGREDIENTS
FOR THE MARINADE:
- 2 teaspoons dried oregano
- 2 teaspoons kosher salt
- 1 teaspoon ground cumin
- 1 teaspoon freshly ground black pepper
- 2 cloves garlic, minced or pressed
- 2 tablespoons lime juice

FOR THE DISH:
- 2 chicken drumsticks and 2 chicken thighs
- 2 tablespoons olive oil
- 1 large onion, chopped
- 1 green bell pepper, chopped
- 3 cloves garlic, minced or pressed
- 1 teaspoon ground annatto seeds, Bijol, or turmeric*
- 1 teaspoon ground cumin
- 1 teaspoon dried oregano
- 2 cups arborio or short grain rice
- 1/2 cup dry white wine
- 3 cups chicken broth
- 1 (14.5-ounce) can diced tomatoes, undrained
- 1 bay leaf
- 1 tablespoon capers, rinsed
- 12 pimento stuffed green olives, sliced
- 1 (6.5-ounce) jar chopped pimentos, drained
- 1 (9-ounce) package frozen baby peas

DIRECTIONS

1. In a small bowl, combine the oregano, salt, cumin, pepper, garlic and lime juice. Rinse chicken and pat dry. Place chicken in a zip lock bag and pour the marinade over chicken. Marinate for at least 2 hours or overnight.

2. Heat a dutch oven over medium-high heat. Add the olive oil and swirl to coat. Remove chicken and pat dry, reserving marinade. Add the chicken and brown on all sides, about 10 - 15 minutes. Remove chicken to a plate.

4. Lower the heat to medium and add the onions and peppers. Sauté until the onions are soft and translucent, about 6 - 8 minutes. Add garlic and sauté 1 - 2 additional minutes. Stir in the annatto, cumin, and oregano and sauté for 1 - 2 minutes. Add the rice and stir to coat.

5. Return heat to high and stir in the wine, broth, tomatoes, bay leaf, and reserved marinade. Bring to a boil then turn heat to low. Press chicken pieces down into the rice. Cover and cook for 20 minutes. Stir in the capers, olives, pimentos and peas and cook for 5 additional minutes.

* Annatto seeds can be found in most spice sections. I grind mine in a coffee grinder and put them back in the jar to use when I want yellow rice. (Sometimes you can find the ground annatto seeds in the spice or ethnic section). If you cannot find annatto seeds, you may be able to find Bijol in the ethnic section of your supermarket. If neither are available, feel free to use ground turmeric. It's not traditional, but it will color the rice.

• CAJUN GRILLED CHICKEN BREASTS •

Another quick dinner. Again, do not over cook the chicken breasts. Remove them from the grill just before it's done to ensure they remain succulent.

PREP: 5 minutes   COOK: 12 minutes

INGREDIENTS
    2 boneless skinless chicken breasts
    1 teaspoon olive oil
    1 teaspoon Cajun or Creole seasoning (or more to taste)
    1-1/2 teaspoons chopped Italian flat leaf parsley

DIRECTIONS
1.   Prepare grill for medium- high heat. Lightly oil grate.

2.   Place chicken breasts between two pieced of wax paper or plastic wrap and pound to an even thickness of about 1/2-inch. Brush chicken with olive oil and sprinkle evenly with Cajun seasoning.

3.   Grill for 4 - 5 minutes then turn and cook for 3 - 4 minutes more until just barely cooked through. Sprinkle with parsley and serve.

Serve with Pan-Roasted Grape Tomatoes and Rice Pilaf.

• CHICKEN FAJITAS •

To keep your veggies from falling through the grill grate, purchase a non-stick basket designed for grills. This accessory will not only keep your veggies from falling into the coals, it will allow you to turn all of the veggies at once. It's also great for fish fillets.

PREP: 10 minutes   MARINATE: 15 minutes
COOK: 15 minutes

INGREDIENTS
    1/3 cup olive oil
    2-1/2 tablespoons fresh lime juice
    1-1/4 teaspoons ground cumin
    3/4 teaspoon chili powder
    2/3 cup chopped fresh cilantro
    2 boneless, skinless chicken breasts or 4 boneless, skinless thighs
    1 large poblano pepper, halved, seeded and cut into 3/4-inch wide strips
    2 red or yellow peppers, halved, seeded and cut into 3/4-inch wide strips
    1 sweet or red onion, peeled and sliced into 1/2-inch rounds
    4 (8-inch) flour tortillas
    Salsa, guacamole, and sour cream to garnish

DIRECTIONS
1. Prepare grill for high heat. Lightly oil grate.

2. In a medium bowl, combine the olive oil, lime juice, cumin, chili powder, and cilantro until well mixed. Add chicken breasts and turn to coat. Marinate for 15 minutes, turning once or twice.

3. Remove chicken to a plate and add the peppers and onions to the bowl. Toss to coat.

4. Place chicken and veggies on grill and cook until well-browned and cooked through, about 5 - 7 minutes per side. Remove chicken and vegetables from grill. Slice chicken into thin strips. Place tortillas on grill and cook until warm and slightly charred, about 1 minute per side.

5. Fill tortillas with chicken and vegetables and garnish with salsa, guacamole, and sour cream.

Serve with Refried Beans and Mexican Rice.

• CHICKEN NUGGETS •

Deep down inside, we all love those bite-sized deep fried pieces of chicken served with a variety of dipping sauces in fast food joints that line our highways. Here's a healthier version that both adults and kids find delicious. I prefer making this with chicken thighs because they tend to be more tender and juicier than the breasts. But if you don't overcook the chicken, breasts will do just fine.

PREP: 5 minutes   COOK: 10 minutes

INGREDIENTS
    1 pound boneless, skinless chicken thighs or breasts, cut into 1-inch chunks
    1 egg, beaten
    1 cup Italian breadcrumbs
    1/4 cup grated Parmesan cheese
    1/2 teaspoon Hungarian sweet paprika
    1/2 teaspoon garlic powder
    Kosher salt and freshly ground black pepper, to taste
    3 tablespoons olive oil

DIRECTIONS
1. In a shallow bowl, lightly beat egg. In another shallow bowl or zip lock bag, combine the breadcrumbs, cheese, paprika, and garlic powder. Season chicken with salt and pepper to taste.

2. Dip the chicken into the egg then dredge in the seasoned bread crumbs (or place into the bag and shake to coat).

3. Heat a 10-inch skillet over medium heat. Add olive oil and swirl to coat. Add chicken and sauté until lightly brown and tender, about 5 minutes.

4. Transfer chicken to a plate lined with paper towels with a slotted spoon to drain.

Serve with your favorite dipping sauce and Savory Oven Fries.

Beef

 # Beef

"Where's the beef?"

Maybe I'm showing my age here by referencing a 1984 TV commercial that featured the crotchety, but loveable, Clara. But I still must ask the question. The beef industry has taken some media hits over the years (some, rightly deserved, but that's for others to write about). For some of us, due to cost or principles, it is rarely, if not ever, found on our tables.

And I'm okay with that.

For the rest of us who enjoy a good burger or steak on occasion, I offer another chapter of great beef recipes. I especially want you to check out "The Classics". These are recipes that have stood the test of time and they've become famous for one reason: they rock. Of course there may be minor variations in how they're prepared, but these are the ways I make them. Feel free to tweak them to make these classics your own.

Unfortunately, beef prices (like so many other prices) are going up. As a result, many of us have kissed the "8, 10 or even 12-ounce serving" goodbye. But that's not a bad thing; it'll certainly be easier on our bank accounts and with the recently recommended 4 or 6-ounce serving, eating beef will be easier on our arteries as well.

And since we're encouraged to eat smaller portions, I find that I can afford to buy better cuts of beef. I hope you will, as well.

In my previous book *Table for Two - The Cookbook for Couples*, I touted the amazing flat iron steak for its tenderness, delicious flavor, and relatively inexpensive cost. Well, evidently the word got out because flat iron steak has been getting harder and harder to find in my local grocery stores (and a number of subscribers to my e-newsletter have also written to let me know how difficult it was to get it, too). Because I promised that the ingredients in my recipes can be easily found in most grocery stores, I thought about leaving the flat irons out this time around. I'm glad I didn't. If you do find them in your local store, do what I do and buy as many as you can afford then freeze them (especially if they're on sale). If you can't find them, substitute NY strip or even top sirloin steak for the flat iron.

• BEEF WELLINGTON •

The last time I ordered this at a fine restaurant it almost cost me…well, never mind. Let's just say one of my kids didn't get the dental work they needed after that date night. Seriously though, I really did enjoy it and I wanted to make this at home. But all of the recipes I found called for a big hunk of filet mignon. That was way too much meat for two and it would also put quite a strain on my wallet. But I was determined to figure out how to make it for just the two of us at a price I could afford. This is what I came up with.

PREP: 20 minutes   COOK: 25 minutes

INGREDIENTS
  2 tablespoons unsalted butter
  6 ounces fresh mushrooms, sliced
  2 tablespoons chopped onion
  1/4 cup dry sherry
  1-1/2 tablespoons chopped fresh Italian leaf parsley
  2 (4 - 6 ounce) beef tenderloin filets
  1/3 (17.5 ounce) package frozen puff pastry, partially thawed
  1-1/2 cups béarnaise sauce
  Chopped fresh parsley to garnish

DIRECTIONS
  1. Preheat oven to 425.

  2. Heat a 10-inch skillet over medium-high heat. Add butter and swirl to coat. Stir in mushrooms, onion, sherry, and parsley and sauté until all the liquid is absorbed and the mixture resembles a paste. Spoon the mixture over each steak.

  3. Meanwhile, partially thaw the puff pastry sheets and roll out pieces thin enough to cover the top, sides and bottom of each steak. Place the steaks on a sheet of pastry and completely wrap each one. Place wrapped steaks on a lightly-oiled baking sheet, cover with plastic wrap and store in the refrigerator until you're ready to cook them.

  4. Bake steaks uncovered in the preheated oven for 25 minutes. (Note: They will be rare but will continue cooking while dish is sitting.)

  5. Prepare a béarnaise sauce (see page 137) or use a premix packet (Knorr's is good). Spoon béarnaise sauce over each steak and sprinkle with parsley to serve.

Serve with Broccoli Cheddar Mashed Potatoes.

• STEAK OSCAR •

Steak Oscar is a variation on Veal Oscar; a dish favored by Sweden's King Oscar II (1829 -1907), hence the name. This dish, like Beef Wellington, utilizes Béarnaise Sauce, which can be tricky to prepare. So I've included a recipe for a simple variation along with the traditional version. Some stores sell Béarnaise Sauce in jars and some in packet mixes. If you choose to go that route, simply find one that tastes good.

PREP: 20 minutes   COOK: 20 minutes

INGREDIENTS

   2 (4 - 6 ounce) beef tenderloin filets, about 1-1/2 inches thick
   1 tablespoon olive or canola oil
   Kosher salt and freshly ground black pepper, to taste
   1/4 cup unsalted butter
   1 (6-ounce) can lump crab meat, drained
   1/2 pound asparagus, tips only (save remaining for soup)
   1-1/2 cups béarnaise sauce

DIRECTIONS

1. Heat a 10-inch skillet over medium-high heat. Brush both sides of filet with oil and season with salt and pepper. Pan fry for 3 - 4 minutes per side for medium-rare (you may also prepare these on the grill or oven-roast them if you want to avoid smoking up the kitchen). Remove fillets to a plate and cover loosely with aluminum foil (or another plate).

2. Meanwhile, melt the butter in a small saucepan over low heat. Gently stir in the crabmeat and simmer while the filets are cooking.

3. Bring a small pot of salted water to boil. Add asparagus tips and cook just until the asparagus tips turn bright green, about 60-90 seconds, Remove and immediately place in a bowl of ice water to stop the cooking process. Drain well.

4. Prepare a béarnaise sauce (see page 137) or use a premix packet (Knorr's is good). Add 2 tablespoons to the crab mixture.

5. To assemble, top each broiled filet with crab meat, then half of the asparagus; spoon Béarnaise sauce, to taste, over all.

Serve with Steamed Broccoli and Roasted Red Potatoes.

SIMPLE BÉARNAISE SAUCE

1 stick unsalted butter, cut up
1 tablespoon lemon juice
1 tablespoon tarragon vinegar (or white wine vinegar)
1 tablespoon minced fresh chives
1/4 teaspoon kosher salt
1/2 teaspoon dried tarragon
2 extra-large egg yolks
Pinch pepper or cayenne
Kosher salt to taste

Combine all ingredients in a saucepan over low heat. Whisk until the butter melts, then whisk constantly until thickened. Remove from heat. Add salt if needed.

• STEAK AU POIVRE •

Although some folks tout the joys of bottled steak sauces, to me, a good steak requires little more than kosher salt and cracked pepper. A lot of cracked pepper. It seems that many people agree, because steak au poivre (steak with pepper) is one of the most popular methods of preparing a good steak. And talk about simple! In its easiest incarnation, the steak is seasoned only with salt and a heaping helping of fresh, coarsely cracked pepper (pressed into the meat with the palm of your hand) before searing it in a hot pan on the stove or on a grill. Some take it to the next level, as I've done here, by preparing a simple sauce. I'm making this with a tenderloin, but you can also make this with a flat iron or New York strip steaks.

PREP: 5 minutes   SET: 30 minutes
COOK: 10 minutes

INGREDIENTS
  2 (4 - 6 ounce) beef tenderloin filets, 1-1/2 inches thick
  Kosher salt to taste
  1 tablespoon whole black peppercorns
  2 tablespoons unsalted butter, divided
  1 teaspoon olive oil
  3 tablespoons chopped shallots
  3 tablespoons cognac
  1/2 cup heavy cream

DIRECTIONS
  1. Remove steaks from the refrigerator 30 minutes to 1 hour
      before cooking.

  2. Sprinkle all sides with salt. Using a mortar and pestle, coarsely crush the
      peppercorns (or you may put them in a small baggie and smack them
      with a kitchen hammer or other heavy object). Spread the peppercorns
      on a plate and press each filet until covered on both sides.

  3. Heat a 10-inch skillet over medium-high heat and add 1 tablespoon
      butter and olive oil. When the butter and oil begins to shimmer, add
      steaks to pan and cook for 4 minutes on each side for medium-rare.
      Remove steaks to a warm plate and tent with foil.

4. Pour off any fat in skillet and add the remaining butter to melt. Add the shallots and sauté until soft and translucent, about 3-5 minutes.

5. Remove skillet from heat*, gently add the cognac and ignite with a long match. (See Table for Two Tip on page: 116). Swirl the cognac until the flame dies. Return the pan to heat and add the cream. Bring the mixture to a boil and whisk until the sauce coats the back of a spoon, approximately 5 to 6 minutes. Season with salt to taste.

6. Return steaks back to the pan, spoon the sauce over, and serve.

Serve with a Baked Potato and Steamed Green Beans.

• COWBOY STEAK •

No, this is not one of the 'creative beef names' that some butchers conjure up to sell less popular pieces of meat that I spoke about in my first book *Table for Two - The Cookbook for Couples* (Sizzler Steaks anyone?) No, this really is a classic dish. A cowboy steak requires a good porterhouse steak (or at the least, a t-bone steak) so this is not the meal to create when the budget's tight. But if you're having a date night at home, this is an excellent choice. (Spurs and chaps are, of course, optional…)

PREP: 5 minutes   MARINATE: 1 hour or overnight
COOK: 20 minutes

INGREDIENTS
   3/4 to 1 pound porterhouse steak, 1-1/2 inches thick
   1/4 teaspoon garlic powder
   1-1/2 teaspoons chili powder
   1-1/2 teaspoons olive oil
   1 teaspoon kosher salt
   1/4 teaspoon cayenne pepper
   1/4 teaspoon freshly ground black pepper

DIRECTIONS
1.   In a small bowl, combine garlic, chili powder, salt, pepper, and oil; stir until it forms a thick paste. Rub paste over the entire surface of the steaks. Wrap each steak in plastic wrap and refrigerate for at least 1 hour or overnight.

2.   Preheat grill for high heat. Lightly oil grate.

3.   Grill steaks for 2 minutes. Flip and continue grilling for 2 more minutes. Move steaks to a cooler part of the grill or reduce heat to medium. Continue grilling until done. About 3 - 4 minutes per side for medium-rare.

4.   Trim meat from bone and divide among two plates.

Serve with Baked Potatoes and Sautéed Zucchini and Onions.

• COFFEE CRUSTED FILET MIGNON •

I'm not sure if this fairly-recent recipe has been around long enough to be considered a 'classic'. But its growing popularity is evidence that it will be one someday.

PREP: 10 minutes   SET: 30+ minutes
COOK: 15 minutes

INGREDIENTS
   1/4 cup medium grind Italian Roast coffee or coarsely ground coffee beans
   2 tablespoons freshly cracked black peppercorns
   2 tablespoons packed dark brown sugar
   2 tablespoons kosher salt
   2 tablespoons granulated garlic
   2 teaspoons cayenne pepper
   2 teaspoons Hungarian sweet paprika
   1 tablespoon peanut or canola oil
   2 (6 - 8 ounce) beef tenderloin filets (1-1/2 to 2-inch thick)

DIRECTIONS
   1.   Preheat oven to 425.

   2.   In a baking dish or pie pan, combine coffee, peppercorns, brown sugar, salt, garlic, cayenne pepper and paprika. Press the steaks firmly into the mixture to coat. Let steaks rest for 30 minutes at room temperature.

   3.   Heat a 10-inch skillet over medium-high heat. Add oil and heat until almost smoking. Add steaks and sear 2 - 3 minutes on each side. Place skillet in the oven and roast for 6 - 8 minutes for medium-rare. Remove steaks to a warm plate and loosely tent with tin foil for 5 - 10 minutes.

Serve with Baked Potatoes and Steamed Asparagus.

• FILET MIGNON WITH GARLIC SHRIMP CREAM SAUCE •

Now we move on to a few more beef recipes. They may not be classics, but they sure are good! This is an interesting take on the classic surf and turf; the shrimp is prepared in a simple cream sauce.

PREP: 10 minutes   COOK: 20 minutes

INGREDIENTS
    2 (4 - 6 ounce) beef tenderloin fillets, 1-1/2 inches thick
    3 tablespoons olive oil, divided
    3 tablespoons unsalted butter, divided
    1 large shallot, minced
    2 tablespoons minced garlic
    1/4 cup white wine
    1/2 pound uncooked large shrimp - peeled, deveined, and cut into 3 pieces
    1/4 cup heavy cream
    1 tablespoon butter
    Kosher salt and freshly ground black pepper, to taste
    Fresh chopped parsley to garnish

DIRECTIONS
    1.   Heat a 10-inch skillet over medium-high heat. Brush both sides of each filet with 1 tablespoon olive oil and sprinkle with salt. Place fillets into the skillet and cook until they start to become firm, about 3 to 4 minutes per side for medium-rare. Remove fillets to a plate and cover loosely with foil or another plate.

    2.   Melt 2 tablespoons butter with the remaining olive oil in the skillet over medium heat until the foam subsides from the butter. Add the shallot and garlic and sauté until the shallot is tender, about 2 minutes. Add wine and sauté until the wine reduces by half, about 3 minutes.

    3.   Add shrimp, cream, remaining, butter, and a pinch of salt and pepper to taste. Cook and stir until the sauce is thickened and the shrimp are pink, about 2 minutes.

    4.   Place fillets on serving plates, and top each with half the shrimp sauce. Season with additional salt and pepper to taste and sprinkle with chopped parsley to garnish.

Serve with Rice Pilaf and Steamed Broccoli.

• PORTUGUESE STYLE BEEF TENDERLOIN •

Red wine, chili paste and garlic are popular ingredients in many Portuguese dishes. They impart flavor and depth to food, especially foods that do not have a pronounced flavor of their own, like beef tenderloin. If your budget doesn't allow for this pricey cut, feel free to use flat iron steak. You can also use the red wine/chili paste on other meats like chicken breasts and pork tenderloin.

PREP: 10 minutes   COOK: 15 minutes

INGREDIENTS
   1/4 cup dry red wine
   1-1/2 tablespoons water
   3 cloves garlic, minced or pressed
   1 teaspoon chili paste
   1/8 teaspoon white pepper
   1/8 teaspoon kosher salt
   1 tablespoon vegetable oil, divided
   2 (4-6 ounce) beef tenderloin steaks

DIRECTIONS
   1.   In a small bowl, combine red wine, water, garlic, chili paste, white pepper and salt. Add beef, and turn to coat evenly.

   2.   Heat 1 tablespoon oil in a 10-inch skillet over medium-high heat. Add steaks and sauté for 2 minutes on each side. Turn heat to medium-low and continue to cook steaks until medium-rare, about 2 more minutes per side. Remove steaks to a plate and cover loosely with aluminum foil (or another plate). Let rest for 5 minutes.

   3.   Meanwhile, add the chili/wine sauce from the bowl to the skillet and bring to a boil for 2 minutes, scraping up any of the brown bits on the bottom. Place each filet on a plate and pour sauce over them.

Serve with Sautéed Zucchini and Tomatoes and Quinoa Pilaf.

• ROASTED SICILIAN STEAK •
WITH BAGNA CAUDA SAUCE

This is one hearty meal. It's a lot of steak so you may not eat it all in one sitting. That just means a delicious lunch the next day.

PREP: 10 minutes   COOK: 15 minutes

INGREDIENTS
    1 cup Italian seasoned panko bread crumbs
    1 cup grated Parmesan cheese
    1 teaspoon seasoned salt
    1 tablespoon garlic powder
    1 teaspoon dried oregano
    1/2 cup olive oil
    2 (8 -10 ounce) t-bone steaks, 1-1/2 inches thick

DIRECTIONS
FOR THE STEAK:
1. Heat the oven to 350°. Lightly oil a broiler pan.

2. In a baking dish or pie pan, combine the bread crumbs, Parmesan cheese, seasoned salt, garlic powder, and oregano. Pour the olive oil into a separate shallow dish. Dip the t-bone steaks in the olive oil on both sides; allow excess to drip off. Press the steaks into the bread crumb mixture then place onto the prepared broiler pan.

3. Bake on the middle rack until medium-rare, about 10 minutes.

FOR THE SAUCE:
    1/4 cup extra-virgin olive oil
    4 cloves garlic, minced or pressed
    4 anchovy fillets
    1-1/2 tablespoons fresh lemon juice
    6 tablespoons butter, cut into pats

1. Heat a small skillet over medium heat. Add the olive oil and swirl to coat. Stir in the garlic, anchovies and lemon juice and sauté until the anchovies have melted away, about 5 minutes. Whisk in the butter 1 pat at a time until combined. Pour sauce over steaks and serve.

Serve with buttered pasta and Sautéed Zucchini and Onions.

• GRILLED FLAT IRON STEAK •
WITH BLUE CHEESE-CHIVE BUTTER

Steak topped with cheese may be a new taste sensation for some people, but the folks who tried my strip steak with Parmesan cheese from *Table for Two - The Cookbook for Couples* wrote in to say it rocked. Now I want you to try this recipe featuring blue cheese. I think you'll find it rocks as well.

PREP: 15 Min   MARINATE: 30+ minutes
COOK: 10 minutes

INGREDIENTS
   2 tablespoons olive oil
   1 tablespoon red wine vinegar
   1 clove garlic, minced or pressed
   1-1/2 teaspoons cracked black pepper
   1/2 teaspoon dried rosemary leaves, crumbled
   1/2 teaspoon dried oregano
   1/8 teaspoon kosher salt
   1 12-ounce flat iron steak
   1-1/2 tablespoons softened unsalted butter
   1/2 ounce crumbled blue cheese
   1-1/2 teaspoons chopped fresh chives
   1/8 teaspoon freshly ground black pepper

DIRECTIONS
   1. In a small bowl, whisk together the olive oil, vinegar, garlic, black pepper, rosemary, oregano, and kosher salt. Place steak in a re-sealable plastic bag and add marinade. Turn to coat and refrigerate for at least 30 minutes, but preferably a couple of hours.

   2. Preheat an outdoor grill for medium-high heat and lightly oil grate. Meanwhile, remove steak from the marinade, shake off excess, and discard the remaining marinade. Allow the steak to stand at room temperature for 15 minutes as the grill heats up.

   3. Mash together the butter, blue cheese, chives, and black pepper; set aside. Cook the steak to desired degree of doneness, about 3-5 minutes per side for medium-rare. Remove steaks to a plate and cover loosely with tin foil or another plate to rest for 5 - 10 minutes.

   4. Slice the steak thinly across the grain and serve with a dollop of blue cheese-chive butter.

Serve with Rice Pilaf and Steamed Corn.

• GRILLED FLAT IRON STEAK •
WITH MAPLE MUSTARD MARINADE

You can also use this recipe for flank steak and even pork chops or lamb chops.

PREP: 5 minutes   MARINATE: 1+ hours
COOK: 10 minutes

INGREDIENTS
   6 tablespoons balsamic vinegar
   5 tablespoons maple syrup
   2-1/2 tablespoons Dijon mustard
   1 12-ounce flat iron steak
   Kosher salt and freshly ground black pepper, to taste

DIRECTIONS

1. In a small bowl, combine vinegar, maple syrup, and mustard. Place steak in a re-sealable plastic bag and add 1/2 cup marinade mixture. Turn to coat and refrigerate for at least 1 hour. Reserve remaining marinade.

2. Remove steak from marinade and pat dry. Season both sides of meat with salt and pepper to taste.

3. Pre-heat your gas or charcoal grill for medium-high. Lightly oil grate. Place the steak on the grill and cook about 3 minutes per side for medium-rare.

4. Meanwhile, pour reserved marinade into a small saucepan and place on medium-high heat. Bring to a boil, then let it cook for 2 minutes to warm and slightly reduce.

5. Take the steak off the grill and let rest 3 - 5 minutes. Cut in half and drizzle warmed marinade over steak to serve.

Serve with Grilled Broccoli with Lemon and Rice Pilaf.

• IRISH WHISKEY FLAT IRON STEAK •

Leave it to an Irishman to include a steak recipe featuring Irish whiskey. If you don't have any Jameson's on hand, you can make this with any brand of whiskey or bourbon.

PREP: 10 minutes   MARINATE: At least 1 hour
COOK: 15 minutes

INGREDIENTS
  1/3 cup olive oil
  2 tablespoons Irish whiskey
  2 tablespoons soy sauce
  2 teaspoons minced green onion, white with some green
  1/4 teaspoon garlic powder
  1-1/2 teaspoons freshly ground black pepper
  2 teaspoons chopped fresh parsley
  1/4 teaspoon dried thyme
  1/4 teaspoon crushed dried rosemary
  1 12-ounce flat iron steak
  2 tablespoons butter, softened

DIRECTIONS
  1. In a small bowl, combine the olive oil, whiskey, soy sauce, green onion, garlic, pepper, parsley, thyme, and rosemary. Place steak in a re-sealable plastic bag and add marinade. Turn to coat and marinate for at least an hour (if longer than an hour, refrigerate). Remove steaks from marinade and discard the marinade. Allow steak to come to room temperature before cooking if it's been refrigerated.

  2. Preheat an outdoor grill for medium-high heat and lightly oil the grate.

  3. Grill steak, turning once, about 3 - 4 minutes per side for medium-rare. Transfer steak to a warm plate and cover with another plate and let rest for 5 minutes. Cut in half and top with softened butter to serve.

Serve with Grilled Asparagus and Bacon Cheddar Mashed Potatoes.

• FLANK STEAK WITH CHIPOTLE SAUCE •

This is one spicy dish. I often make a little extra Chipotle mayo to keep in the fridge. It's a nice way to perk up sandwiches. Remember, though, a little bit of Chipotle goes a long way, so be sure to adjust this to your liking.

PREP: 10 minutes   MARINATE: 8+ hours
COOK: 10 minutes

INGREDIENTS
FOR THE STEAK:
- 1 12-ounce flank steak
- 2 tablespoons soy sauce
- 2 tablespoons olive oil
- 1 tablespoon honey
- 1 clove garlic, minced
- 2 teaspoons chopped fresh rosemary or 3/4 teaspoon dried
- 1 teaspoon coarsely ground black pepper
- 1/4 teaspoon kosher salt

CHIPOTLE MAYO:
- 6 tablespoons mayonnaise
- 1 tablespoon chopped chipotle peppers in adobo sauce

DIRECTIONS
1. Using a sharp knife, score the surface of the steak with shallow diagonal cuts at 1-in. intervals, making diamond shapes

2. In a small bowl, combine soy sauce, olive oil, honey, garlic, rosemary, pepper, and salt. Place steak in a re-sealable plastic bag and add marinade. Turn to coat and refrigerate for 8 hours or over night.

3. Meanwhile, in a small bowl, stir the chipotle peppers into the mayonnaise. Cover and refrigerate.

4. Preheat an outdoor grill for medium-high heat and lightly oil grate. Remove steak and pat dry. Discard marinade. Grill steak turning once for 3 minutes per side for medium-rare.

5. Remove steak to a warm plate, cover and let stand for 5 minutes. Slice thin and serve with chipotle sauce.

Serve with Mexican Corn and Quinoa Pilaf.

• GRILLED FLANK STEAK WITH PEPPERS AND ONIONS •

Perhaps I should've included this with the Classics. Folks have been grilling steaks and onions since forever. This is a great way to cook steak for fajitas.

PREP: 10 minutes   MARINATE: 8+ hours
COOK: 15 minutes

INGREDIENTS
    1 12-ounce flank steak
    1/2 teaspoon kosher salt
    Freshly ground black pepper, to taste
    1 tablespoon olive oil
    2 tablespoons lime juice
    1 clove garlic, minced or pressed
    1 teaspoon oregano
    1 medium onion, peeled and sliced
    1 green bell pepper, seeded and sliced
    1 red bell pepper, seeded and sliced

DIRECTIONS
1. With a sharp knife, lightly score the flank steak in a criss-cross pattern on both sides, about 1-inch apart. Season with salt and pepper.

2. In a small bowl, combine the olive oil, lime juice, garlic, and oregano. Place steak in a re-sealable plastic bag and add marinade. Turn to coat and refrigerate for 8 hours or over night.

3. Preheat an outdoor grill for medium-high heat and lightly oil grate. Remove steak and pat dry. Discard marinade. Place steak, onions and peppers on the grate. Grill steak, turning once, for 3 minutes per side for medium-rare. Turn onions and peppers to slightly char. Remove steak to a warm platter and let stand for 5 minutes. Slice thin and serve with onions and peppers.

Serve with Rice Pilaf.

• GRILLED RIB EYE STEAKS WITH SAUTÉED VEGETABLES •

What could be better than an unadorned, grilled rib eye steak? How about rib eye steak with bacon! Of course you shouldn't eat this every day, bit it is nice on a special occasion.

PREP: 10 minutes   COOK: 10 minutes

INGREDIENTS
    2 (8-ounce) rib eye steaks, 3/4 inch thick
    1 teaspoon kosher salt
    3 thick slices bacon
    2 teaspoons unsalted butter
    1/4 teaspoon Worcestershire sauce
    3/4 teaspoon Dijon mustard
    1/2 medium onion, sliced thin
    1/2 red bell pepper, seeded and sliced thin
    1/2 pound mushrooms, quartered
    2 tablespoons crumbled blue cheese, divided

DIRECTIONS
1. Prepare outdoor grill for medium-high heat. Lightly oil grate. Season the steaks on both sides with salt and let stand at room temperature.

2. Meanwhile, fry bacon in a 10-inch skillet over medium-high heat until crisp. Remove from the skillet and drain on paper towels. Do not drain grease from the pan.

3. Grill the steaks about 4 - 5 minutes per side, for medium-rare.

4. While the steaks are cooking, stir the butter, Worcestershire sauce and mustard into the bacon grease. Cook and stir over medium-high heat until butter has melted. Add the onions, red bell pepper and mushrooms; cook and stir until tender, about 6 - 8 minutes.

5. To serve, place steaks onto plates. Top with bacon, then blue cheese and then the vegetables. Serve immediately.

Serve with Buttermilk Mashed Potatoes.

• BEEF AND ASPARAGUS STIR FRY •

Stir frying is a great way to whip up a meal in no time. Start your rice or noodles before preparing the beef and you'll have dinner on the table in about 20 minutes.

PREP: 10 minutes   COOK: 10 minutes

INGREDIENTS

- 2 teaspoons cornstarch
- 1/2 cup beef broth
- 3 tablespoons dry sherry
- 2 teaspoons soy sauce
- 1 12-ounce top sirloin or flank steak
- 1/8 teaspoon freshly ground black pepper
- 1 tablespoon canola or peanut oil
- 1/2 pound asparagus, cut in 2-inch lengths
- 1-1/2 teaspoons finely chopped fresh ginger
- 1 garlic clove, minced or pressed

DIRECTIONS

1. In a small bowl, combine the cornstarch, beef broth, sherry and soy sauce. Stir to dissolve. Slice beef cross wise into thin strips and season with pepper.

2. Heat a 10-inch skillet over high heat. Add oil and swirl to coat. When oil just begins to smoke, add beef and sauté for 2 -3 minutes. Add asparagus and sauté until bright green, about 2 - 3 minutes more. Add ginger and garlic and sauté for 1 additional minute.

3. Reduce heat to medium and stir in sauce. Cook until slightly thickened, about 2 - 3 minutes.

Serve over Asian noodles, pasta, or Steamed White Rice.

• SESAME BEEF STIR FRY •

Here's another simple stir fry meal that will probably find its way onto your list of dependable weeknight meals. To slice the steak into thin strips, chill it in the freezer for a bit.

PREP: 10 minutes   COOK: 10 minutes

INGREDIENTS
    2 tablespoons soy sauce
    1 tablespoon minced fresh ginger
    1 clove garlic, minced or pressed
    1/4 teaspoon crushed red pepper flakes
    1 teaspoon cornstarch
    1/2 cup beef broth
    1 12-ounce top sirloin or flank steak
    2 tablespoons sesame seeds
    2 tablespoons peanut or canola oil, divided
    3 cups fresh broccoli florets
    1 cup peeled and thinly sliced carrots

DIRECTIONS

1. In a small bowl, combine the soy sauce, ginger, garlic, pepper flakes, cornstarch and beef broth. Stir to dissolve the cornstarch.

2. Slice beef cross-wise in thin strips. Sprinkle beef slices with sesame seeds to coat.

3. Heat a 10-inch skillet over high heat. Add 1 tablespoon oil and swirl to coat. When oil just begins to smoke, add beef and sauté until brown, about 2 - 3 minutes. Remove to a warm plate with a slotted spoon.

4. Add remaining oil to skillet. Add broccoli and carrots and sauté until crisp-tender, about 3 - 4 minutes.

5. Reduce heat to medium. Stir sauce again then add to pan along with beef and accumulated juices. Cook until sauce thickens, about 2 - 3 minutes.

Serve over Asian noodles, pasta, or Steamed White Rice.

• CREAMED CHIPPED BEEF ON TOAST •

This simple dish makes for a quick hot lunch or light dinner. In fact, this also makes a nice breakfast or brunch dish as well. For dinner, serve this with a light salad.

PREP: 5 minutes   COOK: 10 minutes

INGREDIENTS
  2 tablespoons unsalted butter
  3 tablespoons all-purpose flour
  1-1/4 cups warm milk
  1/2 (8-ounce) jar dried beef
  Pinch cayenne pepper
  4 slices toasted bread

DIRECTIONS

1.   Heat a small saucepan over low heat. Add butter and swirl to coat. Whisk in flour all at once and stir for 2 or 3 minutes to form a roux.

2.   Increase heat to medium-high. Whisk in milk, a little at a time, and stir until thickened, about 5 minutes. Stir in beef and cayenne, and heat through. Serve over toast.

• FLORIDA BARBEQUE CHUCK ROAST •

Who would've thought that this inexpensive cut of meat could turn into a deliciously tender meal? I guess it was up to the early Florida cattlemen. And I'm glad they did. This is similar to barbequed beef brisket but in smaller portions and half the price. The important thing is to slice this very thin - it will make a big difference. Oh, and this will make more than enough for two, so feel free to use the thin slices for sandwiches. Simply reheat slices in a little broth or water so they wont dry out.

PREP: 15 minutes   MARINATE: 6 - 8 hours
COOK: 2 hours

INGREDIENTS
    2 pounds chuck roast
    2 teaspoons chili powder
    1/2 teaspoon oregano
    2 cloves garlic, minced or pressed
    1/4 cup red wine
    2 tablespoons red wine vinegar
    1/4 cup olive or canola oil
    1/4 teaspoon freshly ground black pepper
    Mild or spicy prepared salsa

DIRECTIONS
1. In a small bowl, combine the chili powder, oregano and garlic. Pierce the meat at intervals with a fork then rub the chili mixture all over. In the same bowl combine the red wine, vinegar, oil, and pepper. Put the meat in a zip lock bag and add the red wine marinade to coat. Refrigerate for 6 - 8 hours.

2. Prepare a grill for indirect heat. Place a drip pan next to the coals. Lightly oil the grate. Remove the meat from the marinade and place it on the grate above the drip pan. Brush the meat with the marinade. Cover the grill and cook the roast slowly, turning from time to time, brushing with reserved marinade, for about 1-1/2 hours until the roast registers 120° with an instant read thermometer for medium-rare.

3. Remove meat from grill to a platter and cover loosely with tin foil for 15 minutes. Slice very thin and serve with salsa.

Serve with Grilled Corn and Spicy Oven Fries.

Pork

 # Pork

Unlike lamb, I don't need to convince many of you to try pork. Whether it's pork loin, ribs, sausage, bacon or hot dogs, most of us eat pork in some form every week. We eat it roasted, barbequed, stir fried and pulled, making pork one of the most versatile cuts of meat. And the world agrees, because pork consumption worldwide is close to 110 million tons. That's a lot of Porky Pig.

Of course most of us here in the states reach for pork chops when we're in the mood for pork because they're inexpensive and quick to prepare. However, when you walk up to the meat counter, you're likely to find quite an array of cuts labeled 'chops'. Here's a quick list of what you might find. I've arranged them according to their tenderness:

- Pork Loin Chops (also labeled pork loin end chops, loin pork chops, pork center loin chops). These chops will have a t-shaped bone similar to t-bone steaks. These chops are the most tender.
- Pork Rib Chops (also labeled pork rib cut chops, rib pork chops, pork chop end cut)
- Pork sirloin chops (also labeled sirloin pork chops)
- Pork top loin chops (also labeled pork strip chops) are sometimes sold boneless and called pork loin fillets.

Fortunately for our arteries, today's pork chops have much less fat than those of a few decades ago. Unfortunately for our palates, today's pork chops cook up much drier than in days past. The remedy? Brining. Soaking the chops for even 30 minutes will help you cook up tender, juicy chops that are just like the one's grandma used to make.

BRINING PORK CHOPS:
In a medium bowl, combine 1 quart water and 2 tablespoons salt and stir to dissolve. Place pork chops into a 1-gallon zip lock bag and add brining liquid. Let sit for 30 minutes. Remove pork chops and pat dry. Cook as directed.

• SAUTÉED PORK CHOPS WITH SAGE •

Don't let the 40 minute cook time scare you off. Most of the cooking time is unattended allowing you plenty of time to prepare the sides.

PREP: 30 minutes   COOK: 40 minutes

INGREDIENTS
   3/4 teaspoon kosher salt
   1/4 teaspoon dried sage
   1/4 teaspoon ground black pepper
   2 bone-in pork loin chops, 3/4 to 1-inch thick
   1 tablespoon unsalted butter
   1/3 cup beef broth

DIRECTIONS

1.   In a small bowl, combine the salt, sage and black pepper. Heat a 10-inch skillet over medium heat and add the butter. Swirl to coat. Add the chops and sauté until well-browned, about 5 minutes per side.

2.   Add beef broth to skillet and reduce heat to low. Cover and simmer chops for 30 minutes, turning once.

Serve with Lemon Balsamic Broccoli and Roasted Red Potatoes.

Table For Two Tips

HOT PAN, COLD OIL, FOOD WON'T STICK
This mantra has been around for decades. I believe Jeff Smith was the one who popularized it on his Frugal Gourmet show back in the 80's. However, Harold McGee, renowned expert on the chemistry of food and cooking, also states that it's better to heat your pan first and then add your oil or butter.

The oil or butter fills the microscopic hills and valleys of even the most smooth-looking pan to create an even surface on which the food will cook. The longer the oil or butter spends in contact with the hot metal of your pan, the more time it has to break down and become viscous and gummy. Therefore, to better ensure that your food won't stick, heat your pan, add the oil or butter and swirl to coat, then immediately add your meat or vegetables.

• PORK CHOPS WITH BLUE CHEESE GRAVY •

I've prepared beef using blue cheese. They go together quite well. Especially hamburgers. Here's a blue cheese twist for pork chops. The gravy is rich. You'll love it.

PREP: 5 minutes   COOK: 30 minutes

INGREDIENTS
    1 tablespoon unsalted butter
    2 bone-in pork loin chops, 3/4 to 1-inch thick
    1/2 teaspoon kosher salt
    1/4 teaspoon freshly ground black pepper, or to taste
    1/4 teaspoon garlic powder, or to taste
    1/2 cup whipping cream
    1 ounce blue cheese, crumbled

DIRECTIONS
    1. Heat a 10-inch skillet over medium heat. Add butter to skillet and swirl to melt. Season chops with salt, pepper and garlic powder. Add chops and sauté, turning occasionally, until brown and barely pink inside, about 20 minutes.

    2. Remove chops to a plate and cover with another plate to keep warm. Stir the whipping cream into the skillet, loosening any bits of meat stuck to the bottom. Stir in blue cheese. Cook, stirring constantly until sauce thickens, about 5 minutes. Pour sauce over pork chops and serve.

Serve with Steamed Green Beans and Basic Garlic Smashed Potatoes.

• GRILLED BOURBON GLAZED PORK CHOPS •

When you're in the mood for pork on the grill but don't have time to barbeque, you'll be glad you have this recipe. When you purchase molasses for this dish (or any other recipe) look for unsulphured molasses. It's made from sun-ripened sugar cane that's been allowed to grow for 12 - 15 months. It's sweeter than those that have had sulphur added.

PREP: 5 minutes   COOK: 10 minutes

INGREDIENTS
  2 bone-in pork loin chops, 3/4 to 1-inch thick
  1 teaspoon olive or canola oil
  1-1/2 tablespoons cracked black pepper (more coarse than ground)
  1 tablespoon molasses
  1 tablespoon spicy brown mustard
  2 tablespoons bourbon
  1/2 teaspoon Worcestershire sauce

DIRECTIONS
  1. Preheat grill to medium-high heat. Lightly oil grate.

  2. Press cracked pepper onto each side of the chops. In a small bowl, combine the molasses, mustard, bourbon, and Worcestershire sauce.

  3. Grill chops for 2 - 3 minutes until nicely brown on one side. Brush with bourbon molasses mixture and turn. Grill for an additional 4 - 5 minutes, turning and basting often, until the chops are well-glazed and cooked through.

Serve with Grilled Corn and Savory Oven Fries.

• GRILLED PORK CHOPS WITH PEACHES •

In *Table for Two - The Cookbook for Couples* I introduced grilled peaches as a great dessert for cookouts. Then I thought, why not use grilled peaches as part of the entrée? I think it was a good thought. You probably will think so as well.

PREP: 5 minutes   COOK: 10 minutes

INGREDIENTS
   2 large ripe peaches, peeled, halved and pitted
   1/4 cup barbeque sauce
   1 tablespoon cider or white wine vinegar
   1 tablespoon honey
   2 bone-in center cut pork chops, 3/4 - 1-inch thick
   Kosher salt and freshly ground black pepper, to taste

DIRECTIONS
   1.   Preheat grill to medium-high heat. Lightly oil grate.

   2.   Coarsely chop one peach then place in a food processor or blender along with the barbeque sauce, vinegar, and honey. Process until smooth. Set half the sauce aside to serve with the meal.

   3.   Season pork chops generously with salt and pepper to taste. Place pork chops on the grill, brush with half of the remaining barbeque sauce and cook for 4 minutes. Turn the pork chops and brush on the remaining half of the barbeque sauce. Add peach halves to the grill, cut side down. Grill the chops and peaches until the pork chops are medium-rare and the peaches are tender, about 4 minutes.

   4.   Remove the chops and peaches from the grill. Cut each peach half into thirds and serve with chops and reserved barbeque sauce.

Serve with Grilled Asparagus and Bacon Cheddar Mashed Potatoes.

• ROAST PORK CHOPS WITH BACON AND GREENS•

Here's a quick version of the southern staple smothered pork chops and greens.

PREP: 10 minutes   COOK: 20 minutes

INGREDIENTS
   2 bone-in pork loin chops, 1-1/2 inch thick
   3 tablespoons chopped fresh marjoram, divided (or 1 tablespoon dried)
   1/2 teaspoon allspice
   1/2 teaspoon kosher salt
   1/4 teaspoon freshly ground black pepper, to taste
   2 tablespoons olive oil
   2 thick-cut bacon slices
   2 cloves garlic, minced or pressed
   8 cups assorted greens (kale, mustard greens, Swiss chard), stems discarded
   5 teaspoons white wine vinegar
   1/2 cup chicken broth
   2 tablespoons Dijon mustard

DIRECTIONS
   1.   Preheat oven to 475°.

   2.   In a small bowl, combine 2 tablespoons (or 2 teaspoons if dried)
        marjoram, allspice, salt, and pepper. Rub the spice mixture on both
        sides of the chops.

   3.   Heat a 10-inch skillet over high heat. Add oil and swirl to coat. Add
        pork chops and brown on all sides, about 7 minutes. Transfer chops to
        a small rimless baking sheet and roast until they register 145° with an
        instant read thermometer, about 9 minutes.

   4.   Meanwhile, add bacon to the skillet and reduce heat to medium. Sauté
        until brown, about 3 minutes. Add the garlic and sauté for 1 additional
        minute. Stir in greens and sauté until wilted, about 3 minutes. Add 1
        teaspoon wine vinegar and season with salt and pepper to taste.

   5.   Remove greens and most of the bacon from the skillet to a bowl. Add
        broth, mustard and remaining wine vinegar to skillet and simmer until
        slightly thickened, about 4 minutes. Stir in remaining marjoram.

   6.   Divide greens between two plates, top with pork chops and spoon
        sauce over all.

Serve with Boiled New Potatoes.

• SALT AND PEPPER CRUSTED PORK TENDERLOIN •

It can't get any easier than this. But don't let the simplicity of this dish put you off. Go ahead and give it a shot. Then double or triple it for company. They'll think you're a genius. But hey, we both know you are anyway.

PREP: 5 minutes   SET: 15 minutes
COOK: 25 minutes

INGREDIENTS
    3/4 pound pork tenderloin
    2 teaspoons freshly ground black pepper
    1 teaspoon kosher salt
    1 teaspoon rosemary, crumbled
    1 clove garlic, minced or crushed
    1 tablespoon olive oil

DIRECTIONS
1. Preheat oven to 400°.

2. In a small bowl, combine the pepper, salt, rosemary, and garlic. Rub mixture all over pork tenderloin.

3. Heat an oven-proof 10-inch skillet over high heat. Add oil and swirl to coat. Add tenderloin and brown on all sides, about 5 - 6 minutes. Transfer skillet to the oven and roast until pork is cooked through, about 20 minutes. Slice and serve.

Serve with Garlic Roasted Broccoli with Balsamic Vinegar and Sautéed Potatoes with Mushrooms.

• MAPLE-GARLIC MARINATED PORK TENDERLOIN •

I love pork tenderloin because it is so tender, in spite of the fact that it is low in fat, and because it takes to marinating so well. This is another great company dish if you double the ingredients.

PREP: 5 minutes   MARINATE: 8 hours or overnight
COOK: 25 minutes

INGREDIENTS
  1 tablespoon Dijon mustard
  1/2 teaspoon sesame oil
  1/4 teaspoon garlic powder
  Freshly ground black pepper, to taste
  1/2 cup maple syrup
  3/4 pound pork tenderloin

DIRECTIONS
  1. In a small bowl, combine mustard, sesame oil, garlic, pepper, and maple syrup. Place pork in a re-sealable plastic bag and add marinade. Turn to coat and refrigerate for 8 hours or over night.

  2. Preheat grill for medium-low heat. Lightly oil grate.

  3. Remove pork from marinade, and set aside. Transfer marinade to a small saucepan, and cook on the stove over medium-low heat for 5 minutes.

  4. Lightly oil grate. Place pork on grate and grill, basting with reserved marinade, until interior is no longer pink, about 15 to 25 minutes. Watch your heat, you don't want the marinade to burn.

Serve with Steamed Corn and Bacon Cheddar Mashed Potatoes.

• PORK TENDERLOIN WITH HONEY GRAPE SAUCE •

We've prepared chicken and fish with grapes. Why not pork?

PREP: 15 minutes   COOK: 25 minutes

INGREDIENTS
   3/4 pound pork tenderloin
   Kosher salt and freshly ground black pepper, to taste
   3 teaspoons olive oil, divided
   1-1/2 tablespoons minced shallots
   1 teaspoon minced garlic
   2/3 cup seedless red grapes, halved
   1 tablespoon soy sauce
   1 tablespoon honey
   ¼ teaspoon grated fresh ginger
   1/8 teaspoon Asian five-spice powder

DIRECTIONS
1. Cut the tenderloin crosswise into 6 pieces. Place pieces one at a time between two sheets of plastic wrap or wax paper and pound to 1/2-inch thickness to create pork "medallions". Season with salt and pepper to taste.

2. Heat a 10-inch skillet over high heat. Add 2 teaspoons oil and swirl to coat. Add medallions and sauté until brown but still tender, about 2 - 3 minutes per side. Remove to a plate and cover with another plate to keep warm.

3. Turn heat to medium and add the remaining oil to the skillet. Stir in the shallots and garlic and sauté for 2 minutes. Stir in the grapes, soy sauce, honey, ginger and five spice powder and sauté until heated through

4. Return medallions with any juice that has collected to the skillet. Sauté, turning the medallions in the sauce until cooked through, about 8 minutes. Serve medallions with sauce.

Serve with Sautéed Snow Peas and Steamed White Rice.

• KALAMATA PORK TENDERLOIN WITH ROSEMARY •

I know you can buy black olives from California for much less than their Greek cousins, but you'll be selling your taste buds short by doing so. As you've probably already gathered, I do try to cook frugally, but I also use more expensive ingredients if they make a huge difference in the dish. Being frugal does not mean being cheap.

PREP: 10 minutes   COOK: 15 minutes

INGREDIENTS
   3/4 pound pork tenderloin
   1/4 cup all-purpose flour
   1/4 teaspoon kosher salt
   1/8 teaspoon freshly ground black pepper
   3 teaspoons olive oil, divided
   2 teaspoons chopped fresh rosemary
   1 small clove garlic, minced or pressed
   1/4 cup dry red wine
   1/4 cup chicken broth
   1 tablespoon sliced Kalamata olives
   1-1/2 teaspoons grated lemon zest

DIRECTIONS
1. Cut the tenderloin crosswise into 6 pieces. Place pieces on at a time between two sheets of plastic wrap or wax paper and pound to ½-inch thickness.

2. In a shallow bowl, combine the flour, salt, and pepper. Dredge pork in flour to coat. Shake of excess.

3. In a 10-inch skillet, heat 2 teaspoons olive oil over medium-high heat. Add medallions pork and sauté until browned, turning once, about 3 minutes per side. Transfer meat to a plate and cover with another plate to keep warm.

4. Reduce the heat to low and add remaining olive oil. Stir in rosemary and garlic and sauté for 2 minutes. Pour in wine, and bring to a boil. Boil until the liquid is thick. Pour in chicken broth and boil until reduced to about half. Stir in olives and lemon zest and cook until heated through. Spoon sauce over the pork and serve.

Serve with Garlic Roasted Broccoli with Pine Nuts and Greek Style Mashed Potatoes.

• SWEET AND SOUR PORK •

This popular dish is usually deep-fried, but we're trying to cook healthier. So instead of the traditional and fatty pork butt (which, I confess is delicious) and a couple of cups of hot oil for frying, we are going to use pork tenderloin and just a smidgen of oil. Your arteries will thank you and your taste buds won't miss a thing.

PREP: 10 minutes   COOK: 12 minutes

INGREDIENTS
   3/4 pound pork tenderloin, cut into 1-inch cubes
   1-1/2 tablespoons corn starch, divided
   1 teaspoon kosher salt
   1/4 teaspoon freshly ground black pepper
   1 tablespoon soy sauce
   2 tablespoons sugar
   2 tablespoons cider vinegar
   1-1/2 teaspoons ketchup
   3 tablespoons water
   1/4 cup olive oil
   1 slice fresh ginger
   1/4 cup diced green pepper
   1/4 cup diced red pepper

DIRECTIONS
   1.   In medium bowl, combine 1 tablespoon cornstarch, salt and pepper. Add pork and toss to coat. In another small bowl, combine the soy sauce, sugar, cider vinegar, ketchup, water and remaining cornstarch.

   2.   Heat a 10-inch skillet over medium-high heat. Add oil and swirl to coat. Add pork and sauté until golden brown, about 8 minutes. Remove with a slotted spoon to a paper towel on a plate to drain.

   3.   Add ginger to the skillet and sauté until aromatic, about 30 seconds. Remove ginger and add green and red peppers. Sauté for 2 minutes. Add soy sauce mixture to the skillet and bring to a boil, stirring until thickened, about 2 minutes.

   4.   Add pork to skillet and toss to coat.

Serve with Steamed White Rice.

• PORK LO MEIN •

Here is another popular Asian dish. If you aren't able to find dried mushrooms, feel free to substitute baby portobellos. I usually do. And if you can't find lo mein noodles, use regular thin spaghetti.

PREP: 15 minutes   COOK: 20 minutes

INGREDIENTS
    1/2 pound pork tenderloin, cut into thin matchstick strips*
    2 dried Chinese mushrooms (or four baby portobello mushrooms)
    2 teaspoons cornstarch
    1/4 teaspoon kosher salt
    1/2 pound lo mein noodles (or thin spaghetti)
    1 tablespoon peanut or canola oil
    1/2 teaspoon grated ginger
    2 scallions, cut into 2-inch pieces, green parts included
    1/4 cup bamboo shoots
    1/2 zucchini, cut into matchstick strips, or 1 cup snow peas
    1 tablespoon soy sauce
    1 tablespoon oyster sauce
    1-1/2 teaspoons sesame oil

DIRECTIONS
1.   Soak dried mushrooms in 1/4 cup warm water until soft, about 15 minutes. Drain, reserving liquid. Remove stems and discard. Slice caps into shreds. If using baby portobellos, slice into shreds.

2.   In a medium bowl, combine the cornstarch and salt. Add pork tenderloin and toss to coat.

3.   Meanwhile, cook noodles according to directions until just tender or al dente. Drain and rinse under cold water to stop the cooking.

4.   Heat a 10-inch skillet over medium-high heat. Add oil and swirl to coat. When the oil just begins to smoke, add ginger and sauté until fragrant, about 20 seconds. Add pork and sauté until meat loses its pink color, about 3 minutes. Remove pork with a slotted spoon to a small bowl.

5.   Stir in scallions, mushrooms, bamboo shoots and zucchini, and sauté until warmed through, about 2 minutes. Add soy sauce, oyster sauce, reserved mushroom water (or two tablespoons water if using portobellos), noodles and pork. Sauté until noodles are heated through, about 3 - 4 minutes. Drizzle with sesame oil and serve.

*Slice the tenderloin crosswise into thin strips, then stack a few strips on top of each other and slice into matchsticks. If you put the pork tenderloin in the freezer for a bit you will be able to slice it into matchsticks easier.

• BROILED HAM STEAK WITH PLUM GLAZE •

Ham steaks are pre-cooked so you can create a delicious entree in no time. Stock up when they are on sale and keep them in the freezer for those weeknights when you want something nicer than a burger or spaghetti.

PREP: Under 5 minutes   COOK: 15 minutes

INGREDIENTS
    1/4 cup plum preserves
    1 tablespoon Dijon mustard
    1 teaspoon lemon juice
    1/8 teaspoon ground cinnamon
    1 12-ounce ham steak, 3/4 to 1-inch thick
    Kosher salt and freshly ground black pepper, to taste

DIRECTIONS

1. Preheat broiler to high, set rack to 4 inches from the heating elements.

2. Combine the plum preserves, mustard, lemon juice, and cinnamon in a small saucepan. Cook over medium heat until the mixture is slightly thickened, about 3 - 5 minutes

3. Brush one side of the steak with the glaze and broil, glazed side up, for 5 minutes. Turn the steak and brush with glaze. Broil for 5 minutes more.

Serve with Boiled New Potatoes and Pan-Roasted Rosemary Carrots.

Lamb

 Lamb

In my first book, *Table for Two - The Cookbook for Couples*, I did my best to try to convince folks to eat more lamb. For some reason, it still has earned a mixed reputation. Often when I'm doing shows I ask members of the audience if they enjoy lamb. Most say they don't. When I ask them why, they say they don't like the taste. When I ask them when was the last time they tried lamb, most can't remember!

I'm still convinced that they had a bad experience when they were young. Perhaps the lamb was overcooked and slathered with some type of strong, minty, canned green sauce. Who would want to have lamb again if that was the way they had to eat it?

So I'm climbing back up on my soapbox to extol the glory of lamb. Remember, it plays a major role in Mediterranean and Middle Eastern cuisines, not to mention the cuisines of Northern Europe, Australia, New Zealand, Canada, and the British Isles.

Hey…millions of people can't be wrong.

Here's a dozen more recipes for lamb. If you haven't tried it in a while, start with the Pan-Seared Rosemary Lamb Chops. I promise you, that one dish will forever change your thoughts about lamb.

• PAN-SEARED ROSEMARY LAMB CHOPS •

It doesn't get much simpler than this (unless, of course, your palate yearns for raw lamb). Feel free to cook these on the grill, too.

PREP: Under 5 minutes   COOK: 10 minutes

INGREDIENTS
- 1 teaspoon chopped fresh rosemary
- 1/4 teaspoon kosher salt
- 1/8 teaspoon freshly ground black pepper
- 1 clove garlic, pressed or minced
- 4 (3-ounce) rib lamb chops
- 2 teaspoons olive oil
- 2 tablespoons unsalted butter, divided

DIRECTIONS
1. In a small bowl, combine the rosemary, salt, pepper and garlic. Rub mixture over the lamb chops and set aside.

2. Heat a 10-inch skillet over medium-high heat. Add the olive oil and swirl to coat. Add lamb and cook for 3 minutes per side for medium-rare. Remove lamb to a warm plate.

Top each chop with a 1/2 pat of butter and let sit for 5 minutes.

Serve with Roasted Asparagus and Tomatoes and Orzo with Parmesan Cheese.

• BASIC GRILLED LAMB CHOPS •

Once you taste grilled lamb chops, you'll find yourself stocking up when they are on sale.

PREP: 5 minutes   MARINATE: 1+ hours
COOK: 5 minutes

INGREDIENTS
    1 tablespoon olive oil
    2 tablespoons lemon juice
    2 cloves garlic, minced or pressed
    1/2 teaspoon rosemary
    1/4 teaspoon thyme leaves
    Pinch cayenne pepper
    1/2 teaspoon kosher salt
    2 lamb shoulder chops, about 3/4-inch thick

DIRECTIONS
1.   In a small bowl, combine the olive oil, lemon juice, garlic, rosemary, thyme, cayenne pepper, and salt.

2.   Place chops in a re-sealable plastic bag and add marinade. Turn to coat and marinate for at least an hour (if longer than an hour, refrigerate).

3.   Preheat grill to medium-high heat. Lightly oil the grate. Remove bag from refrigerator and let it come to room temperature. Let chops come to room temperature (approximately 20 minutes) before grilling. Remove chops and discard marinade.

4.   Place chops on the grate and grill until bottom of each chop is well browned, about 2 minutes. Turn each chop and cook about 2 more minutes for medium-rare (or 2-1/2 minutes for medium).

Serve with Grilled Asparagus and Italian Style Mashed Potatoes.

• GRILLED SPICED LAMB CHOPS •

Here's another great grilled lamb recipe. It doesn't require any marinating so you can make this one in a jiffy.

PREP: 5 minutes   COOK: 10 minutes

INGREDIENTS
    1/2 teaspoon cinnamon
    1/4 teaspoon freshly ground black pepper
    1/8 teaspoon ground allspice
    1/8 teaspoon cumin
    Pinch of kosher salt
    Pinch of cayenne pepper
    4 (4-ounce) lamb loin chops, 1 to 1-1/2 inch thick
    Lime wedges to garnish

DIRECTIONS
    1.   In a small bowl, combine the cinnamon, pepper, allspice, cumin, salt and
          cayenne pepper. Rub spice mixture evenly over the chops.

    2.   Prepare grill for medium-high heat. Lightly oil grate. Grill chops 4 - 5
          minutes on each side for medium-rare. Garnish with lime wedges.

Serve with Steamed Green Beans and Orzo with Mushrooms.

• GRILLED LAMB CHOPS WITH SOY-SHALLOT MARINADE •

If the chops at the market are thinner than 3/4-inch and more like 1/2-inch, you'll be able to reduce the grilling time by about thirty seconds per side.

PREP: 5 minutes   MARINATE: 30 minutes
COOK: 5 minutes

INGREDIENTS
    2 tablespoons minced shallots
    1 tablespoon minced fresh thyme leaves or 1 teaspoon dried
    1 tablespoon chopped fresh Italian flat leaf parsley
    1-1/2 tablespoons lemon juice
    1 tablespoon olive oil
    1 tablespoon soy sauce
    2 lamb shoulder chops, about 3/4 inch thick
    Kosher salt and freshly ground black pepper, to taste

DIRECTIONS
    1.   Preheat grill for medium-high heat. Lightly oil the grate.

    2.   Mix the first six ingredients in small bowl, then rub both sides of each
          chop with the paste; let stand at least 20 minutes or up to 1 hour at
          room temperature.

    3.   Sprinkle chops with salt and pepper.

    4.   Place chops on the grate and grill until bottom of each chop is well
          browned, about 2 minutes. Turn each chop and cook about 2 more
          minutes for medium-rare (or 2 1/2 minutes for medium.)

Serve with Grilled or Steamed Cauliflower and Lemon Orzo.

• GRILLED BALSAMIC-HONEY LAMB CHOPS •

I offered a dish similar to this using flat iron steak in my first book. If you enjoyed that recipe, I know you're gonna love this one.

PREP: 5 minutes   MARINATE: 1 hour
COOK: 10 minutes

INGREDIENTS
   1/4 cup olive oil
   2 tablespoons balsamic vinegar
   1 clove garlic, minced or pressed
   1-1/2 teaspoons fresh rosemary, chopped
   1-1/2 teaspoons honey
   1 teaspoon Dijon mustard
   1/2 teaspoon dried oregano
   Kosher salt and freshly ground black pepper, to taste
   4 (3-ounce) rib lamb chops

DIRECTIONS
   1.   In a small bowl, combine olive oil, balsamic vinegar, garlic, rosemary, honey, mustard, oregano, salt and pepper. Place chops in a re-sealable plastic bag and add marinade. Turn to coat and marinate for at least an hour (if longer than an hour, refrigerate).

   2.   Preheat grill for medium-high heat. Lightly oil grate. Grill chops for about 3 - 4 minutes per side for medium-rare.

Serve with Pan-Roasted Rosemary Carrots and Smashed Red Potatoes.

• HERB ROASTED LAMB CHOPS •

When you have a craving for chops but the weather won't allow you to fire up the grill, try this roasted lamb chop recipe. I've paired it with roasted asparagus and pancetta rosemary mashed potatoes. It will wow your taste buds.

PREP: Under 5 minutes   MARINATE: 30+ minutes
COOK: 20 minutes

INGREDIENTS
    4 cloves garlic, minced or pressed
    1 tablespoon fresh thyme leaves, lightly crumbled (or 1 teaspoon dried)
    1 tablespoon fresh rosemary leaves, lightly crumbled (or 1 teaspoon dried)
    2 teaspoons kosher salt
    1/2 teaspoon freshly ground black pepper
    2 tablespoons olive oil, divided
    4 lamb loin chops, 1-1/4 inch thick

DIRECTIONS
1.   Preheat oven to 400°.

2.   In a medium bowl, combine the garlic, thyme, rosemary, salt and pepper with 1 tablespoon olive oil. Add lamb chops and turn to coat. Let marinate at room temperature at least 30 minutes and up to 1 hour.

3.   Heat a 10-inch skillet over high heat. Add remaining oil and swirl to coat. Add lamb and cook until nicely browned, about 2 - 3 minutes per side. Transfer skillet to oven and roast lamb chops to desired doneness, about 10 minutes for medium-rare. Transfer lamb to platter, cover, and let rest 5 minutes.

Serve with Roasted Asparagus with Balsamic Butter Sauce and Pancetta Rosemary Mashed Potatoes

• GRILLED LAMB KABOBS •

For some reason, here in the states we are quite keen to skewer chicken, beef, shrimp and veggies, but we rarely use lamb. This is the way that it's traditionally made throughout the Mediterranean, Middle East and North Africa. A great meal in less than half an hour.

PREP: 10 minutes   MARINATE: 10 minutes
COOK: 8 minutes

INGREDIENTS
   1-1/2 tablespoons olive oil
   2 teaspoons red wine vinegar
   1 clove garlic, minced or pressed
   3/4 teaspoon ground cumin
   3/4 teaspoon ground coriander
   1/2 teaspoon cayenne pepper, or to taste
   1/4 teaspoon kosher salt
   1-1/2 pounds lamb shoulder, trimmed, boned, and cut into 1-inch pieces
   4 (8-inch) bamboo skewers soaked in water for 20 minutes (or you can use
      steel skewers)

DIRECTIONS
   1.   Preheat grill for medium-high heat. Lightly oil grate.

   2.   In a medium bowl, combine the olive oil, vinegar, garlic, cumin, coriander, cayenne pepper and salt. Add the lamb and toss to coat. Let stand for 5 - 10 minutes.

   3.   Thread the lamb onto the skewers allowing 1/4 - 1/2 inches between pieces. Grill, turning occasionally, until crusty brown on the outside, but medium-rare on the inside, about 5 - 8 minutes.

Serve with Grilled Mixed Vegetables and Basic Couscous.

• BRAISED LAMB SHANKS WITH VEGETABLES •
AND WHITE WINE

If you make this after an afternoon of snow skiing you will probably eat it all. If not, you'll probably have some veggies left over. If that's the case, save them for tomorrow and simply warm 1 or 2 cups of beef or vegetable broth (depending on how much broth you have remaining from the braised lamb) in a medium saucepan and add the leftovers. Reheat for a quick and healthy lunch.

PREP: 10 minutes   COOK: 2-1/2 hours

INGREDIENTS
    2 (8 - 12 ounce) lamb shanks
    1 tablespoon unsalted butter
    1 small onion, cut into 8 wedges
    3 cloves garlic, minced or pressed
    1-1/2 cups fruity white wine
    1/2 teaspoon kosher salt
    1/4 teaspoon freshly ground black pepper
    1/2 teaspoon oregano
    1/2 teaspoon rosemary, chopped
    1-1/2 teaspoons chopped fresh parsley
    1/4 pound small red potatoes, halved
    1/4 pound turnips, peeled and cut into 1-inch cubes
    1/4 pound carrots, cut into 1-inch pieces
    1/4 pound asparagus, trimmed and cut into 2-inch pieces

DIRECTIONS
1. Heat a Dutch oven over medium-high heat. Add the butter and swirl to coat. Add onions and sauté for 4 minutes. Add garlic and sauté for 1 additional minute. Remove onions and garlic to a medium bowl and reserve.

2. Add lamb shanks to the pan and cook to brown on all sides, about 10 - 12 minutes. Remove from pan and place them in the bowl with the onions. Pour the wine into the pan, scraping to remove the brown bits from the bottom. Return the lamb and onions to the pan and sprinkle with salt and pepper.

3. In a small bowl, combine the oregano, rosemary and parsley. Sprinkle half of the herbs into the pan and stir. Bring mixture to a boil, then reduce heat to medium-low. Cover and simmer until lamb is tender, about 1 hour.

4. Add potatoes, turnips, carrots and remaining herb mixture to the pan; simmer until vegetables are tender, about 40 minutes. Add asparagus and cook until just tender, about 5 minutes.

Serve in warm bowls with a simple salad and plenty of warm crusty bread.

• BRAISED LAMB SHANKS WITH TOMATOES •

Braising takes some time, but it requires little attention. If you want a savory, melt in your mouth entrée, this is the dish for you. And well worth the wait!

PREP: 5 minutes   COOK: 2-1/2 hours

INGREDIENTS
    2 (8 - 12-ounce) lamb shanks
    1 tablespoon olive oil
    1/4 teaspoon kosher salt
    1/8 teaspoon freshly ground black pepper
    2 cloves garlic, minced or pressed
    6 tablespoons dry red wine
    1 (14.5-ounce) can diced tomatoes with Italian seasonings, undrained
    2 tablespoons chopped fresh Italian flat leaf parsley

DIRECTIONS
1. Heat a Dutch oven over medium-high heat. Add olive oil and swirl to coat. Sprinkle lamb with salt and pepper then add to pot. Cook, turning often until well-browned on all sides, about 10 - 12 minutes. Remove lamb from pan and set aside.

2. Add garlic to the pan and sauté for 15 seconds. Pour in the wine and stir, scraping to remove the brown bits from the bottom of the pan. Stir in the tomatoes and cook for 2 minutes. Return the lamb to the pan, reduce heat to medium-low, cover and simmer until 1 hour. Turn lamb and continue to simmer until the lamb is fork-tender, about 1 additional hour.

3. Remove lamb to a warm plate and loosely cover. Skim any fat from the pan and increase heat to high. Bring to a boil and cook until sauce is thickened, about 10 minutes. Stir in parsley. Serve lamb with sauce spooned over.

Serve with Italian Mashed Potatoes.

Vegetarian

 # VEGETARIAN

One does not have to be a card carrying vegetarian to enjoy vegetarian food. I'm not a vegetarian, but because of my faith tradition I eat vegetarian about 6 months out of the year when you add up all of the different meatless days. Take Lent for instance, why, there's almost a month and a half right there!

I think we should all eat vegetarian meals more often, regardless of our faith tradition (or absence thereof).

Why?

Well, it's good for our bodies. We all know we should cut back on our meat intake.

It's good for the earth. It allows herds, flocks and fisheries to replenish themselves.

And it's good for our pocketbooks. Have you compared the price of a pound of beans, veggies or rice to a pound of beef?

To me, at least, these are all very good reasons to give vegetarian meals a shot.

And don't think you'll sacrifice anything in the flavor department. The following recipes, and the several other vegetarian recipes found throughout the book, are ample evidence that you don't have to check your taste buds at the door when you opt for a vegetarian meal.

• CURRIED BROCCOLI COUSCOUS •

When you want a healthy, but quick, dinner or lunch, this will do just fine. Add a simple salad and you're good to go.

PREP: 5 minutes   COOK: 10 minutes

INGREDIENTS
    2 tablespoons olive oil
    1-1/2 cups finely chopped broccoli
    1 teaspoon curry powder
    1 cup canned chickpeas, rinsed
    1/3 cup golden raisins
    1 cup water or vegetable broth
    1/2 teaspoon kosher salt
    3/4 cup couscous

DIRECTIONS
1. In a large saucepan, heat the oil over medium-high heat. Add the broccoli and cook, tossing occasionally until tender, about 2 - 3 minutes.

2. Add the curry powder and stir to combine. Stir in the chickpeas, raisins, water or broth, and salt and bring to a boil.

3. Stir in the couscous, cover, and remove from heat. Let steam 5 minutes, then fluff with a fork.

• QUINOA AND BLACK BEANS •

Here's an interesting twist on what would normally be beans and rice. Once you try quinoa, I know you'll be substituting it for rice in other recipes. If you can, buy it from a store that allows you to buy it loose (as do many natural food stores) because the pre-packaged bags can be pricey.

PREP: 5 minutes   COOK: 30 minutes

INGREDIENTS
    6 tablespoons quinoa
    1 teaspoon olive oil
    1/2 onion, chopped (about 1/2 cup)
    2 cloves garlic, peeled and chopped
    3/4 cup vegetable broth
    1/2 teaspoon ground cumin
    1/8 teaspoon cayenne pepper
    Kosher salt and freshly ground black pepper, to taste
    1/2 cup frozen corn kernels
    1 (15-ounce) can black beans, rinsed and drained
    1/4 cup chopped fresh cilantro

DIRECTIONS
1.   Place the quinoa in a fine mesh strainer, and rinse under cold, running water until the water no longer foams.

2.   Heat a medium saucepan over medium heat. Add the olive oil and swirl to coat. Add the onion and sauté until lightly browned, about 5 - 6 minutes. Add garlic and sauté 1 additional minute.

3.   Stir the quinoa into the saucepan and add the vegetable broth. Season with cumin, cayenne pepper, salt, and pepper. Bring the mixture to a boil. Cover; reduce heat to medium-low, and simmer 20 minutes.

4.   Stir corn and black beans into the saucepan, and continue to simmer about 5 minutes until heated through. Add the cilantro and toss.

• QUINOA WITH CHICKPEAS AND TOMATOES •

This is so substantial; I almost wanted to call it a stew.

PREP: 5 minutes   COOK: 25 minutes

INGREDIENTS
- 1 cup quinoa
- 1/8 teaspoon kosher salt
- 1-3/4 cups water
- 1 cup canned garbanzo beans (chickpeas), drained
- 1 tomato, chopped
- 1 clove garlic, minced
- 3 tablespoons lime juice
- 4 teaspoons olive oil
- 1/2 teaspoon ground cumin
- Kosher salt and freshly ground black pepper, to taste
- 1 teaspoon chopped fresh parsley

DIRECTIONS

1. Place the quinoa in a fine mesh strainer, and rinse under cold, running water until the water no longer foams.

2. Bring the quinoa, salt, and water to a boil in a saucepan. Reduce heat to medium-low, cover, and simmer until the quinoa is tender, 20 to 25 minutes.

3. Stir in the garbanzo beans, tomatoes, garlic, lime juice, and olive oil. Season with cumin, salt, and pepper. Sprinkle with chopped fresh parsley and serve.

• SAUTÉED ASPARAGUS AND TOMATO •

Because this is a stir fry, you want to have all of your ingredients prepared and nearby.

PREP: 10 minutes   COOK: 10 minutes

INGREDIENTS
    6 sun-dried tomatoes (not packed in oil)
    1/2 cup boiling water
    1-1/2 tablespoons olive oil
    2 cloves garlic, minced or pressed
    3/4 pound asparagus spears, trimmed and cut into 2-inch pieces
    1/4 cup dry white wine
    1 large tomato, diced (about 1 cup) or 1 cup drained diced tomatoes
    1-1/2 teaspoons tarragon
    1/2 cup frozen petite peas, defrosted
    Kosher salt and freshly ground black pepper, to taste
    Crumbled feta cheese or grated Parmesan cheese to garnish

DIRECTIONS

1. In a small bowl, cover the dried tomatoes with the water and set aside.

2. Heat a 10-inch skillet over high heat. Add the olive oil and swirl to coat. Add the garlic and sauté for 1 minute. Add the asparagus and sauté for 1 minute. Add the wine, cover, and let steam for a few minutes. Meanwhile, remove the sun-dried tomatoes from the water and coarsely chop.

3. Remove the cover and add the fresh tomatoes and tarragon. Sauté for 2 - 3 minutes to reduce the liquid in the pan. Add the sun-dried tomatoes and peas. Sauté until the asparagus is crisp tender, about 2 - 3 additional minutes. (If the sauté becomes too dry, add a little of the dried tomato soaking water.)

Serve over Steamed White Rice or Couscous. Sprinkle with cheese to garnish.

• THAI VEGETABLES WITH COCONUT •

Here's another stir fry. This one from Thailand.

PREP: 10 minutes   COOK: 15 minutes

INGREDIENTS
    1/3 cup cashews, divided
    1 tablespoon olive or canola oil
    1 medium onion chopped (about 1 cup)
    3/4 cup sliced mushrooms
    2 ounces snow peas
    2 ounces baby corn, halved lengthwise (optional)
    1/2 green pepper, seeded and sliced thin
    1-1/2 teaspoons Thai green curry paste
    3/4 cup unsweetened coconut milk, divided
    2 ounces bean sprouts

DIRECTIONS
1. Heat a 10-inch skillet over medium heat. Add cashews and toast, stirring, until golden brown, about 2 - 3 minutes. Remove to a plate.

2. Add olive oil to the pan and swirl to coat. Add onions and sauté for 3 - 4 minutes. Increase heat to medium-high and add mushrooms. Sauté for an additional 3 - 4 minutes. Stir in snow peas, baby corn, and green pepper. Sauté for 2 minutes.

3. Stir in the curry paste and 2 tablespoons coconut milk. Sauté until well mixed. Stir in the remaining coconut milk and bean sprouts. Cook until the vegetables are tender and the coconut milk has reduced a little. Stir in half the cashews. Serve over Steamed White Rice (use jasmine rice if you have it) and sprinkle remaining cashews on top.

Serve with Steamed White Rice.

• SIZZLING RISOTTO AU GRATIN WITH BABY PEAS •

This may seem to take a long time for a rice dish, but let me tell you, this gloriously sizzling rich dish is worth it. If you're unable to find arborio rice in your grocery store, go ahead and substitute medium-grain rice. You may have to use a little more broth if you do. Just be sure to bite into a grain when you add the last 1/4 cup of broth to make sure the rice is done before proceeding.

PREP: 5 minutes   COOK: 1 hour

INGREDIENTS
    2 cups vegetable broth, divided
    2 tablespoons unsalted butter
    1/4 cup chopped onion
    1 cups arborio rice
    1/2 cup dry white wine
    1/2 cup frozen petite peas, defrosted
    4 ounces fontina cheese, cut in 1/4-inch cubes
    1/2 cup heavy cream
    1 pinch ground nutmeg
    Kosher salt and white pepper to taste

DIRECTIONS
1. Bring vegetable broth to a simmer in a medium saucepan. Lightly butter a 1-quart gratin or baking dish. Preheat oven to 500° and set the oven rack in the top third of the oven.

2. In a large saucepan, melt the butter over medium heat. Add the onion and sauté until soft and translucent, about 3 - 5 minutes. Add the rice; raise the heat to medium-high, and cook, stirring constantly, for 3 minutes. Add the wine, raise the heat to high, and cook until wine is completely absorbed, about 3 - 5 minutes. Add 1 cup of the broth; adjust the heat so that the liquid is simmering briskly, and cook, stirring occasionally, until it is mostly absorbed, about 12 minutes. Add the remaining stock in 1/4 cup increments, stirring constantly, until each 1/4 cup is absorbed before adding the next.

3. Remove the rice from the heat and stir in the peas, cheese, cream, and nutmeg. Season with salt and pepper to taste, then pour the rice mixture into the gratin dish.

4. Place the gratin dish in the oven and bake the risotto until it's sizzling and golden, about 15 minutes. If it's not browning, turn on the broiler for the final minute so that the surface is a rich gold. Serve immediately.

• ORZO WITH VEGGIES •

This is a substantial pasta meal that's great on a warm summer's night. Sometimes I'll add some chopped zucchini or yellow squash if I have some in the fridge.

PREP: 5 minutes   COOK: 10 minutes

INGREDIENTS
    3/4 cup orzo
    3 tablespoons chopped, drained oil-packed sun-dried tomatoes
    3 tablespoons extra virgin olive oil
    2 tablespoons balsamic vinegar
    2 tablespoons chopped Kalamata olives
    1/2 cup chopped radicchio (or baby spinach)
    2 tablespoons toasted pine nuts
    1/4 cup chopped fresh basil
    1/4 cup freshly grated Parmesan cheese
    1 clove garlic, minced or pressed
    Kosher salt and freshly ground black pepper, to taste

DIRECTIONS
Cook orzo until tender and firm to the bite according to package directions. Drain well and transfer to a medium bowl. Stir in the tomatoes, olive oil, vinegar and olives. Toss to mix well. Place in the fridge to cool. Once cool, stir in the radicchio, pine nuts, basil, Parmesan, garlic and salt and pepper.

• STUFFED RED PEPPERS •

In *Table for Two - The Cookbook for Couples* I offered a simple recipe for Stuffed Green Peppers. Here's a variation I know you'll enjoy.

PREP: 10 minutes   COOK: 40 minutes

INGREDIENTS
2 red bell peppers, halved lengthwise, seeds and veins removed
2 tablespoons unsalted butter
1 bunch scallions, sliced thin (including firm green parts)
2-1/2 cups frozen corn kernels, defrosted
2 tomatoes peeled and diced (or 1 cup canned)
1 cup grated mozzarella or Monterey jack cheese
2 tablespoons sliced fresh basil
2/3 cup Italian bread crumbs, divided
Kosher salt and freshly ground black pepper, to taste

DIRECTIONS
1. Preheat oven to 400°. Place the peppers on a lightly oiled rimmed baking sheet.

2. Heat a 10-inch skillet over medium heat. Add the butter and swirl to coat. Add the scallions, corn and tomatoes and sauté until scallions are soft, about 3 - 5 minutes.

3. Remove the skillet from the heat and stir in the cheese, basil and 1/3 cup of the breadcrumbs. Season with salt and pepper to taste. Spoon the vegetable mixture evenly into each pepper, and then sprinkle with remaining bread crumbs.

4. Bake until peppers are soft, about 30 - 45 minutes.

• NOODLES IN THAI CURRY SAUCE •

This dish traditionally uses dried Chinese egg (or Lo Mein) noodles and you can usually find them in the oriental section of your supermarket. However, I've used regular Italian linguini or fettuccine in dishes that call for their Chinese cousins with good success. The curry paste also may be found in the oriental section. It may seem a bit pricey for such a small jar, but a little goes a long way. This will make two big bowls of noodles. I hope you're hungry.

PREP: 5 minutes   COOK: 10 -15 minutes

INGREDIENTS
    1/2 pound Chinese egg noodles (Lo Mein) or linguine
    1-1/2 teaspoons peanut or olive oil
    3 cloves garlic, minced or pressed
    1 teaspoon minced fresh ginger
    2 large shallots, peeled and sliced (or 1/2 medium onion, diced)
    1 (15-ounce) can unsweetened coconut milk
    1 to 3 teaspoons Thai red curry paste (to taste)
    2 tablespoons soy sauce
    2 scallions, sliced (including firm green parts)
    Fresh torn basil or cilantro leaves to garnish

DIRECTIONS

1. Prepare noodles according to instructions on the package. Drain and rinse under cold water to stop the cooking.

2. Heat a 10-inch skillet over medium-high heat. Add the peanut oil and swirl to coat. Heat to just shimmering and about to smoke then add the garlic, ginger and shallots; stir fry for 2 minutes.

3. Stir in the coconut milk, curry paste and soy sauce. Lower heat to medium-low and cook, stirring and breaking up the curry paste until well-blended, about 3 - 4 minutes. Add the noodles and toss to warm through. Serve in warm bowls and sprinkle with scallions and basil or cilantro leaves.

• SZECHUAN NOODLES •

There's something about a big bowl of noodles that makes me feel like a kid again. What pre-teen wouldn't revel in such a messy, noisy dish? I'm sure most of us would feel that way and there are probably psychiatrists out there who have written white papers to explain why that is. However, this potentially incendiary bowl of noodles would probably not appeal to most children. Unless of course they are like my son, Brendan. At which point they will ask, "Please pass the hot sauce."

PREP: 5 minutes   COOK: 15 minutes

INGREDIENTS
   1/2 pound Chinese (Lo Mein) noodles or linguini
   1/4 cup vegetable broth
   1/2 teaspoon cornstarch
   3 tablespoons soy sauce
   1 tbsp ketchup
   1-1/2 teaspoons rice vinegar
   1-1/2 teaspoons chili sauce or Sriracha hot sauce (or to taste)
   1/2 teaspoon sugar
   1/2 tablespoons peanut or vegetable oil
   2 cloves garlic, minced or pressed
   2 scallions, sliced (including firm green parts)
   3 tablespoons unsalted peanuts
   1 small cucumber, sliced thin

DIRECTIONS
   1. Cook noodles according to instructions on package. Drain and rinse under cold water to stop the cooking process.

   2. In a small bowl, combine the broth, corn starch, soy sauce, ketchup, vinegar, chili sauce and sugar. Stir to mix well.

   3. Heat a 10-inch skillet over medium-high heat. Add the oil and swirl to coat. Add the garlic and scallions and stir fry for 2 minutes. Stir in the bowl of sauce and whisk well to combine.

   4. Add the peanuts, cucumber and noodles. Stir until combined and heated through.

• SOUTHWESTERN VEGETARIAN CHILI •

This can be a great weeknight meal if you have a few cans of tomatoes, pinto beans, and sweet potatoes in the cupboard. It is especially welcomed after a soccer or football game when the fall begins morphing to winter.

PREP: 5 minutes   COOK: 15 minutes

INGREDIENTS
    2 tablespoons olive oil
    1 medium onion, diced
    1 medium red or green bell pepper, cut into 1/2-inch pieces
    2 garlic cloves, minced or pressed
    1 tablespoon chili powder
    1 (15.5-ounce) can Mexican-style stewed tomatoes, undrained
    1-1/2 cups diced canned or cooked sweet potatoes
    1 cup frozen corn, defrosted
    1 (15.5-ounce) can pinto beans, drained
    1/4 teaspoon kosher salt
    1/8 teaspoon freshly ground black pepper
    2 tablespoons chopped fresh cilantro

DIRECTIONS

1. Heat a large saucepan or medium Dutch oven over medium-high heat. Add the oil and swirl to coat. And the onions and red pepper and sauté until vegetables begin to soften, about 3 - 5 minutes. Add garlic and chili powder and sauté for 1 - 2 additional minutes.

2. Turn heat to high and add tomatoes, sweet potatoes, corn, beans, salt and pepper. Bring to a boil, then reduce heat to medium-low. Simmer, uncovered, until chili thickens, about 6 - 8 minutes. Remove from heat and stir in cilantro.

A STEW FOR EVERY SEASON

I love stew. In each and every incarnation. However, when most of us think of the word 'stew' our minds (and taste buds) seem to point to Irish stew, fish stew, beef burgundy, pot-au-feu, or any other number of other beef stew dishes. Surprisingly, not many of us think of vegetable stews. And if we don't it will be to our loss. Why? Because vegetable stews can be as filling and as delicious as their carnivorous cousins.

I've included a couple of wonderful options here in the vegetarian chapter. I particularly want you to try these next four. Ones that utilize the vegetables that are abundant in their season. Are they healthy? You bet. I think you'll be surprised by their texture and flavor. Like meat stews, they'll leave you well-satiated. And because they're not made with meat, they'll cook in a fraction of the time and will be easier on your pocket book.

Great tasting. Healthy. Time-saving. Frugal. What's not to like?

Together with a small salad and some warm bread, you'll have a meal that's not only filling, but also good enough to serve company without a lot of fuss.

• SPRING VEGETABLE STEW •

You can improvise with this by substituting or adding additional spring vegetables. Just make sure you simmer until they are done to your liking.

PREP: 10 minutes   COOK: 10 minutes

INGREDIENTS
    6 tablespoons unsalted butter, divided
    1 tablespoon olive oil
    1 bunch scallions, chopped with some green
    4 ounces baby portobello mushrooms, sliced
    5 carrots, peeled and cut 3-inches long, then halved length-wise
    1 clove garlic, minced or pressed
    1 tablespoon chopped fresh basil (or 1 teaspoon dried)
    1 tablespoon chopped fresh chervil (or 1 teaspoon dried)
    1 tablespoon chopped fresh Italian flat leaf parsley
    3 tablespoons fresh lemon juice
    1 cup vegetable broth or water
    1 bunch asparagus, tips only (reserve remainder for another use)
    4 ounces snow peas, strings removed
    1 cup baby spinach or kale, torn into small pieces
    2 cans cannellini or great northern beans, drained
    Kosher salt and freshly ground black pepper to taste

DIRECTIONS
1.   Heat a 10-inch skillet over medium-high heat. Add two tablespoons butter and the olive oil and swirl to coat. Add the scallions and sauté for 1 minute. Stir in the mushrooms, carrots, garlic, basil, chervil, and parsley. Sauté for 3 minutes.

2.   Stir in the lemon juice and broth. Cover and lower the heat to medium-low. Cook until the carrots are crisp-tender, about 2 - 3 minutes. Stir in the asparagus, peas, spinach and beans. Cover and cook for 2 - 3 additional minutes.

3.   Remove the lid and add the remaining butter. Cook, stirring, until the butter creates a nice sauce. Check vegetables for desired doneness then season with salt and pepper to taste.

• SUMMER VEGETABLE STEW •

No one wants to spend a lot of time in a hot kitchen when the sun is shining and the backyard beckons. That's why this stew works; it uses fresh veggies and can be whipped up in minutes. I almost hate calling this a stew because it conjures up images of a big Dutch oven simmering on the stove for hours. So let's call it a Summer Vegetable Mélange. Wow, sounds so much better.

PREP: 10 minutes   COOK: 20 minutes

INGREDIENTS
　　1-1/2 tablespoons chopped fresh Italian flat leaf parsley
　　1-1/2 tablespoons chopped fresh marjoram
　　1-1/2 tablespoons chopped fresh basil
　　1/2 teaspoon grated lemon zest
　　Kosher salt and freshly ground black pepper to taste
　　4 tablespoons unsalted butter, softened
　　1/2 pound green beans (the skinnier the better) trimmed
　　　and cut into 3-inch pieces
　　1 tablespoon olive oil
　　1 small onion, diced (about 1/2 cup)
　　1 clove garlic, peeled and sliced thin
　　1/2 cup water or vegetable broth
　　1/2 zucchini or yellow squash, diced or sliced into rounds
　　1 red pepper, diced
　　1 large tomato, diced
　　3 cups fresh or frozen corn kernels

DIRECTIONS
1.　In a small bowl, combine the parsley, marjoram, basil, lemon zest, salt, pepper and butter. Stir to mix and set aside.

2.　Bring a medium saucepan of water to a boil. Add the green beans and cook for 2 minutes then drain.

3.　Heat a 10-inch skittle or sauté pan over high heat. Add the olive oil and swirl to coat. Add the onions and sauté for 2 minutes. Add the garlic and sauté for 1 additional minute. Add the water and reduce heat to medium-low. Cover and simmer for 5 minutes (add more water if needed).

4.　Stir in the zucchini or squash, red pepper, tomato and corn. Cover and simmer for 10 minutes. Stir in the herb butter to melt. Season with additional salt and pepper to taste.

• FALL MUSHROOM STEW •

Mushrooms are available year-round, but most wild mushrooms (except morels) are in season from late summer through the fall. Now I'm not suggesting that you pack a lunch and go out into the forest to ferret out wild mushrooms; that could turn out to be a fatal outing. No, when I speak of 'wild' mushrooms here, I'm referring to any that are not your typical white button mushroom. Here we'll use some of those as well as the last vestiges of tomatoes from the garden. If you don't have fresh, you can use canned in this recipe.

PREP: 10 minutes   COOK: 30 minutes

INGREDIENTS
  1/4 cup olive oil
  1 large onion, peeled and chopped
  2 cloves garlic, peeled and thinly sliced
  1/2 pound oyster, shiitake, or cremini mushrooms, sliced (keep the oyster
    mushrooms whole if using)
  2 tablespoons chopped fresh parsley
  2 tablespoons brandy or cognac
  1/2 cup chicken or mushroom broth
  2 large ripe tomatoes, peeled and chopped (or 1-1/2 cups canned)
  4 teaspoons chopped fresh marjoram, or 1-1/4 teaspoon dried
  1/3 cup heavy cream
  Kosher salt and pepper to taste

DIRECTIONS
  1. Heat a 10-inch skillet over medium-high heat. Add the oil and swirl to
      coat. Add the onions and sauté until they are soft and translucent, about
      6 - 8 minutes. Add the garlic and sauté for 2 additional minutes. Turn
      heat to high and add the mushrooms; sauté until they begin to brown
      and their liquid evaporates, about 10 minutes.

  2. Remove the pan from the heat and add the brandy. Return the pan to
      the heat and sauté until the brandy evaporates, about 1 minute. Add the
      vegetable broth, tomatoes and marjoram. Lower the heat to medium-
      low and simmer, stirring occasionally, until the tomatoes and mushrooms
      are tender, about 10 minutes. Stir in cream and simmer until warm and
      slightly reduced.

• WINTER VEGETABLE STEW •

We sometimes call this Winter Refrigerator Stew in my house because I often make it with whatever leftover veggies I have in the fridge. So feel free to use this recipe as a guideline, rather than something written in stone. You can use Brussels sprouts, turnips, rutabagas, cauliflower, baby artichokes…well, I think you get my drift. It is after all, similar to what musicians call 'a variation on a theme'. For more 'variation on a theme' recipes, see my book *Cooking Outside the Lines - The Musings of an Extemporaneous Chef*.

PREP: 15 minutes   COOK: 30 minutes

INGREDIENTS
  2 tablespoons olive oil
  2 medium onions, chopped (about 2 cups)
  2 celery stalks, chopped
  2 cloves garlic, coarsely chopped
  1 red pepper, coarsely chopped
  6-ounces mushrooms, halved if large
  2 medium carrots, peeled and chopped
  3 parsnips, peeled and chopped
  4 red potatoes, cut into 1-inch cubes
  1 (10-ounce) box frozen cut green beans
  1 teaspoon dill
  1 teaspoon marjoram
  1 cup vegetable stock (or beer for a nice change)
  1-1/2 cups water
  1 tablespoon Dijon mustard (or more to taste)
  1 tablespoon molasses
  Kosher salt and freshly ground black pepper, to taste

DIRECTIONS
  1. Heat a Dutch oven over medium-high heat. Add the olive oil and stir to coat. Add the onions and celery and sauté until the onions are soft and translucent, about 8 - 10 minutes. Add the garlic and sauté for 1 additional minute. Add the red pepper and mushrooms and sauté for 5 additional minutes.

  2. Add the carrots, parsnips, potatoes and green beans. Stir to mix then stir in the dill and marjoram. Stir in the stock (or beer) and water. Bring to a slow boil then stir in the mustard and molasses. Reduce heat to medium-low and simmer until the potatoes are tender, about 10 minutes. Season with salt and pepper to taste.

Sides

BASIC VEGGIES

• ASPARAGUS •

This wonderful spring vegetable can be found in a variety of colors: green, purple, green and purple, and creamy white. Choose thin stalks - they tend to be younger, and therefore, more tender.

Asparagus has been cultivated and cooked from ancient times and is a good source of folic acid, potassium and dietary fiber.

Many folks coat their asparagus with thick sauces like Hollandaise, but in my book, asparagus needs very little in the ways of seasoning. Simply sprinkle the cooked spears with a little kosher salt and pepper, then drizzle with butter or olive oil and sprinkle with grated Parmesan, pecorino or white cheddar cheese.

To Boil: In a small or medium skillet, bring 5 cups of water to a boil and add 2-1/2 teaspoons salt. Add 1/2 pound asparagus in one layer and return to a boil. Cook uncovered until crisp-tender.

- 4 – 5 minutes for thin spears
- 6 – 7 minutes for medium spears
- 8 - 9 minutes for thick spears

To Steam: Place 1/2 pound asparagus spears in a steamer basket over an inch or two of boiling water. Cover and steam.

- 4 – 5 minutes for thin spears
- 6 – 7 minutes for medium spears
- 8 - 9 minutes for thick spears

To Microwave: Place 1/2 pound asparagus in a microwave baking dish. Add 1 tablespoon chicken stock, wine, or water; cover and cook on high for 4 –9 minutes, stirring halfway through, until crisp-tender. Remove and let stand for 2 additional minutes.

To Roast: Wash and pat dry asparagus and brush liberally with olive oil or butter. Grill over a medium charcoal fire until crisp-tender.

To Sauté: Melt 1-1/2 teaspoons butter and 1-1/2 tablespoons olive oil in a 10-inch skillet over medium heat. Add asparagus and sauté, stirring often until crisp-tender, about 10 minutes. Sprinkle with your choice of sharp cheese.

• BROCCOLI •

This is one of the green cruciferous vegetables that we refused to eat as children, the other being Brussels sprouts. I think the reason was because these, along with most vegetables, were cooked and cooked until they turned into mush. Think school cafeterias, greasy-spoon diners, or all-you-can-eat buffets. But it was to our loss. The American Cancer Society announced years ago that we could reduce our risk of some cancers if we simply added broccoli and other cruciferous vegetables to our diet. Still not convinced? The recipes below will change your view of this nutritious vegetable.

To Boil: In a saucepan, bring 8 cups of water to a boil and add 2-1/2 teaspoons kosher salt. Add 1/2 pound broccoli and return to a boil. Cook uncovered until crisp-tender.

- 2 – 4 minutes for florets
- 6 – 8 minutes for stalks

To Steam: Place 1/2 pound florets or tender stalks in a steamer basket over an inch or two of boiling water. Cover and steam.

- 5 or so minutes for florets
- 10 minutes for stalks

To Microwave: Place 1/2 pound broccoli in a microwave baking dish. If using stalks, arrange in a circle with stalks pointing toward the center. Add 1 tablespoon chicken stock, wine, or water; cover and cook on high for 5 – 8 minutes, stirring halfway through, until crisp-tender. Remove and let stand for 2 additional minutes.

• BRUSSELS SPROUTS •

Brussels sprouts are basically small cabbages. They are among the same family that includes broccoli and cauliflower. Although it contains a good amount of vitamin A, vitamin C, folic acid and dietary fiber, the lowly Brussels sprout was despised by most of us when we were young. Hopefully, the recipes that follow will win you over.

To Prepare: Cut a small x in the bottom of each spout to help them cook quickly.

To Boil: In a saucepan, bring 8 cups of water to a boil and add 2-1/2 teaspoons kosher salt. Add 1/2 pound Brussels sprouts and return to a boil. Cook uncovered until crisp-tender, about 6 - 12 minutes.

To Steam: Place 1/2 pound Brussels sprouts in a steamer basket over an inch or two of boiling water. Cover and steam for 8-15 minutes until crisp-tender.

To Microwave: Place 1/2 pound Brussels sprouts in a microwave-safe baking dish. Add 2 tablespoons chicken stock, wine, or water; cover and cook on high for 6-8 minutes, stirring halfway through, until crisp-tender. Remove and let stand for 3 additional minutes.

Brussels sprouts are excellent with butter and lemon-pepper, Parmesan cheese, toasted breadcrumbs or cheese sauce – many of the same recipes for broccoli.

• CARROTS •

This versatile root vegetable is a great source of dietary fiber, antioxidants and minerals. Delicious raw or cooked, carrots can be found in beverages, salads, soups, main courses, and even desserts.

Dill, parsley, thyme, mint, chervil, ginger, and nutmeg are great additions to carrots as are brown sugar, honey, raisins, oranges, tangerines, and lemons.

Cooked carrots taste great with just a little butter, kosher salt, and pepper. But feel free to experiment with the herbs and spices above.

To Boil: In a saucepan, bring 8 cups of water to a boil and add 2-1/2 teaspoons kosher salt. Add 1/2 pound carrots and return to a boil. Cook uncovered.

- 5 minutes or so for sliced, diced or matchstick cuts
- 8 minutes or so for halved (length-wise) cuts
- 12-15 minutes for whole carrots

To Steam: Place 1/2 pound carrots in a steamer basket over an inch or two of boiling water. Cover and steam.

- 8 minutes for sliced, diced or matchstick cuts
- 16 – 20 minutes for halved or whole carrots

To Microwave: Place 1/2 pound carrots in a microwave baking dish. Add 1 tablespoon chicken stock, wine, or water; cover and cook on high for 5 – 8 minutes, stirring halfway through, until crisp-tender. Remove and let stand for 3 additional minutes.

• CAULIFLOWER •

Though milder in flavor than broccoli, this sister cruciferous vegetable is low in fat and high in dietary fiber, folic acid, and vitamin C.

Cauliflower may be enjoyed with a cheese sauce, toasted almonds, curry powder, nutmeg or mace.

Note: Cauliflower may be substituted for any of the following broccoli recipes.

To Prepare: Cut the head in half or quarters and cut out the tough core. Break the florets into the desired size.

To Boil: In a saucepan, bring 8 cups of water to a boil and add 2-1/2 teaspoons kosher salt and 1-1/2 tablespoons lemon juice. Add 1/2 pound cauliflower and return to a boil. Cook uncovered until crisp-tender, about 3-5 minutes.

To Steam: Place 1/2 pound cauliflower in a steamer basket over an inch or two of boiling water. Cover and steam for 6-8 minutes until crisp-tender.

To Microwave: Place 1/2 pound cauliflower in a microwave baking dish. If using stalks, arrange in a circle with stalks pointing toward the center. Add 1 tablespoon chicken stock, wine, or water; cover and cook on high for 3 – 5 minutes, stirring halfway through, until crisp-tender. Remove and let stand for 2 additional minutes.

• CORN •

Corn is truly one of the simplest side dishes to prepare. I'm always amazed when I see folks boil it until it nearly turns to mush. Corn doesn't really need to be cooked, it just needs to be 'threatened' - The following methods will show you how. Simply add some sweet cream butter and a little salt and pepper for a delightful summertime treat Thanks to our growers in Florida, corn is now available year-round.

To Boil: In a kettle, bring enough water to a boil so that the corn will be covered. Add 1 tablespoon kosher salt for each quart of water. Remove the corn husks and trim the ends (optional). Drop the corn into the boiling water and return to a boil. Immediately turn off the heat and allow the corn to stand for exactly 5 minutes.

To Steam: Place shucked corn in a pot with 1 to 2 inches of boiling salted water. Cover and steam until corn is heated through, about 5 to 10 minutes.

To Grill or Roast: Start a charcoal fire, preheat a gas grill, or preheat an oven to 450°. Peel the corn husks back and remove the silk. Replace husks and grill for 15-20 minutes or roast 20-30 minutes in the oven.

To Sauté: In a small skillet, heat 1 tablespoon olive oil over medium heat. Add 1-1/2 cups corn and sauté for 3-4 minutes.

Variations: Add 1/4 cup of either chopped tomato, red or green bell pepper, onion or lima beans and sauté with the corn.

• GREEN BEANS •

Fresh green beans do not require a lot of preparation – simply rinse and cook. It's that simple. You may trim the ends if that suits your fancy; I prefer them without the strings. Frozen green beans work well in all of these recipes, but as with most vegetables, avoid canned.
Cooked green beans with a touch of butter, kosher salt and pepper would go well with most of the entrees in this book. A pinch of dill, chervil, parsley or mint to taste will make a wonderful addition to this easy to prepare vegetable.

To Boil: In a saucepan, bring 6 cups of water to a boil and add 2-1/2 teaspoons kosher salt. Add 1/2 pound green beans and return to a boil. Cook uncovered until crisp-tender, about 2 – 4 minutes for French style and 4-8 minutes for whole beans, until crisp-tender.

To Steam: Place 1/2 pound green beans in a steamer basket over an inch or two of boiling water. Cover and steam for 5-7 minutes for French style and 8-12 minutes for whole beans until crisp-tender.

To Microwave: Place 1/2 pound green beans in a microwave baking dish Add 2 tablespoons chicken stock, wine, or water; cover and cook on high for 9-13 minutes, stirring halfway through, until crisp-tender. Remove and let stand for 2 additional minutes.

• PEAS •

Most of us don't have the time or inclination to shell fresh peas, so the recipes below use frozen. The exception is snow peas – fresh is ideal, frozen a close second. Green peas may be flavored with butter, kosher salt and pepper. Some choose to sprinkle cooked peas with a little sugar. Spearmint, sage, or thyme adds a nice finishing touch.

• SPINACH •

Spinach is very nutritious, especially when served raw or steamed. It is a rich source of vitamin A, vitamin C, vitamin E, vitamin K, magnesium, and several vital antioxidants. As with most vegetables, fresh and frozen are best. (Sorry, Popeye, canned spinach just doesn't cut it).

To Prepare: Wash thoroughly and dry. Spinach leaves can be left whole, cut into strips, or chopped.

To Boil: Bring 8 cups of water to a boil. Add 10 ounces of spinach and cook until just wilted, about 1 or 2 minutes.

To Steam: Place 10 ounces of spinach in a steamer basket over an inch or two of boiling water. Cover and steam for 3-4 minutes, turning once.

To Microwave: Place 10 ounces of spinach in a microwave baking dish. Add 2 tablespoons chicken stock, wine, or water; cover and cook on high for 5-7 minutes, stirring halfway through, until tender. Remove and let stand for 3 additional minutes.

• YELLOW SQUASH OR ZUCCHINI •

When shopping for yellow squash or zucchini, select the smallest, heaviest and firmest squash available.

To Boil: In a saucepan, bring 6 cups of water to a boil and add 2-1/2 teaspoons kosher salt. Add 1/2 pound sliced or diced squash and return to a boil. Cook uncovered until crisp-tender, about 2 – 4 minutes until crisp-tender.

To Steam: Place 1/2 pound sliced or diced squash in a steamer basket over an inch or two of boiling water. Cover and steam for 5-7 minutes until crisp-tender.

To Microwave: Place 1/2 pound sliced or diced squash in a microwave baking dish. Add 2 tablespoons chicken stock, wine, or water; cover and cook on high for 2-4 minutes, stirring halfway through, until crisp-tender. Remove and let stand for 2 additional minutes.

Summer squash and zucchini are best served with melted butter and a sprinkling of oregano, parsley, basil, marjoram, dill, or rosemary.

BEYOND THE BASICS

• SIMPLE GRILLED ASPARAGUS •

PREP: 5 minutes   COOK: 3 minutes

INGREDIENTS
 1/2 pound fresh asparagus spears, trimmed
 1 tablespoon olive oil
 Kosher salt and freshly ground black pepper, to taste

DIRECTIONS

1. Preheat grill for high heat. Lightly oil grate.

2. Lightly coat the asparagus spears with olive oil. Season with salt and pepper to taste. Grill over high heat for 2 to 3 minutes, or to desired tenderness.

• SUGAR GLAZED GRILLED ASPARAGUS •

PREP: 5 minutes   COOK: 5 minutes

INGREDIENTS
   1/2 pound fresh asparagus, trimmed
   1 tablespoon olive or canola oil
   1-1/2 teaspoons sugar
   1/4 teaspoon freshly ground black pepper, or to taste

DIRECTIONS

   1.   Prepare grill for medium-high heat. Lightly oil grate.

   2.   Brush asparagus with olive oil and sprinkle with sugar and pepper. Place
        asparagus on grill and cook, turning once or twice, until crisp-tender,
        about 3 - 5 minutes.

• ROASTED ASPARAGUS WITH BALSAMIC BUTTER SAUCE •

PREP: 5 minutes   COOK: 12 minutes

INGREDIENTS
   ½ pound fresh asparagus, trimmed
   1 tablespoon olive oil
   Kosher salt and freshly ground black pepper, to taste
   1 tablespoon unsalted butter
   1-1/2 teaspoons soy sauce
   1/2 teaspoon balsamic vinegar

DIRECTIONS

   1.   Preheat oven to 400°.

   2.   Place asparagus in a shallow 8-inch baking dish. Sprinkle with oil, salt,
        and pepper; toss to coat. Roast asparagus until tender, about
        12 minutes.

   3.   Meanwhile, melt the butter in a small saucepan over medium heat.
        Remove from heat, and stir in soy sauce and balsamic vinegar. Pour
        over the baked asparagus to serve.

• ROASTED ASPARAGUS WITH PARMESAN CHEESE •

PREP: 5 minutes   COOK: 12 minutes

INGREDIENTS
   1 tablespoon olive oil
   1/2 pound fresh asparagus, trimmed
   2 tablespoons freshly grated Parmesan cheese
   1/2 teaspoon kosher salt
   1/8 teaspoon garlic powder, or to taste

DIRECTIONS
   1.   Preheat oven to 400°.

   2.   Lightly oil a 9 x 9 casserole dish with olive oil. Place asparagus in the
        dish and toss with olive oil.

   3.   Sprinkle asparagus with Parmesan cheese, salt, and garlic powder.

   4.   Roast until asparagus is tender, about 12 minutes.

• PAN-ROASTED ASPARAGUS AND TOMATOES •

PREP: 5 minutes   COOK: 6 minutes

INGREDIENTS
   1-1/2 teaspoons olive oil
   1/2 pound fresh asparagus, trimmed
   1 cup grape tomatoes
   Kosher salt and freshly ground black pepper, to taste
   1 tablespoon grated Parmesan cheese

DIRECTIONS
   1.   Heat a 10-inch skillet over medium-high heat. Add the olive oil and
        swirl to coat. Add asparagus and sauté for 3 minutes. Add tomatoes
        and sauté, turning occasionally, until asparagus is crisp-tender and the
        tomatoes just start to burst. Season with salt and pepper to taste. Serve
        and sprinkle with Parmesan cheese.

• REFRIED BEANS •

I know you can buy this in a can, but some brands are loaded with fat and salt. You can whip this up in less than 20 minutes and it will be much healthier for you.

PREP: 5 minutes   COOK: 15 minutes

INGREDIENTS
  2 tablespoons olive or canola oil
  1 medium onion, chopped (about 1/2 cup)
  1-1/2 teaspoons ground cumin (or more to taste)
  1 (19-ounce) can pinto or red kidney beans, rinsed and drained
    (about 1-1/2 to 2 cups)
  Kosher salt and freshly ground black pepper, to taste
  1/8 teaspoon cayenne pepper (or more to taste)

DIRECTIONS
  1. Heat a 10-inch skillet over medium heat. Add oil and swirl to coat. Stir in onions and sauté until soft and translucent, about 8 - 10 minutes. Stir in the cumin and sauté 1 additional minute.

  2. Add the beans and mash with a fork or potato masher. Cook, stirring until heated through, about 3 minutes. Season with salt, pepper and cayenne to taste.

• GRILLED BROCCOLI WITH LEMON •

PREP: 5 minutes   COOK: 10 minutes

INGREDIENTS
  4 large fresh broccoli spears   1 lemon, quartered
  1 tablespoon olive oil   1/4 teaspoon kosher salt
  1/8 teaspoon black pepper   Extra virgin olive oil to drizzle

DIRECTIONS
  1. Heat grill to medium heat. Lightly oil grate.

  2. In a medium bowl, toss the broccoli and lemons with the oil and season with salt and teaspoon pepper. Grill, turning occasionally, until tender and lightly charred, about 10 to 15 minutes.

  2. Squeeze the lemons over the broccoli and drizzle with extra virgin olive oil.

• GARLIC-ROASTED BROCCOLI WITH PINE NUTS •

PREP: 5 minutes

COOK: 20 minutes

INGREDIENTS

1/2 pound fresh broccoli florets
3 cloves garlic, minced or pressed
2 teaspoons olive oil
1/4 teaspoon kosher salt

Pinch of crushed red pepper, or
  to taste
2 tablespoons pine nuts
2 teaspoons fresh lemon juice

DIRECTIONS

1. Preheat oven to 450°.

2. In a medium bowl, combine the broccoli, garlic, olive oil, salt and red pepper. Toss to coat.

3. Place on a rimmed baking sheet and bake until browned and nearly tender, about 12 - 15 minutes. Add pine nuts and bake until the pine nuts are toasted, about 2 additional minutes. Remove from oven and drizzle with lemon juice before serving.

• GARLIC-ROASTED BROCCOLI WITH BALSAMIC VINEGAR •

PREP: 5 minutes

COOK: 10 minutes

INGREDIENTS

2 tablespoons olive oil
1 garlic clove, minced or pressed
1/2 pound broccoli spears
Kosher salt and freshly ground black pepper, to taste
1-1/2 teaspoons balsamic vinegar

DIRECTIONS

1. Preheat oven to 475°.

2. In a small bowl, combine the olive oil and garlic. Place broccoli on a rimmed baking sheet. Pour garlic oil over the broccoli and toss to coat. Season with salt and pepper.

3. Roast broccoli until tender and charred at the edges, about 7 - 9 minutes. Transfer to a serving dish and sprinkle with balsamic vinegar.

• LEMON BALSAMIC BROCCOLI •

PREP: Less than 5 minutes

COOK: 5 minutes

INGREDIENTS
1/2 pound broccoli florets
1 tablespoon unsalted butter
1 teaspoon fresh lemon juice

1 teaspoon balsamic vinegar
1/4 teaspoon kosher salt

DIRECTIONS

1. Place florets in a steamer basket over an inch or two of boiling water. Cover and steam until crisp-tender, about 5 minutes.

2. Meanwhile, combine butter, lemon juice, vinegar and salt in a small saucepan over medium-low heat. Cook until butter melts. Pour over broccoli and turn to coat.

• SAUTÉED BROCCOLI WITH TOMATOES AND BACON •

Perhaps you live with someone who does not care for broccoli. Many of us do. And I don't blame them since most of us grew up with the mushy, overcooked broccoli found in school cafeterias and more than a few restaurants. If you do have someone in your household that holds an aversion to this healthy veggie, than I suggest you whip up a plate of this. I'm confident you will win them over. Think of it as a BLT with broccoli instead of lettuce. And who doesn't like a good BLT?

PREP: 5 minutes

COOK: 18 minutes

INGREDIENTS
2 slices bacon, cut into 1-inch pieces
1/2 pound broccoli florets (2 - 3 cups)
1/2 cup halved cherry tomatoes
1/4 teaspoon kosher salt
1/8 teaspoon freshly ground black pepper

DIRECTIONS

1. Heat a 10-inch skillet over medium heat, add bacon and sauté until crisp, about 6 - 8 minutes. Transfer to a plate with a slotted spoon.

2. Add the broccoli and tomatoes to the skillet and sauté, until the broccoli is tender, about 8 - 10 minutes. Season with salt and pepper then sprinkle with the bacon.

• SAUTÉED BROCCOLI WITH RED PEPPERS •
AND ALMONDS

This is also a wonderful way to cook cauliflower.

PREP: Less than 5 minutes   COOK: 10 minutes

INGREDIENTS
    2 tablespoons unsalted butter
    2 teaspoons sliced almonds
    1/4 teaspoon salt
    1/4 teaspoon freshly ground black pepper
    1 clove garlic, minced or pressed
    1 tablespoon white wine
    1/2 medium onion, chopped (about 1/2 cup)
    1/2 medium red bell pepper
    1-1/2 cups chopped broccoli

DIRECTIONS
Heat a 10-inch skillet over medium-low heat. Add butter and swirl to coat. Stir in almonds, salt and pepper and sauté until golden brown, about 2 - 3 minutes. Add garlic and sauté for 1 additional minute. Stir in wine, onion, red bell pepper, and broccoli. Sauté until broccoli is tender, about 5 minutes.

• ROASTED BRUSSELS SPROUTS WITH ORANGE •
(Brussels Sprouts á l'Orange)

PREP: 5 minutes   COOK: 15 minutes

INGREDIENTS
> 1/2 pound Brussels sprouts, halved lengthwise
> 2 teaspoons olive oil
> 1/4 teaspoon kosher salt
> 1/8 teaspoon freshly ground black pepper
> 1/2 teaspoon orange rind
> 2 tablespoons orange juice

DIRECTIONS

1.   Preheat oven to 425°.

2.   Place Brussels sprouts in a medium bowl. Sprinkle with olive oil, salt, and pepper and toss to coat. In another bowl, combine the orange rind and orange juice.

3.   Place Brussels sprouts in a single layer on an oiled baking sheet and roast for 7 minutes. Turn Brussels sprouts over and roast until tender and browned, about 5 - 7 more minutes.

4.   Transfer Brussels sprouts to a medium bowl and drizzle with the orange juice. Toss to coat.

• GRILLED BALSAMIC CARROTS •

PREP: 5 minutes   COOK: 20 minutes

INGREDIENTS
  2 tablespoons unsalted butter, melted
  1-1/2 teaspoons balsamic vinegar
  1/4 teaspoon rosemary
  1/2 pound whole carrots, peeled
  Kosher salt and freshly ground black pepper, to taste

DIRECTIONS

1. Preheat grill to medium heat. Lightly oil grate.

2. In a small bowl, whisk together the butter, balsamic vinegar and
    rosemary. Arrange carrots on the grill or in a grill basket and brush with
    the butter mixture.

3. Grill until carrots are crisp-tender, turning occasionally, about 20 minutes.
    Season with salt and pepper and brush with any remaining butter sauce.

• BOURBON GLAZED CARROTS •

PREP: 5 minutes   COOK: 10 minutes

INGREDIENTS
  1/2 lb carrots, peeled and sliced diagonally into 1/4 inch slices (about 2 cups)
  1/3 cup water
  1-1/2 tablespoons butter
  1-1/2 tablespoons honey
  1-1/2 tablespoons Bourbon
  Kosher salt and freshly ground black pepper, to taste

DIRECTIONS
Combine all ingredients in a 10-inch skillet over medium high heat. Sauté until
carrots are tender and liquid has turned into a glaze, about 10 minutes, stirring
frequently. Season with salt and pepper.

• PAN-ROASTED ROSEMARY CARROTS •

PREP: 5 minutes   COOK: 20 minutes

INGREDIENTS
   1 tablespoon olive oil
   4 carrots, peeled and sliced on the diagonal, 1/2-inch thick
   1/4 teaspoon kosher salt
   1/8 teaspoon freshly ground black pepper
   1/2 cup chicken broth
   1 teaspoon brown sugar
   1 small sprig fresh rosemary
   Kosher salt and freshly ground black pepper, to taste

DIRECTIONS

1.   Heat a 10-inch skillet over medium-high heat. Add oil and swirl to coat.
     Add carrots, salt, and pepper. Sauté until carrots are golden brown,
     about 8 - 10 minutes.

2.   Stir in chicken broth and sugar. Add rosemary sprig and bring to a
     simmer. Reduce heat to medium-low, cover and simmer, stirring gently
     occasionally, until carrots are tender, about 6 - 10 minutes.

3.   Uncover and discard rosemary. Cook until liquid evaporates, about 1 - 2
     minutes. Season with salt and pepper.

• GRILLED CAULIFLOWER •

There is an extra step to grilling cauliflower than most other veggies. You will need to have a grill-safe skillet with a lid on hand to cook the cauliflower after you produce the grill marks. I just use my cast iron skillet.

PREP: 10 minutes   COOK: 25 minutes

INGREDIENTS
    1 tablespoon olive oil
    2 teaspoons brown sugar
    1/2 teaspoon seasoned salt
    1/2 head cauliflower, cut into 3/4-inch thick slices

DIRECTIONS
1. Preheat grill for medium-high heat. Lightly oil grate.

2. In a small bowl, combine the olive oil, brown sugar and seasoned salt. Brush both sides of the cauliflower slices.

3. Grill until char marks appear on both sides of the cauliflower, about 2 - 3 minutes per side. Transfer to a grill safe skillet with a lid and continue to cook until cauliflower is tender, about 15 - 20 minutes.

• GRILLED CORN •
Three Ways

Whether you grill your corn in the husk or in foil, it's important that you soak the corn for at least 30 minutes before grilling. This will keep the husks from catching on fire and it will insure that the kernels are plump and tender if you are grilling in foil or naked (the corn, not you!)

IN THE HUSK:

PREP: 5 minutes   SOAK: 30+ minutes   COOK: 15 minutes

INGREDIENTS
  2 ears corn, in husks
  Unsalted butter to taste
  Kosher salt and freshly ground black pepper to taste

DIRECTIONS

1. Preheat grill to medium-high for indirect heat. Lightly oil grate.

2. Peel back husk and remove silk. Replace corn husk and tie with and extra husk or string to keep intact. Soak corn in cold water for at least 30 minutes.

3. Place corn on grill and cook on indirect heat, turning occasionally, for about 15 minutes. Season with butter, salt and pepper.

IN FOIL:

PREP: 5 minutes   SOAK: 30+ minutes   COOK: 15 minutes

INGREDIENTS
  2 sheets 12" x 12" heavy duty aluminum foil
  2 ears corn, in husks
  Unsalted butter to taste
  Kosher salt and freshly ground black pepper to taste

DIRECTIONS

1. Preheat grill to medium-high for indirect heat. Lightly oil grate.

2. Remove husks and silk from corn and lay each one on a sheet of heavy duty foil (if you don't have heavy duty foil, double two pieces of regular foil). Slather on butter and season with salt and pepper. Wrap each ear up tight and well-sealed (you don't want the butter leaking out).

3. Grill, turning occasionally, for 15 - 20 minutes.

NAKED:

PREP: 5 minutes   SOAK: 30+ minutes   COOK: 10 minutes

INGREDIENTS
   2 ears corn, in husks
   1 tablespoon olive or canola oil
   Unsalted butter to taste
   Kosher salt and freshly ground black pepper to taste

DIRECTIONS

1.   Preheat grill for medium indirect heat. Lightly oil grate.

2.   Remove husks and silk from corn. Soak for at least 30 minutes. Brush
     each ear with olive oil and grill over indirect heat, turning occasionally,
     until slightly charred and tender, about 10 - 15 minutes. Serve with
     butter, salt and pepper to taste.

• SAUTÉED CREOLE CORN •

PREP: 10 minutes   COOK: 20 minutes

INGREDIENTS
  1 teaspoon olive oil
  2 slices bacon, finely chopped
  1/2 green bell pepper, stemmed, seeded and finely chopped
  3 scallions, white part minced, green part sliced thin
  1/4 teaspoon thyme
  1 clove garlic, minced or crushed
  1-1/2 cups fresh or frozen corn kernels
  1/2 teaspoon hot sauce
  Kosher salt and freshly ground black pepper, to taste

DIRECTIONS
  1.   Heat a 10-inch skillet over medium heat. Add olive oil and swirl to coat.
       Add bacon and sauté until crisp, about 8 minutes. Transfer bacon to a
       paper towel with a slotted spoon.

  2.   Add green peppers and scallions to the skillet and sauté until soft, about
       5 minutes. Stir in the thyme and garlic and sauté for 1 additional minute.

  3.   Add corn and sauté until tender and lightly browned, about 5 - 7
       minutes. Remove from heat and stir in reserved bacon and hot sauce.
       Season with salt and pepper to taste.

• CREAMED CORN •

I know you can buy this in a can. I always have a couple in the cupboard to use in chilis or stews when I'm feeling creative. But here's a homemade version I think you'll enjoy.

INGREDIENTS
- 1/4 cup whole milk
- 2 teaspoons all-purpose flour
- 2 teaspoons butter
- 1 cup frozen corn, thawed
- 1/4 cup heavy cream
- 1/4 teaspoon kosher salt
- 1/8 teaspoon freshly ground black pepper
- 1-1/2 teaspoons sugar
- 1 tablespoon freshly grated Parmesan cheese

DIRECTIONS
In a small bowl, whisk together the milk and flour. Heat a medium saucepan over medium heat. Add the butter and swirl to coat. Stir in the corn, cream, salt, pepper, and sugar. Stir in the flour-milk mixture and cook, stirring, until thickened and corn is cooked through, about 10 minutes. Remove from heat, and stir in the Parmesan cheese until melted.

• MEXICAN STYLE CORN •

This is another item that you can find canned. Again, I want you to try this. It only takes a short time to make.

PREP: 5 minutes   COOK: 10 minutes

INGREDIENTS
   1-1/2 tablespoons unsalted butter
   1 cup fresh or frozen corn kernels
   1/2 teaspoon kosher salt (or to taste)
   Pinch freshly ground black pepper
   1 tablespoon finely-chopped green pepper (use jalapeño for more heat)
   1 tablespoon chopped pimento (jarred is fine)

DIRECTIONS
Heat a small saucepan over medium heat. Add the butter and swirl to coat. Stir in corn, salt, pepper and green peppers. Sauté for 10 minutes. Add the pimentos and sauté until heated through.

• ROASTED GREEN BEANS AND ONIONS •

PREP: 5 minutes   COOK: 13 minutes

INGREDIENTS
   1/2 pound fresh green beans
   1/2 cup sliced onion
   1/2 teaspoon dark sesame oil
   1/8 teaspoon kosher salt
   Toasted sesame seeds to garnish (optional)

DIRECTIONS

1.   Preheat oven to 500°.

2.   In a medium bowl, combine the green beans, onions, sesame oil and salt; toss to coat. Place on a lightly-oiled baking sheet and roast for 10 minutes. Stir beans and continue roasting until tender, about 3 more minutes. Sprinkle with toasted sesame seeds, if using, and serve.

• BALSAMIC GLAZED GREEN BEANS •

PREP: 5 minutes   COOK: 15 minutes

INGREDIENTS
    1/2 pound fresh green beans
    1 tablespoon unsalted butter
    1-1/2 tablespoons minced or pressed shallot
    1 garlic clove, minced or pressed
    3 tablespoons balsamic vinegar
    1/4 teaspoon kosher salt
    1/8 teaspoon freshly ground black pepper

DIRECTIONS

1. Place green beans in a steamer basket over an inch or two of boiling
    water. Cover and steam for 8-12 minutes until crisp-tender. (Or place
    1/2 pound green beans in a microwave baking dish. Add 2 tablespoons
    water; cover and cook on high for 9-13 minutes, stirring halfway through,
    until crisp-tender.)

2. Meanwhile, heat a 10-inch skillet over medium heat. Add butter and
    swirl to coat. Add the shallots and garlic and sauté for 2 minutes. Stir in
    balsamic vinegar, salt and pepper and sauté for 1 additional minute. Add
    green beans and toss to coat.

• GREEN BEANS AND SHALLOTS •

PREP 5 minutes   COOK: 10 minutes

INGREDIENTS
   1/2 pound fresh or frozen green beans (defrosted if frozen)
   3 tablespoons water
   1 tablespoon unsalted butter
   1-1/2 teaspoons olive oil
   1 tablespoon chopped shallot
   1/4 teaspoon kosher salt
   1/8 teaspoon freshly ground black pepper

DIRECTIONS
Place the green beans and water in a medium sauce pan, cover and bring to a boil. Cook until most of the moister has evaporated, about 3 - 4 minutes. Add the butter, oil and shallots and cook, stirring, until the shallots have softened, about 3 minutes. Season with salt and pepper.

• DIJON MUSTARD GREEN BEANS •

PREP: 5 minutes   COOK: 10 minutes

INGREDIENTS
   1/2 pound fresh green beans, trimmed
   1 tablespoon unsalted butter
   2 teaspoons Dijon mustard
   1 tablespoon finely chopped Italian flat leaf parsley
   1/2 teaspoon grated lemon zest
   1/4 teaspoon kosher salt (or to taste)

DIRECTIONS
1.   Place 1/2 pound green beans in a steamer basket over an inch or two of boiling water. Cover and steam for 8-12 minutes until crisp-tender. Or place 1/2 pound green beans in a microwave baking dish. Add 2 tablespoons water; cover and cook on high for 9-13 minutes, stirring halfway through, until crisp-tender.

2.   Meanwhile, melt butter in a small saucepan over medium-low heat. Stir in mustard, parsley, lemon zest and salt. Place green beans in a serving bowl, add butter mixture and toss to coat.

• GREEN BEANS AND CHERRY TOMATOES •

PREP: 10 minutes   COOK: 15 minutes

INGREDIENTS
   1/2 pound green beans, trimmed and cut into 2-inch pieces
   1/2 cup water
   1 tablespoon unsalted butter
   2/3 cup cherry tomato halves
   1/8 teaspoon pepper
   1/2 teaspoon chopped fresh basil

DIRECTIONS
1. Place beans and water in a medium saucepan. Cover, and bring to a
    boil. Set heat to low, and simmer until tender, about 10 minutes. Drain off
    water, and set aside.

2. Meanwhile, heat a small skillet or saucepan over medium heat. Add
    butter and swirl to coat. Stir in tomatoes pepper and basil and cook,
    stirring gently, until tomatoes are just soft, about 3 - 5 minutes. Pour the
    tomato mixture over cooked green beans, and toss gently to blend.

• SIMPLE SAUTÉED KALE •

PREP: Less than 5 minutes   COOK: 6 minutes

INGREDIENTS
   2 teaspoons olive oil
   1 garlic clove, minced or pressed
   1/2 pound kale, stemmed and shredded
   2 tablespoons water
   1/2 teaspoon red wine vinegar
   1/8 teaspoon kosher salt
   1/8 teaspoon freshly ground black pepper

DIRECTIONS
Heat a 10-inch skillet over medium heat. Add olive oil and minced garlic and
sauté 1 minute, stirring constantly. Add kale and water; cover and cook 5
minutes or until tender. Remove from heat; stir in vinegar and season with salt
and pepper.

• CREAMED PEAS WITH NEW POTATOES •

PREP: 5 minutes   COOK: 25 minutes

INGREDIENTS
1/2 pound baby red potatoes, quartered
1/2 cup frozen peas
2 teaspoons unsalted butter
1 tablespoon finely chopped onion
2 teaspoons all-purpose flour
Kosher salt and freshly ground black pepper, to taste
1/2 cup milk

DIRECTIONS
1. Bring a large saucepan or medium pot of salted water to a boil over high heat. Add potatoes and boil for 8 - 12 minutes until tender. Drain.

2. Meanwhile, in a medium saucepan, bring 1/2 cup water to a boil. Add peas, then cover and cook for 3 - 5 minutes, or until tender (don't overcook). Drain in a colander.

3. Using the same saucepan, melt butter over medium heat. Add the onions and sauté until soft and translucent, about 3 - 5 minutes.

4. Stir in flour and whisk to make a thick paste; gradually stir in milk and bring to a boil. Cook, stirring constantly until slightly thickened, about 2 minutes. Season with salt and pepper. Add potatoes and peas to the sauce and simmer until heated through.

• STUFFED YELLOW SQUASH •

PREP: 5 minutes

COOK: 25 minutes

INGREDIENTS

2 yellow squash
1 tablespoon minced onion
1 clove garlic, minced or pressed
2 teaspoons olive oil
2 tablespoons dry breadcrumbs

1 tablespoon grated Parmesan
    cheese
1/8 teaspoon kosher salt
Hungarian sweet paprika to
    garnish

DIRECTIONS

1. Preheat oven to 374°.

2. Cut squash in half length-wise and scoop out centers with a spoon. Chop scooped squash and combine with onions and garlic.

3. Heat a small skillet over medium-high heat. Add olive oil and swirl to coat pan. Add squash and onion mixture and sauté for 5 minutes. Remove from heat and stir in remaining ingredients.

4. Stuff squash shells with the mixture and transfer to a lightly-oiled baking sheet. Cook for 20 minutes. Sprinkle with paprika and serve.

• GRILLED YELLOW SQUASH WITH PEPPER JACK CHEESE •

PREP: 5 minutes

COOK: 8 minutes

INGREDIENTS

1 yellow squash, halved length-wise
1-1/2 teaspoons olive oil
Kosher salt and freshly ground black pepper, to taste
3 tablespoon grated pepper jack cheese

DIRECTIONS

1. Prepare grill for medium-high heat. Lightly oil grate.

2. Brush squash with olive oil and sprinkle with salt and pepper to taste. Place squash on grill and cook until tender, about 3 - 4 minutes per side. Remove to a plate, cut side up, and sprinkle evenly with cheese.

• PAN-ROASTED GRAPE TOMATOES •

PREP: Less than 5 minutes   COOK: 10 minutes

INGREDIENTS
 2 teaspoons olive oil, divided
 1/2 pint grape tomatoes
 1/2 teaspoon chopped fresh oregano
 1/2 teaspoon chopped fresh rosemary
 1/8 teaspoon kosher salt
 Pinch of crushed red pepper, to taste

DIRECTIONS
Heat a small skillet over medium-high heat. Add 1 teaspoon olive oil and swirl
to coat. Add tomatoes and cook until they begin to blister, about 3 - 4 minutes.
Remove from heat and add remaining olive oil, oregano, rosemary, salt and
pepper; stir to coat and let stand 3 - 5 minutes.

• HERB CRUSTED BROILED TOMATOES •

PREP: 5 minutes   COOK: 4 minutes

INGREDIENTS
 2 tablespoons panko breadcrumbs
 1 tablespoon grated Parmesan cheese
 1/2 teaspoon dried Italian seasoning
 1/8 teaspoon kosher salt
 1 teaspoon unsalted butter, melted
 1 tomato, halved horizontally

DIRECTIONS
 1. Preheat broiler.

 2. Combine the breadcrumbs, cheese, Italian seasoning salt and butter in
     a small bowl. Sprinkle herb mixture evenly over the tomato halves and
     place on a lightly-oiled baking sheet. Broil until tops are golden, about
     3 - 4 minutes.

• SAUTÉED ZUCCHINI AND ONIONS •

PREP: 10 minutes   COOK: 6 minutes

INGREDIENTS
 1 teaspoon olive oil
 1/2 pound zucchini quartered lengthwise then cut into 2-inch pieces
 1/4 cup chopped onion
 Kosher salt and freshly ground black pepper, to taste

DIRECTIONS
Heat a 10-inch skillet over medium-high heat. Add olive oil and swirl to coat.
Add zucchini and onions and sauté until lightly brown, about 5 - 6 minutes.
Season with salt and pepper.

• SAUTÉED ZUCCHINI WITH BELL PEPPERS •

PREP: 10 minutes   COOK: 7 minutes

INGREDIENTS
 1 tablespoon olive oil
 1 small zucchini, quartered lengthwise then cut into 2-inch pieces
 1/4 cup chopped red bell pepper
 1/4 cup chopped green bell pepper
 1 small clove garlic, chopped
 Kosher salt and freshly ground black pepper, to taste

DIRECTIONS
Heat a 10-inch skillet over medium-high heat. Add olive oil and swirl to coat.
Stir in zucchini and peppers and sauté for 5 minutes. Add garlic and sauté for 2
additional minutes. Season with salt and pepper.

• SAUTÉED ZUCCHINI AND TOMATOES •

PREP: 10 minutes   COOK: 8 minutes

INGREDIENTS
   2 tablespoons olive oil
   1/2 pound zucchini, sliced 1/4-inch thick
   1/2 cup diced tomatoes
   1 small clove garlic, minced or pressed
   1/4 teaspoon herbes de Provence (available in the spice section) or use 1/8
      teaspoon oregano and 1/8 teaspoon basil
   Kosher salt and freshly ground black pepper, to taste

DIRECTIONS

   1.   Heat a 10-inch skillet over medium-high heat. Add oil and swirl to coat.
        Add zucchini and sauté until crisp-tender and lightly brown, about
        5 minutes.

   2.   Add tomatoes, garlic, herbs, salt and pepper. Sauté until tomatoes begin
        to give off their liquid and the zucchini is tender, about 2 - 3 minutes.

• CLASSIC BAKED POTATO •

Some cookbooks recommend that you throw a couple of potatoes in the
microwave for a few minutes to save on time. Well, that will steam your
potatoes, not bake them. To get truly fluffy, melt in your mouth potatoes
you really have to bake them. That's why I always throw in a couple of extra
potatoes. Then I'll have them for soups, stews or breakfast in the coming days.

Preheat oven to 400°. Wash and dry potatoes and pierce with a fork or knife.
Bake for 45-60 minutes or until you can easily poke a hole in them. Season
with salt and pepper and serve with your choice of topping: butter, sour cream,
chives, cheese, etc.

• TWICE BAKED POTATOES WITH ROQUEFORT CHEESE •

Double this recipe for a nice lunch the next day.

PREP: 10 minutes   COOK: 90 minutes

INGREDIENTS
   3 russet potatoes, scrubbed and dried
   1/3 cup Roquefort cheese
   1/4 cup sour cream
   3 tablespoons freshly grated Parmesan cheese
   1 tablespoon unsalted butter, cut into little pieces
   Chopped fresh chives or parsley to garnish

DIRECTIONS
   1.   Preheat oven to 400°.

   2.   Wash and dry potatoes and pierce with a fork or knife. Bake until a
        skewer can be inserted into and removed from potatoes with little
        resistance, about 45 - 60 minutes (do not turn oven off). Remove
        potatoes and cool on plate about 10 minutes.

   3.   Using a kitchen towel or oven mitt to hold the potatoes, cut each one
        in half. Using a dinner spoon, scoop the flesh from each potato into a
        small bowl, leaving 1/8 to 1/4 -inch thickness in each potato. Place the
        4 potato shells on a lightly oiled baking sheet and return to the hot oven.
        Bake until lightly crisp, about 10 minutes. Remove and transfer potato
        skins to a plate. Turn oven to broil.

   4.   Meanwhile, in a medium bowl, mash the scooped potatoes with the
        Roquefort cheese and sour cream. Spoon the potato mixture into the
        shells, creating a mound. Place potatoes on the baking sheet and
        sprinkle with Parmesan cheese and dot with butter.

   5.   Return potatoes to the oven and broil until spotty brown and crisp on
        top, about 10 to 15 minutes. Remove and allow to cool a little. Sprinkle
        with chives or parsley and serve warm.

• SEASONED BOILED NEW POTATOES •

PREP: 5 minutes   COOK: 10 minutes

INGREDIENTS
    1/2 pound small new potatoes
    5 cloves garlic, peeled
    1 small bay leaf
    1/2 teaspoon black peppercorns
    2 tablespoons unsalted butter, or to taste
    Kosher salt and freshly ground black pepper, to taste

Directions

1. Place the potatoes, garlic, bay leaf, and peppercorns in a large saucepan, add cold water to cover by about an inch and season generously with salt. Bring to a boil, lower the heat, and simmer until potatoes are fork tender, about 8 - 10 minutes depending on size.

2. Drain and discard the garlic, bay leaves, and peppercorns. Halve the potatoes, if large, toss with the butter and season with salt and pepper, to taste. Keep warm.

• ROASTED RED POTATOES •

Double this recipe if you'd like to have potatoes in the morning. Just reheat in the microwave.

PREP: 5 minutes   COOK: 30 minutes

INGREDIENTS
    3/4 pound small red new potatoes, halved
    2 tablespoons olive oil
    1/4 teaspoon kosher salt (or to taste)
    Freshly ground black pepper to taste

DIRECTIONS

1. Preheat oven to 450°. Adjust oven rack to lowest position.

2. In a medium bowl, toss potatoes with oil, salt and pepper. Arrange, cut side down, on a rimmed baking sheet. Roast until tender and golden brown, about 30 minutes (check after 20 minutes).

• MASHED POTATOES TEN WAYS •

These recipes call for 1 pound of potatoes. That's probably more than 2 people will eat in one sitting, but I like to make extra to use for breakfast or in soups.

CLASSIC MASHED POTATOES
Cover 1 pound whole russet or Yukon gold potatoes with cold water. Bring to a boil and simmer for about 45 minutes or until you can pierce them easily with a fork. Drain, peel and mash with 2 or 3 tablespoons unsalted butter. Add 1 /2 cup warm milk, and salt and pepper to taste; mash until you reach your desired consistency. Add more warm milk for fluffier potatoes.

Note: To speed things up, you may want to peel (for the Classic Mashed Potatoes) and cut your potatoes into chunks before boiling them. This will reduce your cook time to about half. If you choose this method, be sure to return the potatoes to the pan after draining and shake them over the burner to allow much of the remaining water to evaporate before adding your butter and milk.

NEO-CLASSIC SMASHED POTATOES
Cover 1 pound whole red potatoes with cold water; Bring to a boil then simmer 40 minutes or until you can pierce them easily with a fork. Drain but do not peel. Smash with 2 or 3 tablespoons unsalted butter. Add 1/4 cup warm milk and salt and pepper. Add more milk for a smoother consistency.

TANGY MASHED POTATOES WITH DILL
Make Classic Mashed Potatoes or Neo-Classic Mashed Potatoes. Use 1/2 cup sour cream instead of milk; top with fresh dill.

BACON-CHEDDAR MASHED POTATOES
Cook 1/4 pound chopped bacon until crisp. Make Classic Mashed Potatoes replacing 1 tablespoon of the butter with 1 or 2 tablespoons bacon drippings (optional). Fold in half the bacon and 1/4-pound grated sharp cheddar cheese. Sprinkle the remaining bacon bits on top and garnish with 2 tablespoons chopped fresh chives.

BUTTERMILK MASHED POTATOES
Replace the milk with warmed buttermilk.

PANCETTA-ROSEMARY MASHED POTATOES

Cook 2 ounces diced pancetta in olive oil with 1/8 teaspoon chopped rosemary and 1 crushed garlic clove; drain and spoon over Classic Mashed Potatoes or Neo-Classic Mashed Potatoes

GREEK STYLE MASHED POTATOES

Make Neo-Classic Mashed Potatoes; add 1/4 pound crumbled feta cheese, 2 tablespoons each minced dill, parsley and scallions, and 1 teaspoon minced oregano.

ITALIAN STYLE MASHED POTATOES

Make Classic Mashed Potatoes. Add 1/2 cup grated bagged Italian 6-Cheese (Sargento, Kraft, etc)

BROCCOLI-CHEDDAR MASHED POTATOES

Boil 2 cups broccoli florets (frozen is okay) until tender; drain. Add to Classic Mashed Potatoes with 1/4 pound grated cheddar cheese and fluff.

MASHED POTATOES WITH CARROTS

Add 2 - 3 cups peeled and chunked carrots when you are boiling the potatoes.

• SAVORY OVEN FRIES •
(Pommes Frites)

PREP: 10 minutes   COOK: 45 minutes

INGREDIENTS
   2 baking potatoes cut lengthwise into 1/4-inch-thick strips
   1 tablespoon olive oil
   1/2 teaspoon hot sauce (or to taste)
   1/2 teaspoon dried thyme
   1/4 teaspoon garlic salt
   Cooking spray or oil in a mister

DIRECTIONS
1.   Preheat oven to 500°.

2.   Heat a medium baking sheet in oven for 5 minutes. In a medium bowl, combine potatoes, olive oil, and hot sauce. Add thyme and garlic salt, then toss to coat.

3.   Remove preheated pan from oven. Coat pan with cooking spray. Arrange potatoes in a single layer and bake, turning once, until lightly brown and crisp, about 40 minutes.

• SAUTÉED POTATOES AND MUSHROOMS •

PREP: 10 minutes   COOK: 18 minutes

INGREDIENTS
   3/4 pound Yukon gold or red potatoes
   1/4 cup canola, vegetable or peanut oil
   3 - 4 mushrooms, thinly sliced, about 1/2 cup
   1-1/2 tablespoons unsalted butter
   1 tablespoon chopped shallots
   1 small garlic clove, minced or pressed
   Kosher salt and freshly ground black pepper, to taste
   2 teaspoons chopped fresh Italian flat leaf parsley

DIRECTIONS
   1.   Peel potatoes and cut into 1/4-inch slices lengthwise. Stack them and
        slice them into1/4-inch strips again (like French fries). You should have
        about 2-1/2 cups. Place potatoes in a colander and run hot water over
        them to remove some of the starch. Drain well and blot dry with paper
        towels.

   2.   Heat a 10-inch skillet over high heat. Add oil and swirl to coat. Add
        potatoes and sauté to cook the strips evenly and until they are golden
        brown, about 10 - 12 minutes. Add mushrooms and sauté for about 4
        additional minutes.

   3.   Remove the potatoes and mushrooms with a slotted spoon to a bowl.
        Pour the oil from the skillet and wipe clean with a paper towel. Add the
        butter to the skillet to melt. Add the shallots and garlic and sauté for 1
        minute. Return the potatoes and mushrooms and toss to coat. Season
        with salt and pepper to taste. Sprinkle with parsley and serve.

• SAUTÉED POTATOES WITH LEMON AND PARSLEY •

PREP: 5 minutes   COOK: 15 minutes

INGREDIENTS

    1/2 pound all-purpose or russet potatoes, thinly sliced
    2 tablespoons olive oil
    1-1/2 teaspoons chopped fresh parsley
    1-1/2 teaspoons fresh lemon juice
    1/4 teaspoon lemon zest
    Kosher salt and freshly ground black pepper, to taste

DIRECTIONS

    1. Cook potatoes in a large saucepan of boiling salted water until just
        tender, about 6 - 8 minutes. Drain.

    2. Meanwhile, heat a 10-inch skillet over medium-high heat. Add olive oil
        and swirl to coat. Add potatoes and cook, turning once or twice, until
        light brown, about 7 - 8 minutes.

    3. Stir in parsley, lemon juice, lemon zest, and salt and pepper to taste.

• ROASTED HONEY-GLAZED SWEET POTATOES •

PREP: 5 minutes   COOK: 1 hour

INGREDIENTS

    2 long, slender sweet potatoes, peeled
    2 tablespoons olive oil
    Kosher salt and freshly ground black pepper, to taste
    1/4 cup honey
    Chopped fresh parsley to garnish

DIRECTIONS

    1. Preheat oven to 400°.

    2. Cut peeled potatoes length-wise into quarters. Place in a bowl and
        drizzle with olive oil then toss to coat. Season with salt and pepper.

    3. Place potatoes on a rimmed baking sheet and roast for 45 minutes.
        Brush with honey and roast until tender, about 15 more minutes. Transfer
        to serving dish and sprinkle with parsley.

• BASIC STEAMED WHITE RICE •

PREP: Less than 5 minutes   COOK: 20 minutes

INGREDIENTS
  1 cup water or chicken, beef or vegetable broth
  1/2 cup uncooked long grain white rice
  2 teaspoons unsalted butter or more to taste (optional)
  Kosher salt and freshly ground black pepper, to taste

DIRECTIONS
In a medium saucepan, bring water or broth to a boil over medium-high heat. Stir in rice and return to a boil. Turn heat to low, cover pan, and simmer until liquid is absorbed and rice is tender, about 18 minutes. Stir in butter, salt and pepper and fluff.

• MEXICAN RICE •

PREP: 5 minutes   COOK: 30 minutes

INGREDIENTS
  1-1/2 tablespoons unsalted butter or olive oil
  2 tablespoons chopped onion
  1 small clove garlic, minced or pressed
  1/4 teaspoon ground cumin
  1/2 cup uncooked long grain rice
  1-1/2 teaspoons tomato paste
  1 cup chicken broth

DIRECTIONS

1. Heat a medium saucepan over medium-high heat. Add butter or oil and swirl to coat. Stir in onions and sauté until soft, about 4 - 5 minutes. Add garlic and sauté for 1 additional minute. Stir in cumin and rice and sauté until rice becomes opaque, about 2 - 3 minutes.

2. Meanwhile, in a small bowl or cup, combine tomatoes paste and chicken broth until well combined. Add broth to the rice and bring to a boil. Lower heat to low, cover and simmer until rice is cooked, about 17 minutes. Remove from heat and let stand for 3 - 5 minutes. Fluff with fork and serve.

• RICE PILAF •

PREP: 5 minutes   COOK: 25 minutes

INGREDIENTS
   1 tablespoon unsalted butter, divided
   1 tablespoon minced onion
   1/4 teaspoon minced garlic
   1/2 cup uncooked long grain rice
   3/4 cup chicken or beef broth
   1/2 teaspoon chopped fresh Italian flat leaf parsley
   1/8 teaspoon dried thyme
   Dash of Worcestershire sauce
   Dash of hot pepper sauce
   1 small bay leaf

DIRECTIONS
   1.   Melt half the butter in a small saucepan over medium-high heat. Stir in
        onions and sauté until soft, about 4 - 5 minutes. Add garlic and sauté
        for 1 additional minute. Add the rice and stir briefly until the grains are
        coated and shiny.

   2.   Stir in the broth and add the parsley, thyme, Worcestershire sauce, hot
        pepper sauce and bay leaf. Bring to a boil and cover. Lower heat and
        simmer for 18 minutes.

   3.   Remove cover and discard bay leaf. Stir in remaining butter and fluff with
        a fork.

• RICE PILAF WITH RED PEPPERS AND OLIVES •

This will probably make more than two servings, but it is so good you may be tempted to eat it all in one sitting. If not, this makes for a wonderful omelet, frittata or even a nice snack the next day.

PREP: 10 minutes   COOK: 25 minutes

INGREDIENTS
    1 tablespoon olive oil or unsalted butter
    1/2 medium red bell pepper, chopped
    2 cloves garlic, minced or pressed
    1 cup uncooked long grain rice
    1-1/2 cups chicken or vegetable broth
    1/3 cup sliced pimento-stuffed green olives
    Kosher salt and freshly ground black pepper, to taste

DIRECTIONS
    1. Heat a medium saucepan over medium heat. Add the olive oil and swirl
        to coat. Add bell pepper and sauté until it begins to soften, about 3
        minutes. Add garlic and sauté for 1 - 2 additional minutes.

    2. Add rice and stir to coat the grains. Cook the rice for 1 - 2 minutes,
        stirring constantly. Turn heat to high; add the broth and bring to a boil.
        Reduce heat to low, cover and simmer until rice is done, about
        17 - 18 minutes.

    3. Remove from heat and stir in olives. Season with salt and pepper.

• RICE AND PASTA PILAF •

Many of us know about this San Francisco treat from the ubiquitous commercials featuring cable cars and conductors. My research shows that while this dish may be enjoyed up and down Telegraph Hill, it actually originated in Armenia. Here's my take on it. I think, like me, you'll be making it a lot. It takes about the same amount of time as the boxed version but here you can control the salt and fat content. Oh, and feel free to tweak it with pimentos, green peppers, mushrooms, etc.

PREP: 5 minutes   COOK: 30 minutes

INGREDIENTS
   2 tablespoons butter, divided
   1/4 cup thin spaghetti broken into 1-inch pieces
   1/4 cup diced onion
   1 clove garlic, minced
   1/4 cup uncooked white rice
   1 cup chicken broth
   Kosher salt and freshly ground black pepper, to taste

DIRECTIONS
1.   Heat a medium saucepan over medium-low heat. Add 1 tablespoon butter and swirl to coat. Add spaghetti and stir until golden brown, about 3 minutes. And the onion and sauté until soft and translucent, about 5 - 6 minutes. Add the garlic and sauté 1 additional minute. Add the rice and stir to coat with the butter.

2.   Increase heat to high and stir in the broth. Reduce heat to medium-low, cover and simmer until the rice is tender, about 17 - 18 minutes. Remove from heat and let stand for 3 - 5 minutes. Add remaining butter and fluff. Season with salt and pepper.

• ORZO WITH PARSLEY •

PREP: 5 minutes   COOK: 10 minutes

INGREDIENTS

1/2 cup orzo pasta
2 cups water
1 tablespoon butter
1 tablespoon chopped fresh parsley

1/4 teaspoon kosher salt
1/8 teaspoon freshly ground
    black pepper

DIRECTIONS

1. In a medium saucepan, bring 2 cups water to a boil. Cook orzo in
    the boiling water, stirring occasionally until cooked al dente, about 10
    minutes. Drain.

2. Stir in butter, parsley, salt and pepper.

• ORZO WITH MUSHROOMS •

PREP: 10 minutes   COOK: 20 minutes

INGREDIENTS

1/4 cup butter, divided
2 tablespoons chopped onion
1 small clove garlic, chopped
1/2 cup uncooked orzo pasta
1/4 cup sliced fresh mushrooms
1/2 cup chicken broth or water
1/4 cup dry white wine

Kosher salt and freshly ground
    black pepper, to taste
1/4 cup grated Parmesan
    cheese
2 tablespoons fresh parsley

DIRECTIONS

1. Heat a medium sauce pan over medium heat. Add 2 tablespoons butter
    and swirl to coat. Add onions and sauté until soft and translucent, about
    5 - 8 minutes. Add garlic and sauté 1 additional minute. Stir in orzo,
    mushrooms, and remaining butter. Cook and stir until butter is melted
    and mushrooms are tender, about 5 minutes.

2. Pour chicken broth and wine into the saucepan and bring to a boil.
    Reduce heat to low. Season with salt, and pepper. Cook 7 to 10
    minutes, until orzo is al dente. Stir in the Parmesan cheese and parsley
    to serve.

• ORZO WITH PARMESAN CHEESE •

PREP: 5 minutes   COOK: 15 minutes

INGREDIENTS
- 1/2 cup orzo pasta
- 2 cups water
- 2 tablespoons butter
- 1 tablespoon minced garlic
- 2 tablespoons Parmesan cheese

- 1 tablespoon milk
- 1/4 teaspoon salt and freshly ground black pepper
- 1-1/2 teaspoons chopped fresh Italian flat leaf parsley

DIRECTIONS

1. In a medium saucepan, bring 2 cups lightly salted water to a boil. Cook orzo in the boiling water, stirring occasionally until cooked al dente, about 10 minutes. Drain.

2. Melt butter in a skillet over medium heat; cook and stir garlic in melted butter until lightly browned, about 5 minutes. Stir orzo into garlic mixture and mix in Parmesan cheese, milk, salt, black pepper, and parsley.

• LEMON ORZO •

PREP: 5 minutes   COOK: 18 minutes

INGREDIENTS
- 2 teaspoons olive oil
- 1/4 cup chopped onion
- 1/2 cup orzo
- 1/2 cup chicken broth
- 1/4 cup dry white wine

- 1/8 teaspoon dried thyme
- 1 tablespoon chopped fresh chives
- 1-1/2 tablespoons fresh lemon juice

DIRECTIONS

Heat a medium saucepan over medium-high heat. Add olive oil and swirl to coat. Add onion to pan and sauté 3 minutes. Stir in orzo, broth, wine, and thyme; bring to a boil. Cover, reduce heat, and simmer until liquid is absorbed and pasta is al dente, about 10 - 15 minutes. Stir in chopped chives and lemon juice.

• QUINOA PILAF •

PREP: 10 minutes   COOK: 20 minutes

INGREDIENTS
   1/2 cup uncooked quinoa
   2 teaspoons unsalted butter
   1/2 small onion, finely chopped
   1 clove garlic, minced or pressed
   1 cup chicken or vegetable broth
   1 tablespoon chopped fresh parsley
   3/4 teaspoon chopped fresh thyme
   1/8 teaspoon Kosher salt
   1 dash lemon juice (optional)

DIRECTIONS

1.   Place the quinoa in a fine mesh strainer, and rinse under cold water until
     the water no longer foams.

2.   Heat a medium saucepan over medium heat. Add butter and swirl
     to coat. Add onions and sauté until soft and translucent, about 5 - 6
     minutes. Add garlic and sauté 1 additional minute. Add quinoa and sauté
     until lightly brown, about 5 minutes.

3.   Stir in the broth, parsley, thyme and salt. Bring to a boil, then reduce
     heat to medium-low. Cover and simmer until quinoa is tender, about 15
     minutes. Sprinkle with lemon juice. Toss and serve.

• QUINOA WITH GARDEN PEAS •

PREP: 5 minutes   COOK: 25 minutes

INGREDIENTS
1 teaspoon butter
1-1/2 tablespoons chopped onion
1/2 clove garlic, minced
1/4 teaspoon chopped fresh thyme
1/3 cup uncooked quinoa
2/3 cup chicken broth
1/8 teaspoon black pepper
1/4 cup frozen peas
3 tablespoons Romano cheese, divided
2 teaspoons chopped fresh Italian flat leaf parsley

DIRECTIONS
1. Melt the butter in a medium saucepan over medium heat. Add the onions and sauté until soft and translucent, about 5 minutes. Add the garlic and thyme and sauté 1 additional minute. Stir in the quinoa, and cook 2 minutes until lightly toasted.

2. Add the chicken broth and black pepper. Cover, and let come to a boil. Once boiling, stir in the frozen peas. Re-cover, reduce heat to medium-low, and continue simmering until the quinoa is tender and has absorbed the chicken stock, 15 to 20 minutes.

3. Stir in half of the Romano cheese and the parsley until evenly mixed. Serve the quinoa and sprinkle with the remaining cheese.

• QUINOA AND VEGGIES •

PREP: 10 minutes

COOK: 20 minutes

INGREDIENTS

1/2 cup uncooked quinoa
1-1/2 cups water
Pinch of kosher salt
1-12 tablespoons olive oil
2 cloves garlic, minced or pressed
1/2 red bell pepper, chopped

1/4 cup corn kernels
1/4 teaspoon cumin
1/2 teaspoon dried oregano
Kosher salt and freshly ground
    black pepper, to taste
1 green onions, chopped

DIRECTIONS

1. Place the quinoa in a fine mesh strainer, and rinse under cold water until the water no longer foams.

2. Bring the quinoa, water, and salt to a boil in a medium saucepan over medium-high heat. Reduce heat to medium-low, cover, and simmer until the quinoa is tender, about 20 minutes.

2. Meanwhile, heat a 10-inch skillet over medium heat. Add the olive oil and swirl to coat. Stir in the garlic, and cook for 2 minutes. Add the red pepper, and corn; continue cooking until the pepper softens, about 5 minutes. Season with cumin, oregano, salt, and pepper, and cook for 1 additional minute.

3. Stir in quinoa and green onions. Toss well to mix. Serve hot or cold.

• BASIC COUSCOUS •

PREP: Less than 5 minutes

COOK: 12 minutes

INGREDIENTS

1 tablespoon unsalted butter
1/2 cup couscous
3/4 cup chicken broth or vegetable broth

1/2 teaspoon kosher salt
Freshly ground black pepper
    to taste

DIRECTIONS

1. Heat a medium saucepan over medium-high heat. Add the butter and swirl to coat. When foaming subsides, add couscous and cook, stirring frequently, until grains are just beginning to brown, about 5 minutes.

2. Stir in broth and salt. Remove pan from heat and let stand until grains are tender, about 6 - 7 minutes. Uncover and fluff grains with fork. Season with additional salt and pepper to taste.

• COUSCOUS WITH PINE NUTS AND SPINACH •

PREP: 5 minutes   COOK: 15 minutes

INGREDIENTS
    1 tablespoon unsalted butter
    1/2 cup couscous
    3/4 cup chicken broth or vegetable broth
    1/2 teaspoon kosher salt
    1 tablespoon olive oil
    2 tablespoons pine nuts
    1 clove garlic, thinly sliced
    1 cup baby spinach
    2 tablespoons crumbled feta cheese
    1 tablespoon fresh lemon juice
    Freshly ground black pepper, to taste

DIRECTIONS
1. Heat a medium saucepan over medium-high heat. Add the butter and
    swirl to coat. When foaming subsides, add couscous and cook, stirring
    frequently, until grains are just beginning to brown, about 5 minutes.

2. Add broth, and salt; stir briefly to combine, cover, and remove pan from
    heat. Let stand until grains are tender, about 6 - 7 minutes.

3. Meanwhile, heat a small skillet over medium heat. Add olive oil and swirl
    to coat. Add the pine nuts and garlic and cook until golden, about
    2 - 3 minutes.

4. Stir the pine nuts and garlic into the couscous along with the spinach,
    feta cheese, and lemon juice. Season with additional salt and pepper
    to taste.

Desserts

 # Desserts

For those of you who know me, you're well-aware that I am not a big dessert eater. In fact, I've never been overly fond of sweets. Even growing up. Of course, I was never one to pass up a nice slice of chocolate cake at a birthday party, but by and large, I was usually the kid who saved their salad for last so I would have something to eat while everyone else dove into their dessert.

Perhaps that's why I didn't have many desserts in my first cookbook. And boy, did I hear about if from folks who bought it. Everyone wanted more dessert recipes.

Okay. Here you go!

Because I am offering recipes scaled down for a couple, it could be hard to come up with recipes for desserts like cakes and pies that will only serve two people. I've tried some that other chefs have published and I was unimpressed.

So I'm going to focus on fruit-based desserts and rice puddings. These can be made in a jiffy and are absolutely delicious.

However, if you do have a hankering for cakes or pies, I encourage you to pick up a cookbook that features baking. Just remember that you'll be creating desserts that will be more than enough for two. And if you don't want to bother making something from scratch, do what I often do: purchase a good pie or cake from your local bakery.

But if you want something quick, refreshing and delicious, the following recipes will more than please.

• CARAMELIZED APPLES OVER VANILLA ICE CREAM •

As I mentioned above, it's hard to bake an apple pie for two. But if you have a craving for apples, this is the next best thing. Serve this over a scoop of good vanilla ice cream and I guarantee you'll be in seventh heaven.

PREP: 5 minutes   COOK: 10 minutes

INGREDIENTS
- 2 tart apples (Granny Smith, Braeburn or even McIntosh)
- 1-1/2 tablespoons unsalted butter
- 1/3 cup sugar
- 1/3 teaspoon apple pie spice or cinnamon
- 1/4 cup heavy cream
- 2 scoops vanilla ice cream

DIRECTIONS

1. Peel and core each apple. Cut into quarters lengthwise, then cut each quarter in half lengthwise to make 8 wedges from each apple.

2. Heat a small skillet over high heat and add butter. Swirl to melt and coat. Add apples and sauté until they begin to soften, about 3 minutes.

3. Sprinkle sugar and apple pie spice (or cinnamon) over apples and continue to sauté until sugar begins to caramelize, about 4 - 5 minutes.

4. Add cream and stir until thickened, about 2 - 3 minutes.

5. Place a scoop if ice cream in two dessert dishes and spoon apples and sauce over the ice cream. Serve immediately.

• GLAZED BANANAS OVER COFFEE ICE CREAM •

Did you try the Caramelized Apples over Vanilla Ice Cream? Good, isn't it? Well, here's another fruit and ice cream dessert. Heck, we're on a roll here!

PREP: 2 minutes   COOK: 5 minutes

INGREDIENTS
    4 tablespoons unsalted butter
    1 tablespoon brown sugar
    1/4 cup orange juice
    1 banana, peeled
    2 scoops coffee ice cream

DIRECTIONS
1.   Heat a small skillet over high heat. Add butter and swirl to melt and coat. Add sugar and cook, stirring, until it forms a syrup, about 3 - 5 minutes. Stir in orange juice until will-blended.

2.   Cut banana in half length-wise and then cross-wise. Add bananas to the skillet and cook, turning once or twice, until well-coated and heated through, about 1 - 2 minutes.

3.   Place a scoop of ice cream in 2 dessert dishes and spoon the bananas and sauce over the ice cream. Serve immediately.

• RUM CARAMELIZED ORANGES •

Do you want a delicious dessert in less than 10 minutes? Look no further!

PREP: 10 minutes   COOK: 3 minutes

INGREDIENTS
- 2 navel oranges
- 1-1/2 tablespoons rum
- 1-1/2 tablespoons light brown sugar

DIRECTIONS
1. Preheat broiler.

2. With a sharp knife, peel the oranges taking care to remove the white pith (it is bitter). Slice oranges crosswise into 1/4-inch thick rounds.

3. Butter a 7" x 11" baking dish. Arrange orange slices (overlapping is okay if necessary). Drizzle rum over oranges and sprinkle with brown sugar.

4. Place baking dish 4-inches from heat and broil until sugar is caramelized. About 2 - 3 minutes.

• MIXED BERRY GRATIN •

This is another dessert that's almost too simple for words.

PREP: 5 minutes   COOK: 2 minutes

INGREDIENTS
   1-1/2 cups mixed berries (you can use frozen, defrosted)
   1/2 cup heavy cream
   1 tablespoon sliced almonds
   1 tablespoon powdered sugar

DIRECTIONS
1. Preheat oven broiler. Set rack 3 - 4 inches from broiler.

2. Rinse and dry berries if using fresh. Divide them into two gratin dishes.

3. Lightly whip the cream until somewhat thick and peaks begin to form. Spoon cream over berries then sprinkle with almonds and dust with sugar.

4. Place gratin dishes on rack and broil until golden brown, about 2 minutes. Serve warm.

• MINT JULEP PEACHES •

A true southern dessert. Perfect for Derby Week.

PREP: 5 minutes   COOK: 1 minute
CHILL: 10 minutes

INGREDIENTS
   1-1/2 teaspoons sugar
   1 tablespoon chopped fresh mint leaves
   1-1/2 teaspoons fresh lemon juice
   2 tablespoons water
   2 tablespoons bourbon
   2 peaches, peeled, pitted and sliced
   4 mint sprigs to garnish

DIRECTIONS

1. In a small sauce pan, combine the sugar, mint, lemon juice and water.
    Heat over medium-high heat until sugar dissolves. Pour into a cup or
    small bowl and add bourbon. Place in freezer to chill, about 10 minutes.
    Remove and strain to remove mint.

2. Place peach slices into two stemmed goblets or small glass bowls. Pour
    syrup over all and toss to coat.

• BALSAMIC GRILLED PEACHES •

I'm a big fan of grilled fruit. Try this and you'll know why.

PREP: 5 minutes   COOK: 6 minutes

INGREDIENTS
  1 large firm peach, halved and pitted
  1-1/2 tablespoons balsamic glaze or vinegar, divided
  2 tablespoons crumbled blue cheese
  1/8 teaspoon freshly ground black pepper

DIRECTIONS
  1. Prepare grill for medium-high heat. Lightly oil grate.

  2. Place peach halves cut-side down on grate and grill for 3 minutes.
      Turn peaches and brush tops and sides with 1 tablespoon glaze. Grill
      until tender, about 3 more minutes. Sprinkle with cheese, pepper and
      remaining glaze.

• GRILLED PINEAPPLE •

While we're grilling, I want you to try this grilled pineapple recipe. If you are pressed for time, simply salt the pineapple and brush with melted butter than grill as directed.

PREP: 5 minutes   MARINATE: 30+ minutes
COOK: 5 minutes

INGREDIENTS
   4 pineapple slices, 3/4-inch thick
   Kosher salt to taste
   3 tablespoons melted unsalted butter
   1/4 teaspoon honey
   Dash of hot pepper sauce

DIRECTIONS

1.   Lightly sprinkle pineapple slices with salt. In a small bowl, combine the butter, honey and hot sauce. Place pineapple slices in a re-sealable plastic bag and add the butter mixture. Seal bag, and shake to coat evenly. Marinate for at least 30 minutes, or preferably overnight.

2.   Preheat an outdoor grill for high heat, and lightly oil grate.

3.   Grill pineapple for 2 to 3 minutes per side, or until heated through and grill marks appear.

• BLUEBERRIES IN ORANGE-CREAM SAUCE •

This simple no-cook dessert can also be made with raspberries, blackberries and even strawberries. Use whatever berries are available and on sale!

PREP: 5 minutes

INGREDIENTS
- 1 (3-ounce) package cream cheese, softened
- 1/3 cup frozen orange juice, undiluted
- 1/3 cup milk
- 2 tablespoons orange liqueur (Curacao, Grand Marnier, Cointreau, or triple sec)
- 1-1/2 cups fresh blueberries, or other fresh berries (if using strawberries, hull and quarter)

DIRECTIONS

1. Place first 4 ingredients into a blender or food processor and process until smooth.

2. Rinse and dry berries then place into 2 dessert dishes. Spoon sauce over berries and serve.

• SAUTÉED RASPBERRIES IN PORT •
OVER VANILLA ICE CREAM

Feel free to use fresh blackberries in this dish for a nice change.

PREP: 5 minutes   COOK: 5 minutes

INGREDIENTS
1-1/2 cups fresh raspberries
2 tablespoons unsalted butter
1 tablespoon sugar
1/4 cup port
2 scoops vanilla ice cream

DIRECTIONS
1. Rinse berries and pat dry.

2. Melt butter in a small skillet over medium-high heat. Add berries and gently stir until coated. Sprinkle with sugar and add port. Simmer until warmed through, about 2 minutes.

3. Place a scoop of ice cream in 2 dessert dishes and spoon the berries and sauce over the ice cream. Serve immediately.

• GRAPEFRUIT AND BLUEBERRIES •
WITH MINT AND FETA

This wonderful dessert also makes a wonderful breakfast. Feel free to mix and match raspberries and blackberries if you have them in the fridge.

PREP: 5 minutes

INGREDIENTS
    1 large red or pink grapefruit, peeled, sectioned and cut into chunks
    1/2 lb fresh blueberries
    1 tablespoon fresh mint, chopped
    1 teaspoon sugar
    1 tablespoon crumbled feta cheese (or more to taste)

DIRECTIONS
Section and cut the grapefruit slices into chunks over a small bowl (to capture any juice.) In a medium bowl, add the grapefruit chunks, blueberries and mint. Pour any juice you captured over the fruit then sprinkle with the sugar and toss. Spoon fruit into two small bowls and sprinkle with the feta.

Breakfast

Breakfast

It's been said that breakfast is the most important meal of the day. That's probably true. To me, breakfast is one of my favorite meals of the day. In fact, I can eat a breakfast meal for lunch and dinner and often do.

You'll need two pieces of kitchen gear if you're going to get serious about breakfast. A cast iron skillet and a non-stick omelet pan. You'll need the skillet for items like bacon, sausage and potatoes. If you season it well and care for it correctly, you will have a virtual non-stick skillet that you can even put in the oven. And if you purchase a non-stick omelet pan (its really the only non-stick pan I have in my kitchen) you will save yourself a lot of headaches when you prepare eggs.

And speaking of eggs, in *Table for Two - The Cookbook for Couples* we covered scrambled eggs (yes, there is a wrong way and a right way to make them) and frittatas, as well as some cool ways to make some of our favorite sides, mouthwatering items like Maple Glazed Canadian Bacon.

We're going to continue with this train of thought as we look at Fried Eggs, Eggs Benedict and Classic French Toast. Then we'll look at some different ways we can take some of these to the next level.

Hopefully, this will get your breakfast mojo working just like it did mine. Once it does, you'll find yourself tweaking and experimenting with all manner of traditional breakfast fare.

Even if you're whipping them up at 7 P. M.

• BASIC FRIED EGGS •

I'd say a majority of folks fry their eggs by melting some butter in a skillet, cracking the eggs open (usually against the edge of the skillet) and then cooking them to their desired doneness. We're going to make our eggs a little different here by cracking the eggs into a bowl first (to ensure that they will not break when adding them to the pan) and then cooking them in a pan with a lid. I think you'll be pleased with the results.

PREP: 5 minutes   COOK: 2 minutes

INGREDIENTS
    2 teaspoons canola or vegetable oil
    4 large eggs
    Kosher salt and freshly ground black pepper, to taste
    2 teaspoons unsalted butter, cut into 4 pieces

DIRECTIONS

1. Heat oil in a 10-inch skillet over low heat for 5 minutes (this will ensure that there are no 'hot spots' in the pan). Meanwhile, crack two of the eggs in a small bowl and the other two eggs into another small bowl. Season eggs with salt and pepper to taste.

2. Increase the heat to medium-high and heat until the oil shimmers. Add butter to the pan and swirl to coat. Pour 1 bowl of eggs in 1 side of the pan and the other bowl in the other. Cover and cook for 1 minute. Remove skillet from heat and let stand, covered, for 15 - 45 seconds for runny yolks; 45 - 60 seconds for soft and barely-set yolks; and 2 minutes for medium-set yolks.

• FRIED EGGS WITH BACON •
AND HONEY GLAZED POTATOES

This may seem like a lot of ingredients and a lot of work for breakfast, but it really isn't. You can cook this homey meal in less than 30 minutes, even less if you've got some cooked potatoes wedges in the freezer. If using fresh potatoes, I recommend soaking them in water for a few minutes to remove some of the starch, but it's not absolutely necessary.

PREP: 5 minutes   SET: 10 minutes
COOK: 20 minutes

INGREDIENTS
   1 large Idaho potato
   4 slices thick-cut smoked bacon
   2 tablespoons olive oil, divided
   1 clove garlic, sliced thin
   1 tablespoon soy sauce
   2 tablespoons honey
   2 tablespoons chopped fresh Italian flat leaf parsley
   1/8 teaspoon thyme
   Hungarian sweet paprika to garnish
   2 large eggs (use 4 if you're really hungry)
   Kosher salt and freshly ground pepper, to taste

DIRECTIONS
   1.   Wash potato well and peel off some of its skin. Cut potatoes into
        wedges 1/6-inch wide. Place potatoes in a bowl and add cold water to
        cover. Let sit for 5 minutes, drain and repeat. (This will remove excess
        starch from the potatoes.) Drain potatoes and pat dry.

   2.   Meanwhile, chop bacon into 1/2-inch squares. Heat a 10-inch skillet
        over medium-high heat. Add 1-1/2 teaspoons olive oil and swirl to coat.
        Add bacon and sauté until it begins to crisp, about 4 minutes. Remove
        bacon with a slotted spoon and set aside.

3. Add 1 tablespoon olive oil and potatoes to the skillet. Sauté over medium-high heat, turning occasionally, until slightly brown, about 15 minutes. Add garlic and sauté 2 minutes. Stir in the soy sauce and honey and bring to a simmer. Reduce heat to medium low and simmer for 5 minutes. Stir in the parsley and thyme and toss to coat. Add bacon back to pan and toss until bacon is re-warmed. Sprinkle with paprika.

4. While the potatoes are cooking, heat 1-1/2 teaspoons oil in an omelet pan over low heat for 5 minutes. Meanwhile, crack the eggs in a small bowl and season with salt and pepper.

5. Increase the heat to medium-high and heat until the oil shimmers. Add butter to the pan and swirl to coat. Pour eggs into the pan; cover and cook for 1 minute. Remove skillet from heat and let stand, covered, for 15 - 45 seconds for runny yolks; 45 - 60 seconds for soft and barely-set yolks; and 2 minutes for medium-set yolks.

Divide potatoes evenly between two plates and slide eggs on top.

• CHAKCHOUKA •

This colorful and spicy Tunisian vegetable and fried egg dish is a great way to start your day. It also makes for a wonderful brunch or supper.

PREP: 10 minutes   COOK: 20 minutes

INGREDIENTS
   2 tablespoons olive oil
   1 medium onion, chopped (about 1 cup)
   1 green pepper, cut into thin strips
   1 red pepper, cut into thin strips
   1 teaspoon ground cumin
   1/2 teaspoon ground coriander
   1/2 teaspoon Hungarian sweet paprika
   Dash hot red pepper sauce (or to taste)
   3 cloves garlic, minced or pressed
   1 (15.5-ounce) can diced tomatoes, undrained
   Kosher salt and freshly ground black pepper, to taste
   4 large eggs

DIRECTIONS
1.   Heat a 10-inch skillet over medium-high heat. Add the olive oil and swirl to coat. Add the onions and sauté until they begin to soften, about 5 minutes. Add the peppers, cumin, coriander, paprika and hot sauce. Sauté until peppers soften, about 5 more minutes. Add the garlic and sauté 2 additional minutes.

2.   Meanwhile, drain the tomatoes and reserve the juice. Add the tomatoes and 1/2 cup juice to the skillet and stir.

3.   When the tomatoes are hot and simmering, make 4 evenly-spaced indentations in them and crack an egg into each indentation. Turn heat to medium-low, cover and cook until the egg whites are cooked and the yolks are soft-cooked, about 3 minutes. Serve in shallow bowls.

• BASIC POACHED EGGS •

PREP: 5 minutes   COOK: 8 minutes

INGREDIENTS
  4 eggs
  1-1/2 teaspoons white vinegar
  1 teaspoon kosher salt

DIRECTIONS
Pour water into a 10-inch skillet until it is 2/3's full and bring to a boil over
medium-high heat. Add vinegar and salt, then reduce heat to medium-low and
let water return to a simmer. Crack each egg into a cup or small bowl and gently
pour into the water, careful that the eggs don't touch. Cook until the whites are
set and the yolk has filmed over, about 4 minutes. Remove eggs (trim ragged
edges if desired) and serve on toasted bread or English muffins.

• POACHED EGGS WITH ROASTED CHERRY TOMATOES •

PREP: 5 minutes   COOK: 30 minutes

INGREDIENTS
1 pint cherry tomatoes (10-ounces)
1 tablespoon extra-virgin olive oil
Kosher salt and freshly ground black pepper, to taste
1 tablespoon fresh thyme leaves (or 1 teaspoon dried)
4 large eggs
2 English muffins, split and toasted

DIRECTIONS
  1. Preheat oven to 425°.

  2. Arrange tomatoes, single layer, in a baking dish. Drizzle with olive oil then
      season with salt, pepper and thyme. Toss to coat. Place baking dish
      in the oven and roast until tomatoes start to burst, about 20 minutes.
      Scrape tomatoes and juice into a small bowl and let cool a bit.

  3. Poach eggs as in the above recipe. Place an egg on an English muffin
      half and season with additional salt and pepper to taste. Top each egg
      with the roasted tomatoes.

• EGGS BENEDICT WITH CRAB •

This elegant dish is traditionally made with hollandaise sauce, which can be tricky to make, especially in small portions. I've tried the bagged products found near the salad dressings with okay results. But since we're trying to use ingredients that are not over-processed as much as possible I'm going to introduce this method to you. Feel free to use this whenever a recipe calls for hollandaise sauce. And although I've listed the chives and tarragon as optional garnishes, they really do make the meal.

PREP: 10 minutes   COOK: 10 minutes

INGREDIENTS
FOR THE SAUCE:
1/3 cup buttermilk (you can use low-fat if you prefer)
1/3 cup mayonnaise
1/2 teaspoon grated lemon zest
1 tablespoon fresh lemon juice
1-1/2 teaspoons Dijon mustard
1/4 teaspoon freshly ground black pepper
1-1/2 teaspoons unsalted butter

FOR THE EGGS:
1-1/2 teaspoons white wine vinegar
4 large eggs
2 English muffins, halved and toasted
4 ounces lump crab meat, divided
Freshly ground black pepper to taste
1 tablespoon chopped fresh chives to garnish (optional)
1 tablespoon chopped fresh tarragon to garnish (optional)

DIRECTIONS
1. In a small saucepan over low heat, combine the buttermilk, mayonnaise, lemon zest, lemon juice, mustard and pepper. Add butter and swirl until butter melts. Keep warm while you prepare the eggs.

2. Pour water into a 10-inch skillet until it is 2/3's full and bring to a boil over medium-high heat. Add vinegar then reduce heat to medium-low and let water return to a simmer.

3. Break each egg into a custard cup or small ramekin then gently pour into the skillet. Cook for 4 minutes or until the desired degree of doneness.

4. Place 1 muffin, cut side up, on each of two plates. Spoon crab evenly among the muffins. Spoon 1 tablespoon of the sauce on top of the crab. Remove eggs from the skillet with a slotted spoon and place 1 egg on top of each muffin. Spoon 3 tablespoons of sauce over each egg and sprinkle with cracked pepper, chives and tarragon.

• POACHED EGGS WITH SAUTEED • MUSHROOMS AND TOMATOES

PREP: 10 minutes   COOK: 10 minutes

INGREDIENTS
1 tablespoon plus 1 teaspoon olive oil
1 medium tomato, sliced into 4 rounds
Kosher salt and freshly ground black pepper, to taste
1/2 pound mushrooms, sliced
1-1/2 teaspoons fresh thyme leaves (or 1/2 teaspoon dried)
4 large eggs
2 English muffins, split and toasted
3 tablespoons grated Parmesan cheese
1 tablespoon chopped fresh chives, to garnish

DIRECTIONS
1. Heat a 10-inch skillet over medium-high heat. Add 1 teaspoon oil and swirl to coat. Add the tomatoes, season with salt and pepper, and cook until just tender, about 1-2 minutes per side. Transfer to a plate.

2. Add the remaining tablespoon oil to the skillet and add the mushrooms, thyme, and salt and pepper. Sauté until golden brown and tender, about 6-7 minutes.

3. Meanwhile, poach the eggs as above.

4. Top each English muffin half with the tomatoes, mushrooms, eggs, Parmesan, and additional salt and pepper. Sprinkle with the chives to garnish.

• CHORIZO BREAKFAST TACOS •

It's become popular for fast food restaurants to offer breakfast tacos and burritos. I guess they're popular because you can eat them with one hand while driving. If eating breakfast while driving is not on your agenda today, try this version of breakfast tacos. It packs a little more punch than the fast food variety. If you would like a milder version, substitute regular breakfast sausage for the chorizo.

PREP: 10 minutes   COOK: 10 minutes

INGREDIENTS
    1 teaspoon olive oil
    4 (6-inch) corn tortillas
    1 cup grated extra-sharp white cheddar cheese (or cheddar cheese of choice)
    4 large eggs
    4 tablespoons chopped fresh cilantro, divided
    Kosher salt and freshly ground black pepper, to taste
    8 ounces fresh chorizo sausages, casings removed
    4 green onions, sliced
    Sour cream to garnish (optional)
    Hot sauce to garnish (optional)

DIRECTIONS
1. Char tortillas over your stove's gas flame or directly on the electric burner coil turning with tongs until blackened in spots. Remove tortillas to a large, lightly-oiled skillet in one layer. If you don't have a large skillet, remove to a warm plate and sprinkle evenly with cheese and loosely cover with tin foil or a pot lid (don't let lid touch cheese).

2. Whisk eggs with 2 tablespoons cilantro, salt and pepper in a medium bowl. Heat a 10-inch skillet over medium-high heat and add the chorizo. Sauté, breaking up the sausage, until cooked through, about 5 minutes. Add the green onions and sauté 2 minutes. Add the eggs and stir until barely set, about 1 minute.

3. Meanwhile, heat the large skillet over high heat until tortillas begin to crisp but are still pliable, about 1 minute. (If you don't have a large skillet, use a small skillet and proceed in two batches). Spoon egg mixture evenly among the tortillas and sprinkle with the remaining cilantro. Fold the tortillas and serve with sour cream and hot sauce if desired.

• CREAMY SCRAMBLED EGGS •

The House of Sea and Sun is a delightful bed and breakfast in St. Augustine Beach that we've stayed at more than a few times. (Yes, I know, it's just a hop, skip and a jump from where we live, but hey, sometimes you don't have to go far to get away, eh?). Rooms are cozy and well-appointed and the breakfasts are simple, yet delicious - like these creamy scrambled eggs.

PREP: Under 5 minutes   COOK: 10 minutes

INGREDIENTS
    4 large eggs
    2 ounces cream cheese, cut into 1/2-inch pieces, softened
    Kosher salt and freshly ground black pepper, to taste
    2 tablespoons unsalted butter
    1/3 cup finely chopped scallions, white and green parts
    Chopped fresh scallion tops or chives to garnish

DIRECTIONS
1.   In a medium bowl, whisk the eggs to blend. Whisk in cream cheese and salt and pepper.

2.   Heat a 10-inch skillet over medium heat. Add butter and swirl to coat. Add scallions and sauté until soft, about 5 minutes.

3.   Turn heat to medium-low and stir in eggs. Cook until barely set, about 4 minutes. Divide eggs between two plates and sprinkle with chopped scallion tops or chives to garnish.

• CREAMY SCRAMBLED EGGS WITH SMOKED SALMON •

Here we'll take the ultra-simple scrambled eggs with cream cheese and turn them up a notch. Feel free to substitute smoked trout or smoked whitefish in place of the salmon. You can double this for company. I guarantee you'll impress them!

PREP: Under 5 minutes   COOK: 10 minutes

INGREDIENTS
    4 large eggs
    1/2 (4.5-ounce) package smoked salmon fillets, cut into 1/2-inch pieces
    2 ounces cream cheese, cut into 1/2-inch pieces, softened
    2 teaspoons chopped fresh dill
    Kosher salt and freshly ground black pepper, to taste
    1/4 cup chopped scallions, white and green parts
    Dill sprigs to garnish (optional)

DIRECTIONS

1. In a medium bowl, whisk the eggs to blend. Whisk in the salmon, cream cheese, dill and salt and pepper.

2. Heat a 10-inch skillet over medium heat. Add butter and swirl to coat. Add scallions and sauté until soft, about 5 minutes.

3. Turn heat to medium-low and stir in egg mixture. Cook until barely set and still moist, about 4 minutes. Divide eggs between two plates and garnish with dill sprigs.

• CREAMY SCRAMBLED EGGS ON ASPARAGUS •

This elegant looking breakfast belies the fact that it is extremely simple to make. You almost want to save this for a special occasion. But since everyday can be a celebration, why not serve it often? Simply add some nice buttered toast or English muffins, a glass of orange juice, and a hot cup of good coffee or tea and you will feel like you were dining in a cozy bed and breakfast.

PREP: Under 5 minutes   COOK: 10 minutes

INGREDIENTS
   4 large eggs
   1/4 cup prepared garlic and herb cheese (I like Boursin®)
   1-1/2 teaspoons fresh chopped basil
   1/2 pound thin asparagus spears, trimmed
   2 tablespoons unsalted butter, divided

DIRECTIONS
   1.   Whisk eggs in a medium bowl and set aside. In a small bowl, whisk together the herb cheese and basil; set aside.

   2.   Place asparagus in a small skillet and add water to barely cover. Bring to a boil and cook until just tender, about 3 minutes. Drain water and return asparagus to the skillet.

   3.   Heat a 10-inch skillet over medium heat. Add 1 tablespoon butter and swirl to coat. Add eggs and stir with rubber spatula until barely set, about 1 - 2 minutes. Add cheese mixture and stir until the eggs and cheese are set but still soft, about 2 minutes.

   4.   Meanwhile, add remaining butter to the skillet with the asparagus and stir until the asparagus is heated through. Divide the asparagus among 2 plates and spoon eggs over to serve.

• BROILED PORTOBELLOS AND SCRAMBLED EGGS •

Here's a delicious breakfast recipe for mushroom lovers.

PREP: 5 minutes   COOK: 10 minutes

INGREDIENTS
   2 large portobello mushroom caps
   2 tablespoons olive oil
   1 garlic clove, minced or pressed
   1/4 teaspoon kosher salt
   Pinch freshly ground black pepper (or to taste)
   4 large eggs
   1-1/2 tablespoons freshly grated Parmesan cheese
   1/2 teaspoon chopped fresh rosemary (1/8 teaspoon dried)
   3 tablespoons unsalted butter, divided

DIRECTIONS
   1.   Preheat broiler.

   2.   Brush mushrooms liberally with olive oil and place gill side up on a lightly
        oiled baking sheet. Sprinkle with garlic, salt and pepper. Set baking
        sheet about 4-inches from the heat and broil mushrooms until they begin
        to soften, about 3 - 5 minutes. Turn mushrooms and broil until they are
        easily pierced with a knife, about 5 - 7 additional minutes.

   3.   Meanwhile, in a medium bowl, whisk the eggs, half the cheese, rosemary
        and additional salt and pepper to taste.

   4.   Heat a 10-inch skillet over medium-low heat. Add 2 tablespoons butter
        and swirl to coat. Add egg mixture and cook, stirring frequently, until
        barely set, about 4 minutes. Dot eggs with remaining butter.

   5.   Place hot mushrooms on a plate, gill side up, and top with eggs.
        Sprinkle with remaining cheese.

• JOE'S SPECIAL •

This is one of those 'serve-anytime-meals'. Legend has it that this dish was created in a restaurant called "New Joe's" in San Francisco in the 1920's. Why "New Joe's"? Perhaps they wanted to differentiate themselves from the countless other Joe's Diners that dotted the landscape at the time. Whatever the origin, this is true diner comfort food. Thank you, Joe, whoever you are!

PREP: 5 minutes   COOK: 15 minutes

INGREDIENTS
   4 eggs
   1 tablespoon olive oil or unsalted butter
   1 small onion, finely chopped
   2 garlic cloves, minced
   1/2 pound lean ground beef
   1/2 package (10-ounce) frozen chopped spinach, thawed and drained or 1 (5-ounce) bag fresh baby spinach leaves (chop or leave whole)
   1/2 teaspoon dried basil
   1/4 teaspoon dried oregano
   1/4 teaspoon nutmeg
   2 tablespoons grated Parmesan cheese
   Kosher salt and freshly ground black pepper, to taste

DIRECTIONS

1.   Beat eggs in a small bowl.

2.   Heat oil in a 10" skillet over medium-high heat. Add onion and sauté until soft, about 5 minutes. Add garlic and sauté for 1 additional minute.

3.   Add beef and cook, stirring, until browned and all moisture evaporates, about 10 minutes.

4.   Add spinach, basil, oregano, and nutmeg. Cook, stirring, until heated through, about 2 minutes.

5.   Add eggs and cook, stirring, until eggs are cooked and mixture is slightly dry, about 4 minutes. Season with salt and pepper to taste and sprinkle with Parmesan.

Serve with warm, crusty bread.

• BAKED EGGS IN CRISPY HAM CUPS •

This is one elegant dish that makes for a delightful breakfast or brunch. It's also a great way to impress house guests, especially if you let them help prepare them. Just be sure to jot the recipe down because I know they will want to create these at home on a lazy Saturday or Sunday morning.

PREP: 10 minutes   COOK: 20 minutes

INGREDIENTS
  4 slices smoked deli ham slices
  2 tablespoons unsalted butter, divided
  1/4 cup frozen petite peas, defrosted
  4 large eggs
  2 teaspoons cream or half and half, divided
  1/2 teaspoon kosher salt, divided
  1/4 teaspoon freshly ground black pepper, divided
  2 English muffins, halved and toasted
  12 ounces mushrooms, sliced
  2 tablespoons sour cream
  1-1/2 teaspoons Dijon mustard
  1 teaspoon chopped fresh tarragon or Italian flat leaf parsley
  Hungarian sweet paprika to garnish

DIRECTIONS
  1. Preheat oven to 400°.

  2. Lightly butter 4 muffin cups with 1 tablespoon butter. Place 1 slice of ham in each cup, allowing the edges to extend over the edges. Place 1 tablespoon peas in each cup then crack one egg into each cup. Drizzle 1/2 teaspoon cream over each egg and sprinkle with salt and pepper.

  3. Place cups into the oven and bake until eggs are almost set, about 15 - 18 minutes.

  4. Meanwhile, heat a 10-inch skillet over medium-high heat. Add the remaining butter and swirl to coat. Add mushrooms and season with remaining salt and pepper. Sauté until mushrooms release their liquid, about 5 minutes. Stir in sour cream, mustard and tarragon. Cook until heated through.

  5. Place two muffins cut side up on each plate. Spoon mushrooms over the muffin halves and sprinkle with paprika. Top each muffin with a ham cup and serve.

• CLASSIC FRENCH TOAST •

PREP: 5 minutes   COOK: 12 minutes

INGREDIENTS
  2 large eggs
  1/2 cup milk or half & half
  1 teaspoon pure vanilla extract
  1/4 teaspoon cinnamon
  4 slices challah, or any hearty white bread
  4 teaspoons unsalted butter
  Maple syrup, plain yogurt, whipped cream (optional)

DIRECTIONS

1. In a small bowl, lightly beat the eggs together with the milk, vanilla and cinnamon. Pour into a baking dish large enough to hold all four slices of bread. Soak the bread for 1 minute on each side. Using firm slotted spatula, pick up bread slice and allow excess milk mixture to drip off. Place slices on a baking sheet.

2. Heat a 10-inch skillet over medium-low heat. Add 2 teaspoons butter and swirl to coat. Add 2 slices of bread and cook, turning occasionally, until nicely brown and crisp, about 5 - 6 minutes. Remove to warm plate and cover to keep warm. Add the remaining butter to the skillet and cook the other two pieces of bread.

Serve with warm maple syrup, yogurt or whipped cream.

• FRUIT-FILLED FRENCH TOAST •

Now we take our classic French toast recipe up a notch. Be sure to use all-fruit spread with no sugar added. I like challah bread but if you cannot find it in your local supermarket, feel free to use any hearty white bread, just be sure it is 1-inch thick.

PREP: 10 minutes   COOK: 12 minutes

INGREDIENTS
    4 slices challah, or any hearty white bread, sliced 1-inch thick
    4 generous tablespoons fruit spread of choice
    2 large eggs
    1/2 cup milk or half & half
    1 teaspoon pure vanilla extract
    1/4 teaspoon cinnamon
    4 teaspoons unsalted butter
    Plain yogurt or whipped cream (optional)

DIRECTIONS

1. Cut each slice of bread horizontally to within 1/2-inch of the edge to make a pocket. Spoon 1 tablespoon fruit spread into each pocket.

2. In a small bowl, light lightly beat the eggs together with the milk, vanilla and cinnamon. Pour into a baking dish large enough to hold all four sliced of bread. Soak the bread for 1 minute on each side.

3. Heat a 10-inch skillet over medium-low heat. Add 2 teaspoons butter and swirl to coat. Add 2 slices of bread and cook, turning occasionally, until nicely brown and crisp, about 5 - 6 minutes. Remove to warm plate and cover to keep warm. Add the remaining butter to the skillet and cook the other two pieces of bread.

Serve plain or topped with yogurt or whipped cream.

• MAPLE MUSTARD-GLAZED CANADIAN BACON •

PREP: Under 5 minutes   COOK: 5 minutes

INGREDIENTS
    1/2 tablespoons Dijon mustard
    1 teaspoon maple syrup
    Pinch cayenne pepper, or to taste
    1/4 pound thinly-sliced Canadian bacon

DIRECTIONS
Preheat broiler. In a small bowl, stir together the mustard, maple syrup and
cayenne pepper until well combined. Arrange bacon slices on a lightly oiled
baking sheet and brush with the maple mustard mixture. Place the baking sheet
4 inches from the heat and broil until golden around the edges, turning once,
about 5 - 6 minutes total. Serve glazed side up.

• CARAMELIZED SLAB BACON •

It's nice to have a toaster oven for this so you don't have to use your big one.

PREP: 5 minutes   COOK: 15 minutes

INGREDIENTS
    1/3 cup golden brown sugar
    1/4 pound bacon slices

DIRECTIONS
Preheat oven to 350°. Place sugar in a shallow bowl. Add bacon strips and turn
to coat completely. Place bacon on a rimmed baking sheet and bake, turning
once, until dark golden brown, about 14 - 16 minutes total.

• SWEET POTATO HASH •

PREP: 10 minutes   COOK: 15 minutes

INGREDIENTS
  2 cups diced peeled sweet potato (about 1/2 pound)
  1 cup diced red potato
  2 tablespoons olive oil
  1/2 cup diced Canadian bacon (about 4 ounces)
  1/2 cup chopped green bell pepper
  1/2 cup chopped onions
  1/2 teaspoon kosher salt
  1/4 teaspoon celery seed
  1/4 teaspoon freshly ground black pepper
  Pinch grated nutmeg
  2 tablespoons chicken broth or water
  1-1/2 teaspoons cider vinegar

DIRECTIONS

1. Place potatoes in a medium saucepan, and cover with water. Bring to a boil. Reduce heat, and simmer until tender, about 5 minutes. Drain.

2. Heat a 10-inch skillet over medium heat. Add oil and swirl to coat. Add bacon and sauté for 4 minutes. Add bell pepper and onions and sauté for 2 minutes. Add potatoes, salt, celery seed, pepper, and nutmeg; sauté for 4 minutes. Stir in broth and vinegar. Toss gently until liquid is absorbed.

**COOK YOUR POTATOES AHEAD OF TIME
FOR BETTER BREAKFAST POTATOES**

When you bake or boil potatoes, make extra and freeze them to make great home fries, hash browns and other breakfast potatoes. In fact, I think you'll find cooking your potatoes ahead of time, even if it's just the night before, will create better breakfast sides. Here's how: Whenever you are baking or boiling potatoes, throw a couple of extra in. When done, set the extras aside to cool, then dice, cube or mash as desired. Place potatoes in a zip lock freezer bag; remove as much air as you can, then lay them flat in the freezer. (They'll be good for about a year.) When you're ready to use them, defrost them in the microwave then cook as directed, except your cooking times will be shorter.

• CLASSIC HOME FRIES •

PREP: 5 minutes   COOK: 20 minutes

INGREDIENTS
    2 tablespoons unsalted butter, divided
    2 tablespoons olive oil, divided
    1 small yellow onion, thinly sliced
    1 lb. red potatoes, peeled and cubed
    1/2 teaspoon Hungarian sweet paprika
    1/4 teaspoon ground cumin
    Kosher salt and freshly ground black pepper, to taste

DIRECTIONS
1.   Heat a 10-inch skillet over medium-high heat. Add 1/2 tablespoons butter and 1/2 tablespoons olive oil and swirl to coat. Add onions and sauté until soft and barely brown, about 7 - 8 minutes. Transfer onions to a small bowl and set aside.

2.   Add the remaining butter and olive oil to the skillet. Add the potatoes and sauté until nicely brown on all sides, about 10 minutes. (Add more oil if potatoes start to dry out).

3.   Return the onions to the skillet and sprinkle with paprika, cumin, and salt and pepper. Cook, stirring and scraping the bottom of the skillet with a spatula, until the potatoes form a golden brown crust.

• POTATOES O'BRIEN •

PREP: 10 minutes   COOK: 25 minutes

INGREDIENTS
   1 tablespoon unsalted butter, divided
   1 tablespoon olive oil, divided
   1/2 cup chopped onion
   1/4 cup diced green bell pepper
   1/4 cup diced red bell pepper
   1 pound red potatoes, peeled and cubed
   Kosher salt and freshly ground black pepper, to taste
   1 tablespoon chopped fresh parsley

DIRECTIONS
1.   Heat a 10-inch skillet over medium-high heat. Add 1/2 tablespoons
     butter and 1/2 tablespoons olive oil and swirl to coat. Add onions and
     sauté until soft and barely brown, about 6 - 8 minutes. Add the green
     and red peppers and sauté until they begin to soften, about 3 - 5
     minutes. Transfer onions and peppers to a small bowl and set aside.

2.   Add the remaining butter and olive oil to the skillet. Add the potatoes and
     sauté until nicely brown on all sides, about 10 minutes. (Add more oil if
     potatoes start to dry out).

3.   Return the onions and peppers to the skillet and turn the heat to high.
     Season with salt and pepper to taste then sauté until warmed through.
     Remove from heat and stir in the parsley.

• CHEESE GRITS •

A southern staple. If you only have one of the cheeses on hand, use 1/2 cup of whatever you have.

PREP: 5 minutes   COOK: 8 minutes

INGREDIENTS
    2-2/3 cups water
    1/4 teaspoon salt
    2/3 cups quick-cooking grits (not instant)
    1/4 cup shredded sharp cheddar cheese
    1/4 cup shredded Monterey jack cheese
    3 tablespoons half-and-half
    1 teaspoon unsalted butter
    Pinch freshly ground black pepper

DIRECTIONS

1. Bring 5 water and salt to a boil in a medium saucepan over medium-high heat. Gradually whisk in grits and bring to a boil. Reduce heat to low, and simmer, stirring occasionally, for 5 minutes. Stir in cheese and remaining ingredients until cheese is melted. Serve immediately.

NOW, WHAT ABOUT THE LEFTOVERS?

Some of these recipes call for only 1/2 a can of chopped tomatoes, or 1/2 a package frozen vegetables. Some call for just a tablespoon of chopped fresh parsley or other herb. Perhaps you found some meat on sale and cooked up a batch. What do you do with the rest? Don't toss it. Here are some delicious and frugal ideas for your leftovers:

VEGGIES:

Soups: Bring two cups of beef, chicken, or vegetable broth to a boil and add the leftover veggies, tomatoes, and/or potatoes. Reduce heat and add 1/4 teaspoon dried thyme, oregano, basil or other herb of choice. Simmer until everything is cooked or warmed through. Salt and pepper to taste.

- Add diced cooked beef, chicken, or pork if you have it on hand and heat through.
- Add leftover beans or rice.
- Stir in a handful of pasta to the boiling broth and cook until ál denté. Then add veggies and cooked meat and heat through.

Breakfast or Brunch: Use leftover veggies to create a unique omelet, frittata, or scrambled egg dish. For something a little more elegant use left over veggies in baked eggs.

Stir Fry: Use broccoli, cauliflower, carrots, or squash to create a stir-fry.

FRESH HERBS: Chop herbs and place one tablespoon into each square of an ice cube tray. Add water to cover and freeze. Remove cubes and place in a labeled freezer bag. Add frozen cubes to soups, stews, gratins, sauces, and other dishes.

MEATS: Thinly slice beef or pork and reheat in a bit of broth to make sandwiches. Slice leftover beef or pork into thin strips for stir-fries. Dice leftover beef or pork and add to soups.

Heat a can of drained red or black beans in 1/2 cup broth. Add diced beef or pork, and season with oregano and chili powder to taste for a quick chili lunch. Add leftover diced tomatoes if you have them.

FISH AND SHELLFISH: Diced cooked fish and whole shrimp can be served over a bed of greens with your choice of salad dressing. Bring a cup of fish or clam broth and cream to a simmer and add some sautéed onions and diced, cooked fish or shrimp for a quick chowder. Throw in some cubed potatoes if you have them.

Index

CPSIA information can be obtained at www.ICGtesting.com
Printed in the USA
LVOW03s1229060414

380509LV00008B/235/P

9 780980 156874